Praise for *All in the Best Possible Taste*

'Bromley's box of recollections, peppered with amusing detail, reads like the real thing . . . his unashamed love for television makes his book an engaging primer for 1980s TV, from *Dallas* to *Danger Mouse*, which will have you stacking up a whole new YouTube play list' *Metro*

'Good fun. Bromley makes an entertaining guide to the viewing habits of a typical middle-class family of the period . . . full of diverting stories and odd facts . . . Gradually you realise that the way television changed and developed in the Eighties was like a series of well-positioned dominoes: push one and the whole lot fall over.' *Daily Mail*

'An enjoyable slice of nostalgia' *Choice*

'. . . and often hilarious' *Press Association*

'. . . warm and nostalgic account of growing up in the decade in which television irrevocably changed.' *Yorkshire Post*

D1079705

Also by Tom Bromley

Crazy Little Thing Called Love
Half a World Away
Rock and Pop Elevens (co-author)
We Could Have Been the Wombles
The Encyclopaedia of Guilty Pleasures (co-author)
Shopping While Drunk (co-author)

All in the Best *Possible* Taste

Growing Up Watching Telly in the Eighties

TOM BROMLEY

SIMON &
SCHUSTER

London · New York · Sydney · Toronto

A CBS COMPANY

First published in Great Britain in 2010 by Simon & Schuster UK Ltd
This paperback edition published by Simon & Schuster UK Ltd, 2011
A CBS COMPANY

1 3 5 7 9 10 8 6 4 2

Simon & Schuster UK Ltd
1st Floor
222 Gray's Inn Road
London
WC1X 8HB

www.simonandschuster.co.uk

Simon & Schuster Australia
Sydney

A CIP catalogue copy for this book is available
from the British Library.

ISBN: 978-1-84983-058-4

Typeset by Hewer Text UK Ltd, Edinburgh
Printed and bound in Great Britain by CPI Cox & Wyman, Reading, Berks RG1 8EX

For Mum, Dad, Joff, Helen and Katherine

'I love it when a plan comes together'

Colonel John 'Hannibal' Smith

Contents

Introducing . . .

This book could begin with a blue and yellow globe going round and round and round. Or a white number 2 in the middle of a black screen, flanked by two pairs of orange stripes, Adam Ant-style. Depending where you are in the country, you might (like me) have seen a golden chevron rising from a pool of liquid gold; or possibly a silver knight on horseback holding a flag; or a shot of the London skyline, reflected as if in the river below (though only on Monday to Friday). It might begin with a multicoloured number 4 collapsing into pieces before magically reassembling itself. Should you have the facilities to watch this on VHS or Betamax cassette, this is the point at which Radio One DJ Simon Bates will turn up to warn you about the potentially offensive content of the following feature: 'sexy scenes' and 'some of the milder swearwords', for example.

Actually, there aren't really any 'sexy scenes' here for Simon to get hot under the collar about. This is my story of growing up in front of the television set in the 1980s, and I'm sorry to say that the good women of my hometown were sensible enough to spurn my advances for the entire duration of the decade. This was, as you might imagine, a bitter disappointment to my teenage self. But, with no majorly 'sexy scenes' to write about, there is no need to pepper this book with those red triangles that Channel 4 used to put in the corner of the screen whenever they showed an explicit film. With no red triangles required, my publisher hasn't had to splash out on colour printing and has only needed to pay for the equivalent of a black-and-white licence.

I should probably advise you that there is some strong language in what you are about to read, some of which is what Simon Bates might refer to as 'sexual swearwords'. In addition I should make it clear that, while many programmes are mentioned in this book, other television shows from the period are also available. Although I definitely watched a lot of telly in the eighties – and no doubt more than my parents would have liked – I by no means watched everything that was on. If I haven't included certain programmes you watched, this is probably because: a) you had more taste than I did; b) you were allowed to go to bed later than I was; or c) you had the luxury of a TV set in your own room. In other words, be grateful for your own good fortune rather than taking it out on me.

Anyway . . . Having mentioned that later on in the evening Lorraine Chase and Willie Rushton are among the celebrity guests joining Terry Wogan on *Blankety Blank*, the continuity announcer will attempt to hide his disdain as he reveals the next programme: *Now we have the first in a new series. With a light-hearted look back over the highs and lows of television in the eighties, it's time to join our host for* All in the Best *Possible* Taste . . .

Episode One

'This attic's full of memories for me'

If Bruce Springsteen was born to run and Madonna was born to flirt, then I was born to watch television. I wouldn't say I was completely obsessed by the box, but my first word was not 'mummy' or 'daddy'; it was 'two', which I uttered one day when I spotted a swan in the park. The shape of the curve of the swan's neck obviously echoed that of the number 2, and BBC 2 was the channel on which my favourite programme, *Play School*, was shown at eleven o'clock every morning. I can't remember whether I thought that *Play School* might miraculously appear out of the pond, but I gave the swan a good hard stare anyway – just in case.

In my early years I saw *Play School* in everything. I christened my maternal grandmother Granny Mima because I thought she looked a bit like the *Play School* doll Jemima. The biggest crisis that happened in my very young world, and for which my parents soon learned to steel themselves, was the annual party-political conference season, when Humpty Dumpty and Hamble were shunted off in favour of Willie Whitelaw and Shirley Williams. My response, apparently, was to do an impression of the little white dot that marked the end of the day's telly (basically, I'd lie on the floor and scream).

My earliest memories are all television-related. When I was four we went to a garden fete where, among the cakes and 'guess the name of the dolly', the guest of honour was Johnny Ball. That fair messed with my head, I don't mind telling you. Soon afterwards, my parents took me to see the touring show of the Wombles. I'm not entirely sure what I thought my orange heroes might do to me (was I about to be recycled?) but my response, I'm ashamed to say, was to wet myself.

To some degree, everyone is convinced that the telly they watched as they grew up was brilliant and that everything that came afterwards was rubbish. I don't suppose it's any different in my case but, at the same time, I do feel lucky that my early years coincided with the Oliver Postgate era. Postgate was the poet laureate of children's television in all but name, and the creator of such programmes as *Ivor the Engine*, *Bagpuss* and *The Clangers*. His shows had a homespun, homemade feel to them, which came partly from the warmth of Postgate the storyteller and partly from the inventiveness of Postgate the animator: his was a self-taught, self-created style, all lovingly filmed in a converted cowshed.

Everything about Postgate's programmes was wonderfully British: *Ivor the Engine* was set in the 'top left-hand corner of Wales', where Jones the Steam would make tea from Ivor's boiler and Dai Station would worry about things being against regulations; *Bagpuss*, meanwhile, featured mice 'making' chocolate biscuits and a soundtrack of English folk music. Postgate himself had come from a political background (his grandfather was the Labour Party leader George Lansbury) and this worldview seeped into his stories: in one episode of *Ivor the Engine*, Ivor helps a fox escape the hunt (the huntsmen have terribly posh voices and are called things like Carruthers); in another Postgate programme, *Noggin the Nog*, the recipe (or formula) for 'firecake' (or nuclear power) is discovered, complete with mushroom-cloud consequences; the Clangers find themselves puzzling over the concept of money, with Postgate's voiceover telling them how silly it all is — and Postgate even made a special edition of the show for the 1974 election, in which the Clangers are taught the inadequacies of party politics.

There were many other programmes that I ravenously consumed as well – *Camberwick Green* and *Fingerbobs* (complete with bearded Yoffy) also followed the folksy, finger-picked, animated template. But Oliver Postgate was undoubtedly the standout figure: a person whom nobody in children's TV since has ever come close to eclipsing; someone, too, whose humane left-leaning take on the world became quietly, subtly, embedded within me. Proof, if proof were needed, of the huge influence that television can have on a young mind — a fact that would probably have exercised my parents a lot more had they not been in agreement with pretty much everything that Oliver Postgate was saying.

My family were middle class. Indeed, with a father who was a doctor and a mother who was a teacher, I would be hard pressed to pretend that we were anything else. I would say that I make no apologies for that but, being middle class, I am of course terribly sorry about the whole thing. My mother was a feminist, going so far as to do an MA in Women's Studies. The middle-class nature of her political views were encapsulated when York went Conservative in the 1983 general election: my mother 'celebrated' by drawing a moustache on the picture of our triumphant new Tory MP in the local paper — something she strangely omitted to mention when she had a cup of tea with him after church the following Sunday. My dad, meanwhile, very much felt that his political views were between him and the ballot box, a stoical code of proud silence somewhat spoiled by my mother leaning over and advising the tellers exactly how he was voting.

I can't really have many complaints about my childhood. We lived in one of the nice parts of York, which in itself is one of the nice parts of the north of England. York — if you were never forced to go there on a school trip — is rich in all sorts of history, from its Roman walls to the Jorvik Viking Centre to York Minster. (No, I'm not entirely sure why it's a minster and not a cathedral either.) The city is one of those locations that people always describe as 'a nice place to bring up children', which translates as either family-friendly and full of decent schools or just a bit dull. So middle class was our particular street that it had chestnut trees all the way down each side, which was great for conkers until the council came along and hacked them back. Our house, in the middle of our middle-class street, was suitably semi-detached, with the other half occupied by the local vicar.

There were six of us in our family. In television terms, I was Bromley Boy Child One; two years younger was Bromley Boy Child Two, my brother Jonathan — or Joff, as he was called; then there was the Independent Third Version, my sister Helen; and, finally, having arrived in the early eighties like Channel 4, was my youngest sister, Katherine. It was (is) a big family and, barring the usual arguments of growing up, a happy one: if you're looking for a fictional comparison for the Bromleys, the nearest I can think of is probably the Griswolds, the cinematic brood whom Chevy Chase leads in various abortive attempts at vacations (with mildly amusing results) in the *National Lampoon's* series. Indeed, the only abuse I can report my parents for is the middle-class sort of sending us to bed early and dressing us up in Clothkits. Clothkits, for those lucky enough not to know, was a sort of early version of Boden — the main difference being that customers weren't sent the finished article, but instead a load of material and instructions so they could sew the whole thing together themselves. You could always spot Clothkits kids a mile off: they were the ones looking slightly embarrassed in their badly stitched orange dunga-rees, complete with block brown patterns of sunflowers and rocking horses.

There is one other member of the Bromley family I should prob-ably introduce you to, and that, of course, is the television set. It lived in the sitting room, on some shelves to the left of the fireplace. The sitting room itself was decorated, as you might expect, in Habitat and Laura Ashley: the lampshade was one of those white paper globes, while the curtains were dark green and florally patterned. Seating options for watching television were a brown Ercol sofa and armchair, a bright-green beanbag, or warming oneself in front of the fire. We had a proper working fire in those days; a daily job in the morning was to sweep out the grate and refill the coal scuttle.

Our television, it is fair to say, was not the newest model that was available on the market. It didn't have a newfangled remote control, nor one of its cousins, the not-so-remote control that stretched out on a piece of wire. Instead, changing channels involved getting up and pressing the buttons on the set. Or, more specifically, getting the smallest child in the room to get up and do it for you. Above the television, in an elevated position that echoed my mother's views on culture, were books – shelf after shelf of poetry and literature – all looking condescendingly down on their electronic rival.

So there we were, the Clothkits Griswolds (minus our not-yet-born sister Katherine), settling down to watch to watch a new decade of television. I can't remember much about the actual ushering in of the eighties, bar the images of Soviet tanks invading Afghanistan on Christmas Day the week before. The only other thing I remember is the Village People performing their new single on Noel Edmonds' *Multi-Coloured Swap Shop*. The song was one of their lesser-known numbers, 'Ready for the 80s', which they performed on '8' and '0' podiums in their usual collection of outfits from the dressing-up box. As it happened, the eighties weren't quite so ready for the Village

People's upbeat 'everything is going to be great' message and, a bit like Afghanistan, the single took a tanking. It is certainly possible that the song failed to 'trouble the Forty' because it failed to capture the mood of the time: far from looking forward to the eighties, there was a national nervousness about such minor things as mass unemployment and nuclear war. My own theory, for what it is worth, is that the song didn't chart primarily because it was shit.

One of the difficulties in writing a chapter about children's programmes of the eighties is that so many of the shows were repeats. Series that you might have watched in the eighties, and feel are very much part of the decade's firmament, on closer inspection turn out to have belonged to someone and some-*when* else. Many of the Hanna-Barbera cartoons of which I was a massive fan had actually been knocking around for donkey's years: *Hong Kong Phooey* dates back to 1974, *Scooby Doo* began in 1969 and *Wacky Races* first aired in 1968; even older were the likes of *Touché Turtle* (1962), *Top Cat* (1961) and the *Flintstones* (1960).

The same was true of British programmes: Oliver Postgate's *Ivor the Engine* and *Noggin the Nog* had both originally been made in black-and-white in the sixties, before being remade into colour; countless other firm favourites, such as *Chorlton and the Wheelies*, the *Flumps*, *Bod*, *Rentaghost* and *Jamie and the Magic Torch* were all much-repeated seventies shows. *Jamie and the Magic Torch* I used to particularly love, with its 'Pinball Wizard'-style power chords as Jamie's torch created a helter-skelter for him and his dog, Wordsworth, to slide down into a slightly trippy, Yellow Submarine-type world. If one wanted to get all Freudian about things, one might wonder whether Jamie playing with his 'magic torch' was actually a reference to another sort of teenage nocturnal activity. But I won't bring that up here, in case I spoil the memory for you.

It was this sort of quality product – regularly repeated but being discovered for the first time – that the new programmes of the eighties found themselves up against. It's a tall order: the equivalent of Spandau Ballet pitching up to find themselves competing for chart places against the Beatles and the Rolling Stones. In other words, the fact that a lot of children's TV in the eighties seemed a bit rubbish wasn't entirely because it lacked merit. New programmes were juxtaposed with the best of the best, and often seemed second rate by comparison: *Henry's Cat*, for example, was no *Roobarb & Custard*; while *Button Moon* was essentially *The Clangers* remade with kitchen implements.

Having said that, it didn't help that a number of the new shows came across as part children's programme, part advert for the associated merchandise. This trend perhaps took its lead from George Lucas, who had in the late seventies famously kept hold of the merchandising rights to his *Star Wars* trilogy. He'd been able to do this because the studio hadn't considered them to be worth anything (at the time, science-fiction films were not known to be profitable); as it turned out, there were dollars to be made by the bucket-load. Consequently, anyone with an idea for a children's programme now also had several further ideas about tie-in videos, books and figures.

One such example was *Postman Pat*, which over the years has shifted twelve million books, four million videos and DVDs, and has been translated into every language from Persian (*Pat-e Postchi*) to Italian (*Il Postino Pat*). Postman Pat, a little like Mr Spoon on *Button Moon*, got the gig because they needed a name to rhyme in the theme tune – in Pat's case, it had to rhyme with 'black-and-white cat'. Pat and said pet, Jess, delivered both the post and a series of gentle japes in Greendale, a Lake District-like part of the world that, to me, felt only a couple of postcodes along from Peter's mail round in *Camberwick Green*. I've always found it a useful rule of thumb in life to steer clear of people with personalized number plates and Pat (with his 'Pat 1' postal van) is no exception. I'm all for keeping rural post offices open but, if cuts did have to be made, Pat would be my first choice for a P45, given how rubbish he is at the essentially simple task of posting a letter through someone's front door. Back in the eighties, rare was the episode where something or other didn't go wrong on Pat's round. And when Pat got promoted in the recently revamped series – *Postman Pat Special Delivery Service* – his 'special' form of delivery continued, even though he now had a helicopter and other high-tech devices to help him. A second-class show, in my book. Which, of course, this is.

Thomas the Tank Engine and Friends was the ITV adaptation of the train-based children's books written by the Reverend W. Awdry (the W stands for Wilbert). As children's books go, the Thomas books are not universally popular – Ian Jack, the former editor of *Granta*, suggests that 'the real charm of the books lies in the illustrations' and that the stories are 'plain little things, with jerky little sentences that are hard to read aloud'. There is also something a little old-fashioned and moralistic in these tales of stuck-up engines and troublesome trucks, which I guess fits in with the steam-train setting and is why they made a comeback in the 1980s. For the TV series the 'jerky little sentences' were given to former Beatles drummer Ringo Starr to read; Starr was to check himself into detox for alcoholism a couple of years later, which led to lots of predictable jokes about Ringo the Red-Nosed Engine and so forth. Not that this stopped the merchandising going full steam ahead: if you allowed your children to eat TV dinners, you could even serve them Thomas the Tank Engine pasta shapes while they watched the programme.

Going one better, or possibly one worse, was *He-Man and the Masters of the Universe*, which was a toy first and a cartoon series second. The toy manufacturer Mattel came up with the idea in 1980 and, by the mid-1980s – with a little help from the accompanying show – had shifted $500 million worth of their He-Man toys, and made a further $500 million by the licensing of He-Man toothbrushes, He-Man alarm clocks and He-Man underwear.

He-Man was in real life (if one can use 'real life' to describe a cartoon drawing) Prince Adam of Eternia. Prince Adam was a bit wet, as princes go, a fact that could be detected by the pink waistcoat in which he swanned about ('girly-pink', as Arnold Schwarzenegger would call it). All changed when, on his eighteenth birthday, the Sorceress gave He-Man his magic sword (are we in magic-torch territory here?) and, by the power of Grayskull . . . He! Had! The! Power! As if by magic, Prince Adam was completely transformed into, well, pretty much still Prince Adam, actually, except he was now dressed like Hunter from *Gladiators*. As makeovers went, we weren't exactly in Spider-Man or Incredible Hulk territory. Despite this, He-Man's nominal love interest, Teela, never quite worked out that Prince Adam and He-Man were the same person. It didn't seem to cross her mind that whenever He-Man appeared Price Adam just happened to vanish, and that — silly costumes aside — the two different men *looked exactly the same*. Even Clark Kent bothered to put a pair of glasses on.

While He-Man was flashing his sword around, his pet, a cowardly green-and-yellow striped tiger called Cringer, became the 'mighty Battle Cat'. He-Man then proved he was the most powerful (if not the brightest) man in the universe by punching the television screen. His main enemy was Skeletor, essentially a skull in a hoodie who combined all the classic evil-villain stereotypes: laughing manically at his own brilliance while failing to see even the most basic flaws in his plans, etcetera. He wasn't helped by his poor selection of sidekicks, a motley crew of complete morons such as Beast Man (he looked a bit like a beast), Mer-Man (a bit like Beast Man, but more fishy) and Triclops (a supposed 'Master of Vision', despite only having one working eye). There was also the Sorceress of the Night; you'd be forgiven for thinking she might be called Black Magic or Moon Woman, but she actually went under the name of Evil Lyn. One can only assume there was some similarly named primary-school teacher on whom the writer wanted revenge.

He-Man himself had a twin sister, the equally subtly titled She-Ra, Princess of Power. If you thought Skeletor's posse had bad names, well . . . She-Ra's friends included Castaspella (she could cast spells), Flutterina (she could flutter like a butterfly) and Netossa (she could toss nets). And that's not to mention She-Ra's sworn enemy, Hordak, whose horde of horribles included Catra (she was a bit like a cat), Scorpia (she was a bit like a Scorpion) and Camilla (she was a bit like a horse). I might have made the last one up.

At the end of each episode one of the characters would give viewers a patronizing little lecture based on the moral lessons to be learned from that show's story – a Jerry Springer-style 'Final Thought' in the days when Springer was still digesting the fact that being mayor of a major American city and hiring prostitutes is not always a vote-winning combination. I don't remember He-Man ever cautioning against that, though (*'A word of advice, Jerry: next time don't pay by cheque!'*). Instead he focused his attention on the importance of being wary of strangers, of believing in oneself, and of not falling for what was essentially a corporate-driven marketing exercise thinly dressed up as a children's cartoon.

One message that He-Man did impress strongly was the value of truthfulness. For all that he might have had a point, one of the most significant discoveries kids make when growing up is that adults aren't always completely honest in their dealings with them. I still remain scarred from the experience of having a letter read out on Radio One by Bruno Brookes, who then said, and I quote: 'I'll send you a pen in the post, mate.' Did Bruno ever send me said pen in the post, thus providing me with the proof needed to convince my sceptical class-mates I'd been on the radio? No, Bruno, 'mate', you didn't.

The ones who really lie to you, of course, are your parents. Some of the lies are born of the desire to avoid difficult questions – things like telling you that Fluffy the rabbit has gone away on holiday or that babies come from storks or off the back of lorries. Other lies are forced on to parents by convention – the existence of the tooth fairy, the Easter Bunny and Father Christmas. I have to say, I was on to the

12

latter fairly early as our 'Santa' couldn't be bothered to take the price tags off the stocking presents. Not only that, but he also appeared to do his shopping at the local newsagent's. I briefly considered challenging my parents on the sheer duplicity of proceedings, but I figured I quite liked getting the presents so kept my mouth shut instead.

There is a third kind of parental lie: the sort that plays on the blind gullibility of young children and their predilection to believe whatever their mother and father tell them. For me, the head hoodwinker was undoubtedly my dad. And his big fib concerned the popular children's-television presenter Rolf Harris. Rolf, my dad repeatedly claimed, had ended up on British screens because he'd been forcibly deported from his home country.

'Nobody liked him in Australia,' Dad explained convincingly. 'In fact, everyone hated him so much that he was asked to leave the country.'

Because it was told to me at just the right impressionable age, the Rolf Harris story stuck in my mind for many years to come. Indeed, I once had a heated argument on the subject with someone at university. Certainly to my seven-year-old self the deportation myth did not seem completely far-fetched. After all, in the late 1970s and early 1980s York was one of many places to take its share of 'boat people' – Vietnamese refugees who had risked everything to escape their war-ravaged country. My mother taught English to some of the families, who by all accounts weren't particularly chuffed to be in York. I guess if you'd been promised the sunshine of California and ended up in a run-down council estate in the north of England you wouldn't be completely thrilled either. With my mother returning from her teaching sessions with extraordinary stories of the families' journeys – storms on the high seas, being chased by pirates – my father's Rolf story took on a life of its own. I imagined him sat at the helm of an overcrowded boat, making a Rolf-type shivering noise, and clutching his paintbrush and wobble-board close to his chest.

13

'Oh yes,' Dad would tell me, having really warmed to his theme, 'we were the only country stupid enough to let him in. Rolf Harris, with his ridiculous songs and his rubbish painting.'

'Two Little Boys' was on our cassette of Ed Stewart's *Junior Choice*, much to my father's dislike. Every time the song played it was accompanied by his running commentary about how useless Rolf was. And whenever Rolf got the paintbrush out on one of his many TV shows and asked, 'Can you tell what it is yet?' Dad couldn't resist answering . . .

'I can tell what it is. It's another one of your lousy pictures.'

Rolf himself might be a little surprised by my father's revisionist history of his early years. He actually came to England in the late 1950s of his own volition in order to study art. From there it was a career of cartoons and records and television shows. By the start of the 1980s he was hosting *Rolf on Saturday OK?* and he remained a mainstay throughout the decade with his various cartoon clubs, first on the BBC and then ITV. (His *Animal Hospital* and cover of 'Stairway to Heaven' are, sadly, beyond the remit of this book.)

Quite what beef my father had with Rolf I was never entirely sure. Dad takes offence at very little, so it's a little odd that something as harmless as a man crinkling his face up and going 'hoohahooha-hooha' should so get his goat. But if his plan was to evict Rolf from our house, it backfired a little. Rather than following my father's lead in loathing Rolf, the seven-year-old me felt that he deserved the same sympathy as the Vietnamese boat people my mother was teaching. Thus, to my father's quiet disgust, rather than watching less Rolf I actually ended up watching more. All of which probably tells you more about the consequences of lying than *He-Man* ever did.

Rolf on Saturday, OK or not, was just one of the weekend's many children's programmes. Saturday morning, of course, was where most of these could be found, though what was on was not quite as good as what had been on the decade before. While *Multi-Coloured Swap Shop* and *Tiswas* (both of which ceased to air in 1982) had been fresh, funny and innovative, it says much that the most memorable moment of Mike Read's *Saturday Superstore* was when a caller – named Simon, I believe – told pop band Matt Bianco 'You're a bunch of wankers.' Similarly, the standout incident from *Going Live!* was when someone called Eliot phoned in to ask the equally risible Five Star 'why they're so fucking crap?'

Of course, not everything on children's TV in the eighties was feeble: *Grange Hill* was great (a programme I'll return to in a later chapter); *Danger Mouse* was always good squeaky fun, with David Jason as the world-saving mouse, and Terry *'and June'* Scott as his sidekick Penfold; *Willo the Wisp* had lots of fans (if not me) thanks to the voice of Kenneth Williams; *Jigsaw* I always liked, even though it was all rather weird – characters included Jigg the jigsaw piece, a pterodactyl called Ptery, and Noseybonk, a slightly nightmarish masked man with a huge white nose.

Perhaps the greatest contribution that eighties television gave to children's TV was in its selection of foreign cartoons and dramas, often adapted from classic books, that went on for what seemed like eternity. I might be wrong, but I'm assuming that what happened was that a commissioning editor from the BBC had lunch with one of his chums from French or German or Japanese TV and, after one too many glasses of wine, returned to the office with a carrier-bag full of video cassettes and the schedule sorted for the next six months. Which might have made life easy for him, but was hell for those viewers who didn't like the shows.

One such programme was *Heidi*, a Swiss-German drama series that was so dreary and went on for months and months. *Heidi* was the adaptation of Johanna Spyri's novel *Heidi's Years of Wandering and Learning*. And years of Heidi wandering about there certainly seemed to be. Oh look: there's Heidi in the Alps with her grandfather and Peter the goatherd! Here's Heidi in Frankfurt with sickly Clara, dreaming of the fresh mountain air! Oh no! Now Heidi's all feeble and sleepwalking! Better get her back to the mountains and reading to Peter's blind grandmother! What's this? Clara has come to join Heidi in the Alps? But wait, Peter has pushed her wheelchair down the mountain! Don't worry – it turns out that Clara can walk after all!

The lack of anything even remotely interesting happening was not helped by the sort of dubbing that appeared to be suffering from a satellite-style delay. So Heidi's lips would be going ten to the dozen, asking, I don't know, '*Entschuldigen sie bitte, wie komme ich am besten zum bahnhof?*' and three seconds later a dismembered voice would say, 'Hello, goat boy.' So bad was the delay – and I think I remember this rightly – that the final episode was just a black screen as they caught up with thirty minutes of missing dialogue.

Meanwhile, someone in Spain had the bright idea of doing a cartoon version of Alexander Dumas' *The Three Musketeers*. But – get this – rather than doing the cartoon with people, all the characters would be canine! So the musketeers became 'muskehounds' and D'Artagnan became Dogtanian! I'm sure whoever came up with all this was very pleased with themselves, but, while *Heidi* traded in tedium, *Dogtanian* went for irritation as its calling card: the lead character, one of literature's most dashing heroes, was now a Scrappy Doo-style puppy with a Postman Pat ability to get himself into scrapes. And as for the 'One for all and all for one' theme tune, I can only apologize if that is now going round in your head.

This anthropomorphizing of world classics continued with *Around the World with Willy Fogg*, in which both the puns and the eighty days' time restriction were dropped but the dressing up of animals continued. Less irritating, but still not very good.

A far better idea was to adapt Homer's *Odyssey* and set it in the future: the result was *Ulysses 31*. Ulysses (or 'Ulysee-ee-ee-es' as the theme tune had it) handily rhymed with galaxies, which (like Postman Pat and Mr Spoon) was probably why he got the part. Ulysses had hacked the Gods off royally in an incident that involved killing a sci-fi version of Cyclops and freeing various enslaved children in the process – among them his son, Telemachus. Which doesn't strike me as a particularly bad thing to have got up to, but the net result was that Ulysses was sentenced to travel among unknown stars, and to have the way back to Earth wiped from the ship computer's memory: cue another batch of endless adventures. With his flowing locks and full beard, Ulysses looked very much like a late-period Beatle. Except that rather than Ono the irritating Japanese girlfriend he had to make do with Nono the equally annoying small robot.

The *War and Peace* of these adaptations was not, in fact, *War and Peace* – probably a good thing, as I'm not sure the world was ready for nineteenth-century Russians re-imagined as rabbits and foxes. Instead, the book was Scott O'Dell's 1960s children's novel, *The King's Fifth*. This might not immediately ring any bells, but probably sounds more familiar when I tell you it concerned a sixteenth-century Spanish boy called Esteban, who joined a ship sailing for the New World in the search of shiny treasure.

The Mysterious Cities of Gold was so long it put all the other foreign series in the shade: while most of the others here clocked in at a not-inconsiderable twenty-six episodes (or, put another way, a full half year of Thursday evenings), *The Mysterious Cities . . .* ran at thirty-nine consecutive episodes. I could tell you in detail what happened but we'd be here for the rest of the book. In a nutshell, a Spanish explorer called Mendoza was searching for said golden cities; accompanying him were Esteban (in search of his father), Zia (the kidnapped daughter of an Inca priest, there to help with the translation), and Tao (the irritating last living descendant of some underwater, Atlantis-style civilization).

I can only assume that Mendoza must have been kicking himself for leaving Spain without bringing his map with him, because the characters then proceeded to undertake the sort of endless American tour that has been the breaking point of many a British rock band. In that slightly annoying way, finding a mysterious city was not the end of the programme: there was also the collapse of ancient civilizations to deal with, along with a whole race of strange creatures frozen underneath a mountain, some sort of nuclear-power system that the ancients had come up with, and a giant bird-type plane called the *Golden Condor* (it was apparently solar-powered, which I'm sure can't be a great way to run a plane).

I'm carping slightly because I watched *The Mysterious Cities of Gold* religiously, despite the religion being some kind of new-wave mumbo-jumbo. Like *Ulysses*, the series felt fresh in its foreignness: Japanese-style animation through a French translation filter. Hanna-Barbera cartoons were great, but they never (to my knowledge) attempted anything with this sort of range. Things have regressed a little since then: these days everything is now English-originated (besides the odd drama on BBC4, the same is true of adult programmes too). It might be cheaper in terms of translation costs, but it presents a narrower, more Anglo-centric worldview as a result. It's not so much that the past is another country; more, in the context of children's television, that other countries are now part of the past.

The nearest the eighties had to an Oliver Postgate figure was probably Raymond Briggs. Briggs is primarily a children's author and illustrator, and his books *Fungus the Bogeyman* and *Father Christmas* were extremely well-thumbed favourites in our school library. He has a political touch too: *When the Wind Blows* is about the effects of a nuclear attack, while his picture book *The Tin-Pot Foreign General and the Old Iron Woman* concerns the Falklands War. Given his popularity, it is no surprise that a number of his books have been adapted for film and TV, none more famously so than the Channel 4 version of *The Snowman*.

The Snowman was first shown in December 1982, shortly after Channel 4 had launched, and was one of the station's early successes: it won that year's BAFTA for Best Children's Programme and was nominated for an Oscar. Perhaps its biggest prize was to become a staple of Christmas television, being regularly repeated every festive season since. The cartoon itself is a fairly faithful adaptation of Briggs' original book: the story of a young boy who builds a snowman that magically comes to life at night. The two major additions for the TV adaptation were the inclusion of David Bowie, who in the opening scene played the young boy in adult life, looking back through an attic of memories, and the song 'Walking in the Air', which accompanies the scene where the snowman and the boy fly through the night sky (the song, incidentally, was sung by choirboy Paul Auty; Aled Jones' subsequent hit single was just a cover).

Right from the off, *The Snowman* had the look and feel of a children's classic. And, unlike some of its more sanitized and moralistic rivals, this was a cartoon that didn't pull its punches. Because, for all of the cuteness of the choirboy singing and the carefree relationship between child and snow, it ended with the boy waking up the following day to discover that the snowman had melted into a pool of mush. Even now, I don't think I'm the only person to have found myself in a similar position on the sofa as a result. That's partly to do with the shock of a sad finale among the usual sea of happy endings, but the programme also tugs the strings because it touches on something bigger. I don't know if this was the intention, but I've always understood the melting of the snowman to be a metaphor for the end of childhood innocence – the sort of complex emotional subject that very few children's programmes from the eighties were brave enough to tackle. It is this bravery that goes some way to explaining why, of all the children's programmes from the eighties, *The Snowman* is virtually the only one that is still regularly repeated, and still resonates today.

After the break, we head north to meet a man having problems with a ferret, meet another with a bare bottom and a teddy bear, and a third with his hand up a cow's posterior . . .

Ad Break

The Leeds

Down to the dogs now, where a popular dodgy dealer is trying his hand at greyhound racing. No, not Del Boy: the other one – Arthur Daley. There's no sign of his minder today, mind: just his dog, Gonzalez, triumphing in all the races and Arthur taking his winnings down to his building society, the Leeds. The account is called 'Liquid Gold', which may or may not be the same molten pool from which the Yorkshire TV chevron rises. Anyway, it feels slightly surprising to find Daley in a building society at all, let alone in a Yorkshire one, as you'd half expect him to keep his money in a fat roll under the mattress. I guess Arthur is streetwise enough to know that Yorkshire people are – how can I put this? – careful with their money, which is probably why they needed so many building societies: the Leeds, Bradford & Bingley, the Halifax and so on.

In one of life's little ironies, the one time Arthur makes money out of something legit, he gets done over himself. While he is sat in the pub sipping his pint, Gonzalez is lured away, in true Daley fashion, by a man with a string of pork-and-beef sausages. Well, two can play at that game: when Gonzales returns to the greyhound track under a different guise, Daley is there in the crowd with something to distract him – a tiny poodle called Fifi. I don't speak greyhound myself, but like to imagine that Gonzalez is crooning in her ear: '*I could be so good for you . . .*'

Episode Two

'I'd like to apologize to our viewers in the north'

I had something of a Hovis childhood. I wasn't Yorkshire born but was very much Yorkshire bred. I'd actually been born many miles further south, in Salisbury, but we'd moved up to York when I was two. Those very early childhood years were not something I could remember, and their existence was something I learned not to bring up in conversation, polite or otherwise. Yorkshire was a place for Yorkshire people, and the fact that you were actually a 'soft southerner' was not the sort of revelation to win you many friends.

There's a classic comedy sketch called 'The Four Yorkshiremen', performed by Monty Python in their 1982 film *Live at the Hollywood Bowl* but originally part of another, late-1960s series called *At Last the 1948 Show*. In the sketch, the four Yorkshiremen take turns to boast about how difficult and terrible their respective childhoods

23

were, going to increasingly ridiculous lengths to lord it over the previous speaker: 'Cardboard Box? Luxury!' It was funny because of the truth behind the joke – it combined the feeling that everything someone from Yorkshire did had to be bigger and better with the idea that proper Yorkshire people both *were* tougher and *had it* tougher than anyone else.

This sense of pride and self-belief was reinforced by a sense of separateness from the rest of the country. In a sketch from Victoria Wood's television show, her spoof television announcer, played by Susie Blake, says, 'I'd like to apologize to our viewers in the north. It must be awful for them.' This perception was backed up by that of the county's then most successful football team, 'Dirty Dirty' Leeds United. Leeds fans would regularly chant about how everyone didn't like them – and about how they didn't care. All of which served to foster a strong local pride and a strange dislocation whereby the rest of the country looked down on Yorkshire and Yorkshire looked down on the rest of the country.

Nowhere was this philosophy about Yorkshire more engrained than in its policy towards cricket. Yorkshire County Cricket Club had a very simple rule when it came to who was allowed to represent them: only those born within the 'historic borders' of Yorkshire were eligible to play. People would go to great lengths to achieve the necessary status. I had one friend at school whose mother during labour was driven fifty miles over the border so her child-to-be might one day represent his county. The agony of her contractions as the car screeched up the M1 to Sheffield was not entirely without reward: fortunately, she gave birth to a son. Unfortunately, though, spectatorship turned out to be his main sporting prowess.

There was an unspoken problem with the 'Yorkshire-born' policy: that being that seemingly everyone who was born within the county – Geoffrey Boycott aside – was crap at cricket. The other counties, who had adopted the slapdash policy of not caring where their players came from, had the pick of the best players and walloped Yorkshire accordingly. The once-great county team hadn't won anything for years and spent their seasons bumping along at the bottom of the league.

Geoffrey Boycott, sometimes known as GLY or Greatest Living Yorkshireman, summed up much of what being from Yorkshire was all about. One of the cricketing greats, he was, depending on who you talked to, either brilliant or obstinate, single-minded or self-obsessed. Geoffrey was famous for scoring runs at a snail's pace and not giving his wicket away: once he was in, he could stick it out at the crease for as long as it took, playing forward-defensive shot after forward-defensive shot for what could seem like days, weeks, even months. In one test match, so legend has it, Ian Botham was sent in on team orders to run his team mate out so things could be speeded up a bit.

I met Boycott once, in the late eighties, when I was working in a bookshop where he was doing a book-signing.

'Come on, lad, get cracking,' he said to me. Given the number of his innings I'd been forced to sit through, this felt a bit rich.

Pride in all things Yorkshire could be stretched to incredible lengths. If Geoffrey Boycott was the Greatest Living Yorkshireman, then the Worst was the county's second-most famous inhabitant: Peter Sutcliffe, the 'Yorkshire Ripper'. For the best part of a decade Sutcliffe had gone about his horrific business of assaulting or murdering numerous women – some of them prostitutes and some of them not – in particularly unpleasant ways. In 1981, after several false starts, the police finally caught up with Sutcliffe after a chance encounter over a driving charge, and he was put away for life.

Clearly he was not a nice person and psychologically a few cans of Double Diamond short of a six-pack. And yet his Yorkshire moniker was difficult to completely ignore. After all, how many other counties could lay claim to having their own Ripper? Exactly. Consequently there was a sense of grim pride in him being 'our' Ripper: *I tell thee, lad, people can say what they like about that Sutcliffe, but he grafted for them murders . . .*'

In television terms, Yorkshire's identity was reinforced by the region-alization of ITV. Just as no other county had their own Ripper, so no other county had their own television area: it was all Southern this, or Central that. Yorkshire Television, along with its golden emblem, shone out. Broadcasting out of Leeds, it pre-empted a number of the big television changes of the 1980s: in the late 1970s, YTV ran a trial breakfast-television programme, five years before the launch of *TV-am* and the BBC's *Breakfast Time*; it launched a quiz show called *Calendar Countdown* before Channel 4 was born; and in the mid-1980s became the first ITV region to broadcast through the night.

The host of *Calendar Countdown* was Richard Whiteley, who of course later hosted Channel 4's *Countdown*. Prior to the launch of Channel 4, Whiteley was best known for an incident involving him and a ferret on our local news programme. In every way, this was a piece of television that could only happen in Yorkshire: where else would you find a ferret fancier plus ferrets invited into a television studio? With an unerring sense of inevitability (though it's possible I think that simply because I've seen the clip so many times) the ferret Whiteley was holding locked its teeth on to his left hand and refused to let go. So far, so *It'll Be Alright on the Night*. But what makes the scene a 'Yorkshire' one is the ferret fancier's disinterested response.

'Put it on the floor,' he told Whiteley in a matter-of-fact way. 'It won't hurt you.'

Richard Whiteley clearly disagreed, and the best part of a minute later the ferret was still biting down hard. With a continued air of indifference, the fancier finally prized the ferret's jaw open and set Whiteley free.

'If that meant business it would have been through to the bone,' he said, making clear what a big girl's blouse Whiteley was being. As if to reinforce the point, he then added: '*She*'s playing with you.'

Like I said, only in Yorkshire.

*

Whatever you might think of the people, Yorkshire has stunning countryside on offer. From the North York Moors to the Yorkshire Dales, the coastline of Whitby and Robin Hood's Bay to three Peaks, there's a lot to see. And, every Sunday, I saw a lot of it. My parents, like all upstanding middle-class folk, saw the seventh day not as a day of rest but as a day of improvement. Following church in the morning and a roast for lunch, Sunday afternoon was set aside for either a bracing country walk or, more likely, a visit to one of Yorkshire's stately homes or historical relics.

The jewel in Yorkshire's crown was Castle Howard, a 300-year-old stately home that wasn't actually a castle at all but a palatial structure topped off with a St Paul's-style dome. It boasted enormous and well-manicured lands, including an impressively large fountain and a mausoleum, an ice house (disappointingly not actually made of ice), and the 'Temple of the Four Winds', which was just a bit exposed.

On separate occasions, both Joff and I disgraced ourselves at Castle Howard. For my brother it was by stepping over one of those purple ropes separating the furniture from the tourists. He'd done so after a prolonged discussion between us as to what would happen if the rope was crossed. What happened was that an alarm went off, and we got one of those stiff talkings-to you get from the sort of sour-faced wardens who don't like being woken from their slumber in the corner.

My own crime was having the temerity to sit down in a chair. In my defence, I was feeling a little tired – something I put down to the soporific effect that the humidity in such buildings has on me (and, I'm ashamed to say, still does). Unfortunately, the chair I chose to sit on was the best part of 300 years old.

In 1981, Castle Howard was one of the most famous buildings on television, though it was better known by another name, Brideshead Castle – it being the setting of ITV's adaptation of Evelyn Waugh's *Brideshead Revisited*. This wasn't just any old adaptation: costing £10 million to make, and at more than twelve hours long, this was one of the biggest and most lavish drama series ever made in Britain. It might seem odd now to think that it was ITV, rather than the BBC, who made such a show. In more ways than one it was a case of the commercial broadcaster quite literally parking their vehicles on the BBC's lawn – Castle Howard was owned by George Howard, then Chairman of the BBC.

Ten million pounds is a lot of dough for a television series even today; thirty years ago, it was an enormous sum of money. What ITV got for their money was a veritable *Who's Who* of British actors: Laurence Olivier, John Gielgud, Claire Bloom and Stephane Audran were just some of the famous names to take part. The stars of the programme, however, were the then relatively unknown Jeremy Irons, who played Charles Ryder, and Anthony Andrews, who was given the role of Sebastian Flyte.

Brideshead Revisited begins during the Second World War, when soldier Charles Ryder is posted to Brideshead Castle. This is the 'revisiting' of the title, as Brideshead was once the home of his close friend Sebastian Flyte, whom Ryder met as a student at Oxford. The story follows their relationship in the years before the war: living it up at Brideshead together; Charles' infatuation with Sebastian's sister, Julia; Sebastian's fun-loving outlook descending into alcoholism; Julia's ultimate rejection of Charles in favour of her belief in Catholicism.

As well as Brideshead and Oxford, the story takes the characters to Venice, where Charles' father (Laurence Olivier) lived, to Morocco (where Sebastian ends up) and on an ocean liner bound for America (where Charles is reacquainted with Julia). And, although all these locations were faithfully and expensively filmed (the liner sequences were filmed on board the *QE2* as she steamed across the Atlantic), it was Castle Howard as Brideshead that captured the audience's imagination as much as it did the main character's.

It would be stretching the point to suggest that I sat rapturously throughout what Anthony Burgess described as 'the best piece of fictional television ever made'. The sorry truth is that it didn't take me long to clock that Brideshead was the place with the chairs you weren't allowed to sit down on and promptly declare I was going to watch no such thing. I was wrong to be so dismissive, of course, and also in the minority. The only person besides myself who didn't fall in love with the programme was Clive James, then television critic for the *Observer*. And admittedly his criticisms were a touch more sophisticated than mine. James considered the adaptation to be 'windier' than Waugh's original novel, and not just the scene where Charles and Sebastian were buttock-naked: 'very worthy, even estimable, but still inexorably enslaved to the stylistic beauty of the original text . . . the series is a Fabergé curate's egg,' he eloquently concluded.

In the outside world Clive James was, like me in the Bromley household, a lone voice. The series pulled in an audience of nine million viewers, which is the same sort of number that *The X Factor* pulls in today. It partly owed its success to a great cast, a great setting and a great original novel. But two other factors helped it really stand out, the first of which was the timing of the programme's release. In a documentary about the making of *Brideshead*, producer Derek Granger suggested that, 'The beginning of the eighties was Thatcherism and a new kind of affluence. The stock market was booming and we were out of those gloomy, frozen seventies. There was a kind of feeling that people wanted luxury. And I think this big, luxuriant, opulent, hugely expensive show, showing wealth and ostentation, just hit a nerve.'

I also think its sheer length was beneficial. To condense a novel into a feature film or a two- or three-part drama usually involves ripping out most of the story bar the nuts and bolts of the main narrative. Allowing the story to spread out over many more hours lets an adaptation really breathe, and avoids losing anything important. I was once fortunate enough to hear Anthony Minghella speak about the making of *The English Patient*. His original cut of the film, which included everything from the novel he wanted to keep in, was eight hours in length.

This makes one consider the success of such critically acclaimed modern American drama series as *The Wire*, *The Sopranos* or *Mad Men*, because surely the latitude of these extended series allows the characters and stories the extra dimension that makes the programmes so popular. Of course, the size of the US means the potential audience for quality drama is larger than in the UK, which in turn means the budget is greater and it's possible to make the shows more expansive. In the UK, where the equivalent audience is smaller and budgets therefore likewise, programmes like *Brideshead Revisited* are the exceptions to the norm: usually our series are shorter, with all the narrative constraints that implies.

Castle Howard was not the only place in Yorkshire being turned into a film set during the eighties. The West Yorkshire village of Holmfirth was the setting for the long-running sitcom *Last of the Summer Wine*; Esholt, near Bradford, was better known as the location for *Emmerdale Farm*; a quiet corner store in a Doncaster sidestreet was turned into Arkwright's, Ronnie Barker's shop in *Open All Hours*; and, high in the Yorkshire Dales, Askrigg became Darrowby, the fictional home of *All Creatures Great and Small*.

Last of the Summer Wine I always found a little corked. Compo, Foggy and Clegg were the three ageing amigos who, for half an hour on a Sunday evening, would get involved in some sort of minor jaunt or scrape that would all be resolved quite happily by the time the credits rolled. To me, it made Yorkshire look like some sort of flat-capped Eternity: a place where the only things to ever die are jokes.

Emmerdale, meanwhile, was very much *Emmerdale Farm* back then. The show wasn't the only thing to change its name: the village itself was originally called Beckindale. If *Last of the Summer Wine* specialized in 'proper' surnames, like Dewhurst and Utterthwaite,

Emmerdale went for right-classic Christian names, such as Seth and Amos. The characters would wander around the fields worrying about the lambing season before retiring to the Woolpack for a pint of real ale and a chorus of 'Nay, Mr Wilks'.

Should anyone be in any doubt as to just how Yorkshire they were, the characters were given the sort of facial hair that can be grown only by having worked on the land since 1873. Amos Brearly, the local land-lord, brandished a set of sideburns that made Noddy Holder's efforts look little more than teenage bum fluff. Poacher Seth Armstrong, meanwhile, had the sort of moustache that would take one dismiss-ive look at Tom Selleck and say, 'Now this, sunshine, is a moustache.' So twirling was his nasal topiary that from certain angles it looked as though he was blowing black steam out of his nostrils.

One wonders why, when they found a sheep bleating about a sore neck, the owners of Emmerdale Farm never gave Skeldale House in Darrowby a ring and asked for the services of James Herriot. The North Riding town of Darrowby was home to his veterinary practice in *All Creatures Great and Small*. Actually, probably the reason that James Herriot never got such a call was that his programme was, like *Brideshead Revisited*, set before the war. It was based on a series of bestselling books by James Herriot (the pen name of real-life vet Alf Wight), called things like *If Only They Could Talk* and *It Shouldn't Happen to a Vet*, which had been bundled up into a single volume for the US market: *All Creatures Great and Small*. This was originally made into a film starring, among others, Anthony Hopkins. I haven't seen it, so can't confirm whether he pan-fried a newly born calf with some fava beans and a bottle of Chianti. The film might not have set the world on fire, but did enough for the BBC to consider adapting the books for a TV show.

All Creatures Great and Small starred Christopher Timothy as James Herriot, Robert Hardy as the eccentric Siegfried and Peter Davison as Tristan. Timothy's wife was first played by Carol Drinkwater (who went on to write books about making olive oil) and then Lynda Bellingham (who went on to make gravy). The programme's title was a little misleading: Darrowby was not exactly bustling with a Noah's ark of animals. Rather, the 'all creatures' were actually 'all the creatures you might find on a 1930s Yorkshire farm', with the 'great' being a prize cow and the 'small' being Tricki-Woo, an irritating pet Pekinese.

The programme offered up what always struck me as a curious combination of rolling Yorkshire countryside, the gentlest of Sunday-night comedy and the sight of Peter Davison with his hand stuck up a cow's backside. That, let's be honest, is what everyone remembers from the programme. That and putting the mug of Mellow Bird's back down on the table because it suddenly didn't seem quite so appetizing. Despite knowing what was about to happen, you were never quite able to tear your eyes away from the screen. In fact, the opposite was usually the case.

'Quick!' I'd shout as whichever vet on duty rolled their sleeve up and dunked their forearm in a bucket of cold water. 'He's going in!'

Whereupon my brother would rush into the sitting room and we'd utter a collective, 'Eeeuw!'

The secret to sticking your arm up a bovine bottom (should you ever find yourself in such a situation) is apparently to make your hand flat, like a fish, and then wiggle it up the channel. The reason the vets went to such lengths – apart from to show off – was usually to do with a cow being with calf. A skilled practitioner could feel around, find the foetus and from its size predict how far gone Ermintrude was. One had to be extremely careful in one's rummaging: a less skilled vet would find their groping around becoming just plain groping. Believe me, that can lead to an acutely awkward silence in the meadow the following morning.

The final episode of the original run pulled in 16 million people. There followed a succession of Christmas specials (where the cow was substituted for a turkey) before a further three series took the story beyond the Second World War. Not that you'd really know: like the facial-hair fashions in *Emmerdale Farm*, one got the feeling that nothing ever really changed.

Christopher Timothy wasn't actually from Yorkshire (he was born in Wales) and indeed neither was James Herriot (Alf Wight was born in Scotland). But the success of *All Creatures Great and Small* led to them being made 'Honorary Yorkshiremen' in the early 1990s. From a county not renowned for its love of outsiders, this was something of an accolade. Their place in local culture was cemented when Alf Wight died in 1995 and more than 2000 people turned up to his funeral in York Minster.

By the start of the nineties Yorkshire was beginning to change. *Emmerdale Farm* was now just *Emmerdale* and its rural plotlines were being swapped for more raunchy ones. In 1993, to ram the 'we've changed' point home, a Lockerbie-style plane crash in the village cleared out about half the cast. Even Yorkshire Cricket Club altered its rules with an embarrassed cough. Now you could play for the county even if you hadn't been born there – you just had to have gone to school there. This meant that a bright young batting prospect called Michael Vaughan, born (gasp!) in Lancashire but educated in Yorkshire, was eligible for selection.

It also meant that I, too, could play for the county. *Could* being the crucial word. I had by now found my role in a cricket team, which was to come in to bat at number nine. Nothing wrong with that, you might think, for a bowler. Except that I didn't bowl either. I remain almost unique in cricketing circles: a non-bowling, tail-order specialist batsman, a position sometimes known as 'making up the numbers'.

To anyone outside Yorkshire the degree to which 'being Yorkshire' mattered, growing up, might seem odd. Similarly, I can understand someone who watched these programmes might wonder what it was about them that bothered me so much. After all, the Yorkshire that television decided to show was either about old people in the present day or young people in the olden days. It was nostalgic and old fashioned – a white-rose-tinted take on small, close-knit communities the modern world had somehow passed by. Even *Brideshead Revisted*, a non-Yorkshire show with a very Yorkshire setting, was a tale about clinging on to a past that was no longer really there. It's a depiction of Yorkshire that continues to be lapped up: in 1992 the ITV drama *Heartbeat* began. That show, based in another fictional Yorkshire village (this time Aidensfield), was originally set in 1964; given that we're now in 2010, the show should by now have reached the early 1980s – but instead it remains stuck in a television time-warp.

I wonder if the problem I have with some of these programmes is that they suffered from Sunday-night syndrome: *Heartbeat, All Creatures Great and Small, Open All Hours* and *Last of the Summer Wine* all found their home on the Sunday-evening schedules, nestling alongside such other thrilling rollercoaster rides as *Songs of Praise* and *Antiques Roadshow*. As a child in the Bromley household, Sunday night meant bath night – hair washed, and early to bed for school the following morning. These programmes for me, then, are forever associated with the drudgery of that, and the fact that the weekend was winding down to a close. It did cross my mind more than once that my parents had done a deal with the TV schedulers – to get them to put on a series of soporific shows to reduce the level of household arguments on a Sunday. When the alternative was watching Compo, Foggy and Clegg roll down a hillside in an old tin bath, having a bath yourself didn't seem such a bad option after all.

That still leaves the question as to why it is Yorkshire itself that is so often considered the ideal home for these sleepy shows. I can only guess that the producers once saw Geoffrey Boycott bat.

After the break, we visit a country overrun by innuendo, meet a man who has had his microphone bent and discover the dangers of not looking when you lean against the bar . . .

Ad Break

Maxell Cassette Tapes

To the outside of a café, where a man is recreating the bit from the Bob Dylan film *Don't Look Back* where his Bobness holds up the words to his song 'Subterranean Homesick Blues' on large pieces of card. Except this chap isn't grooving along to 'Subterranean Homesick Blues', but to the 1960s hit 'The Israelites' by Desmond Dekker and the Aces. Except the words written on the cards he's holding up aren't the lyrics to 'The Israelites', but to a similar-sounding song apparently called 'My Ears are Alight'. In fact, none of the lyrics he holds up are quite the same as what we're listening to. So this poor chap is hearing things like 'Cheese head' and 'Why find my kids' . . .

So what is going on? Is the guy a little bit deaf? Does he require a Morrissey-style hearing aid in order to work out what the lyrics are? As it turns out, the problem is not his hearing: it's that he didn't record the song on a Maxell cassette tape. (Note to younger readers: cassette tapes were what we in the eighties used to record the Top 40 and our vinyl records on. What's that? You don't know what the Top 40 or vinyl records are either . . . ?)

Episode Three

'I think we're on a winner here, Trig'

As with many middle-class parents, my mum and dad were suspicious of the television and its potential for pernicious influence. 'Auntie' Beeb was considered preferable to 'Uncle' ITV but even so, time in her company was strictly rationed. Any sign of dissent over what we were and weren't allowed to watch, and my parents would pull out examples of even more hardcore middle-class behaviour to shut us up.

'Of course, the Joneses only let their children watch one programme a week,' my dad warned.

'Do you remember the Shelleys? They don't even have a set at all,' my mother would say with a sigh. 'Their children prefer to spend their evenings reading poetry and listening to Radio Four.'

Television take-up was by no means universal in the early eighties, and to make matters worse, my parents seemed to be friends with every family in York who had decided to opt out. I think the sitting around reading poetry bit was probably a figment of my mother's imagination: from what I could glean, what actually happened was that the children in these families went round to 'play' at other friends houses – friends who had TVs in their rooms and could thus watch whatever crap they wanted.

My parents' concerns about the power of television were not helped by the way that Joff and I chose to watch it. As we gradually got older, so we shuffled closer towards the screen, with my hand reaching out to turn the volume ever higher. From the vantage point of the sofa it must have looked as though we were literally getting drawn in, mesmerized by what we saw.

'Thomas!' my mother would shout from behind her copy of *The Madwoman in the Attic*. 'Will you *please* sit back from the television, and turn that sound down!'

'What?' I'd reply, not taking my eyes off the screen.

'And don't say "What"! If you want someone to repeat something say "Pardon".'

'What . . . ?'

If hearing, or trying to, was my excuse for sitting so close to the screen, my brother's justification was his bad eyesight (a very typical early-childhood split that, sharing out the impaired senses between us). After a trip to the local optician's it was concluded that Joff had what was colloquially called a 'lazy eye'.

This being the early 1980s, the cure for a lazy eye was suitably Thatcherite. Joff was given a pair of glasses with a plaster stuck over the lens of the eye that was working properly. With that one out of action, so the theory went, the work-shy, benefit-scrounging eye would have no choice but to stop being so bone-idle and start doing some bloody work for a change. Joff wasn't that happy to have a patch, and neither was his school. He was meant to be a king in the school nativity that year, but the headmistress decided he looked more like Horatio Nelson than a wise man and demanded its removal.

The cause of my hearing problems, meanwhile, was simple and slightly sticky: snot. Like most small children, my nose seemed to be permanently running for the formative years of my existence. So much so that even my handkerchief and shirt sleeve couldn't quite keep up. But that was OK, because I came up with a Baldrick-type cunning plan to get rid of the stuff. Sniffing.

'You shouldn't do that,' my father would say. 'Isn't that right, Carole?'

'Hmmm? Oh yes.' My mother, who was enjoying a far easier washing load, was slightly more relaxed on the issue.

'You'll get a build-up,' my father would continue. 'In your ears.'

'In my ears? You're saying the snot is going to go from my nose to my ears?' I'd laugh.

Having been hoodwinked by father over Rolf Harris, I simply wasn't going to fall for his whole nose-ear story. A direct link between my nose and my ears? It was such a preposterous claim that it was obviously a lie – a bit like the one about having to be good or 'Father Christmas' wouldn't come to visit. Admittedly, I wasn't completely sure where all the snot was going, but if I had to put my pocket money on its whereabouts I preferred the theory that it just disappeared – a bit like the three of hearts in a Paul Daniels magic trick.

Then I started waking up with earache.

The pull of popular culture is at its strongest when it becomes entwined with your own life. This is especially the case with music, where a particular song can capture a romantic moment or bring back memories – something that was at the heart of Simon Bates' 'Our Tune' feature, which went out at eleven every weekday morning on Radio One. I never wrote in to Simon Bates myself – I was still a bit scarred by the whole Bruno Brookes thing, to be honest – but found myself creating a similar sort of personal association with the sitcom *Porridge*. Being unable to get to sleep because my ears hurt, I would stumble downstairs in throbbing pain. There my parents would be sat, watching the television, which more often than not was the latest rerun of this Ronnie Barker comedy.

'Why is it called *Porridge?*' I once asked between throbs.

'It's slang for "prison",' my father replied, still watching the screen.

'I thought it was bad to use slang?'

My mother looked at my father. He shrugged.

'You're the English teacher,' he said.

'It's justified within the context of the social setting of the programme,' my mother sighed. 'It's the sort of language that people inside prison use.'

'So bad people use slang?'

'Exactly.'

'If I use slang, will I end up in prison?'

'You might.'

'How's your ear?' my father asked.

'Still hurting,' I said. 'I reckon it'll be better in another twenty minutes or so. Could I have one of your crisps?'

'Oh, they're very bad for ears,' my father said. 'All that crunching.'

Ronnie Barker tickled my dad something rotten. One of his favourite scenes, which he'd repeatedly regale at length, was from *Going Straight*, the *Porridge* follow-up series, in which Ronnie Barker's character, Fletcher, had finished his sentence and was back home. Upon leaving prison, Fletcher went to a cobbler's to pick up a pair of shoes that he'd put in to be repaired seven years previously.

'And the cobbler looked at Ronnie Barker's ticket . . .' My dad would already be creasing up in anticipation of the punch-line . . . 'and said, "Oh yes, ready Thursday".'

Porridge was the first adult comedy I remember watching with any regularity, albeit in the slightly painful circumstances of my ongoing earache. The association has stayed: even now, re-watching all those prison doors slamming shut at the beginning still gives me a psychosomatic twinge. Although Ronnie Barker is hailed as one of the comic greats, my earache memories mean I've always had the hearing equivalent of a blind spot to his charms. Consequently I never really got on with either him or his partner in crime, Ronnie Corbett, and particularly not with their unholy trinity of eighties programmes: *The Two Ronnies*, *Open All Hours* and *Sorry!*

Open All Hours starred Ronnie Barker as Arkwright, a corner-shop keeper, doing battles with his nephew Granville (played by a young David Jason) and an appalling stammer (in b-b-b-both senses). Then there was his love interest, Nurse Gladys Emmanuel (Lynda Baron), on whose 't-t-t-Morris Minor' Arkwright spent most of the programme trying to get his hands. There was a funny till that tried to take your fingers off as it snapped shut, and that was about it. Arkwright's shop didn't even open all hours.

It crossed my mind more than once that Ronnie Corbett's sitcom *Sorry!* was so-called as a literal pre-emptive apology for the following thirty minutes of television 'humour'. Ronnie Corbett played Timothy ('Timothy!'), a forty-year-old librarian, still living at home and unable to escape the clutches of his domineering mother ('Mother!'). That didn't seem like comedy to my childhood self: that was a nightmare.

'Don't worry,' my mother would say, 'as soon as you are legally old enough, you're out the door.'

Not even my *Porridge*-adoring Dad laughed that much during *The Two Ronnies*. The show was book-ended with spoof news stories and sprinkled with marginally funny sketches, seldom-funny songs, a bit of dressing up in drag and Ronnie Corbett sitting in a chair and taking ten minutes to tell a joke that he could have done in thirty seconds (and wasn't that funny anyway). Obviously there was the 'Fork Handles' sketch, and the '*Mastermind*' one, where the contestants gave the answer to the question before, but as far as I was concerned these were very much the exceptions that proved the rule. If that wasn't bad enough, at the end of the programme Joff and I would be packed off to bed.

'And it's goodnight from me,' my dad would say.

'And it's goodnight from him,' my mum would add, before pointing us towards the door.

Much of television comedy in the early 1980s was a bit like Terry Wogan's knitting-needle microphone on *Blankety Blank*: thin, straight and – one couldn't help thinking – ever so slightly affected. To those of us watching in the north, it also felt as though the home counties was home and everywhere else was very much away. Sitcom land, it seemed, was nothing more than a notch on London's commuter belt. It was from there that Reggie Perrin (Norbiton), Jerry Leadbetter (Surbiton) and Terry Medford (Purley) would all catch their respective trains into the city. Tom Good used to commute in too, until he decided to turn his back garden into a working farm. Then he spent his days kicking around the suburbs with his wife, Barbara, Jerry's wife, Margo, Reginald's Elizabeth and Terry's other half, June. The M25 might still have been being tarmacked back then, but it was as if the BBC had already drawn a ring around the capital, beyond which no sitcom was allowed to stray.

In fact, with the notable exception of *Bread* (which I always found a bit stale, myself), the only comedies allowed to roam beyond the reach of London seemed to be those set in the past. *Hi-de-Hi!* was set in a late-1950s holiday resort and ran for most of the decade. It starred Paul McShane as Ted Bovis, a Hoffmeister 'Follow the Bear' sort of ageing Teddy Boy, Ruth Madoc as pouting Gladys Pugh and Su Pollard as Peggy 'But Miss Cathcart!' Ollerenshaw. Peggy dreamed of being a Yellowcoat, a role which, as far as I could work out, seemed to involve wearing a yellow jacket, short white shorts and being told off for having your hands in your pockets. Ruth Madoc, who woke the holidaymakers up with a cheery Welsh cry of 'Morning, campers!' had a thing for her boss, Jeffrey Fairbrother. Played by Simon Cadell (and looking as though he ought to be in a spy novel) Jeffrey seemed to prefer girls who couldn't keep their hands out of their pockets. Gladys' protestations would thus fall about as flat as whatever that day's entertainments were meant to be. Then someone, usually Spike Dixon, would end up falling in the swimming pool.

If the jokes in *Hi-de-Hi!* were as old as its setting, it seemed positively modern compared to that other eighties stalwart, *'Allo 'Allo*. Set in rural France during the Second World War, it starred Gordon Kaye as René Artois, owner of the imaginatively titled Café René. René looked and sounded like a sort of gone-to-seed Inspector Clouseau. For reasons I could never quite understand, he was considered irresistible by the café's far-better-looking waitresses, Yvette and Maria, both of whom were well up for a bit of René-ravishing and -ravaging whenever his wife's back was turned.

The France of *'Allo 'Allo* was occupied not by the Nazis but by innuendo, and suffered sustained attack from wave after wave of bad jokes. Resistance, a bit like that in the programme, was futile. There was Officer Crabtree, a British agent pretending to be a *gendarme*, who said hilarious mispronounced things like 'Good Moaning!' and 'I was Pissing by the Door'. There was a phalanx of comedy Nazis, called things like Herr Flick and Lieutenant Gruber, who spent most of their time searching for a painting called *Fallen Madonna with the Big Boobies*. There was a bedridden mother-in-law called Madame Fanny. And Maggie, the Resistance leader who said, 'Listen very carefully, I shall say zis only once,' about sixteen times an episode. Such was the success of the show that René and Yvette released a single, a cover of the Serge Gainsbourg and Jane Birkin classic 'Je T'Aime . . . Moi Non Plus'. However, the viewing public didn't *je t'aime* all the 'Oooh, Rrrrené's' and it stalled at number 57. The German occupation of France may only have lasted five years but it took almost double that for the BBC1 schedule to be liberated from the show. Like so many of its sitcom stable mates of the time, it was something of a low, a low.

*   *   *

Not every eighties sitcom was as conservative as the government and as laboured as the opposition. The Bromleys were big fans of *Dear John*, about a man who got a 'Dear John' letter, both literally and metaphorically, in which his wife told him she was leaving him for his best friend. John ended up joining the 1-2-1 Club, a group for recently divorced and separated people. Which doesn't sound that funny so far, but the group, run by the slightly sex-obsessed Louise, contained a whole menagerie of oddballs and misfits. Most memorable was the character of Kirk, an apparently confident and cocky ladies' man who, it transpired, was nothing of the sort and lived at home with his mum. Then there was Kate, a lovely if fragile young thing, who John took a shine to in that classic will-they-won't-they sort of a way. *Dear John* was the sort of comedy that was laced with a bit of emotional punch: there was something sad as well as something funny about its take on relationships, a bit like the joke at the end of *Annie Hall* about needing the eggs.

Broader comedy was apparent in *Brush Strokes*, meanwhile. This was the programme that made actor Karl Howman, who, in the days before he turned his hand to advertising Flash, felt like a fresh and funny presence. Ushered in by Dexys Midnight Runners' 'Because of You' theme tune, the sitcom starred Howman as Jack the Lad Jacko, a painter whose patter was as smooth as his plastering. Jacko spent most of the programme winding up his well-to-do boss Lionel, flirting with Lionel's wife, Veronica, and trying to persuade their secretary, Sandra, to go out with him. When he wasn't doing that, he was hanging out with his lumbering mate Elmo, who ran the inevitable Putney wine bar. *Brush Strokes* might not have been the most groundbreaking comedy every written, but, like the character Jacko, at least its heart was in the right place.

Meanwhile, in another trendy wine bar on the opposite side of London, a couple of likely men were eyeing-up a pair of attractive young things sipping wine and smoking at a table. The taller of the two men was wearing a bright-blue suit, and looking a little awkward holding his glass of red. The shorter and older of the two, sporting a full-length grey raincoat, and leaning on the end of the bar, was extremely confident of some action.

'I think we're on a winner here, Trig,' Del Boy was saying to his friend, standing up and adjusting himself before leaning back down on to the bar . . . But what Del hadn't noticed was that the barman had lifted up the ledge in order to get out — and, as Del carried on telling Trig to play it cool, he fell through the gap and kept falling, behind the bar, flat out of sight.

This is just one of many memorable moments from *Only Fools and Horses*. I could easily have picked out the miracle of the weeping Virgin Mary statue, which turned out to be a drip from the church ceiling. Or the day trip to Margate, when Del Boy's dodgy car radio caught fire and caused the bus to blow up. Or when Rodney won a holiday in an art competition, except he only did so because Del entered him in the under-fifteens category. Or the moment when Del and Rodney were hired to clean chandeliers and detached the wrong one from the ceiling.

Only Fools and Horses starred David Jason as Del Boy and Nicholas Lyndhurst as his brother, Rodney, who — as Trotters Independent Trading ('New York–Paris–Peckham') — dreamed of becoming millionaires this time next year. The chances of Del Boy's schemes failing were about as reliant [reliant means dependent, not reliable] as his three-wheeled van: these included selling hairdryers that turned out to be paint-strippers, digital watches that could play thirty-six different national anthems, portable compact-disc players that flung the CDs out as though they were clay pigeons, and 'Made in Britain' dolls that sang a full repertoire of Chinese lullabies.

Del Boy and Rodney lived in a council flat high up in Nelson Mandela House in Peckham. The flat was originally shared with their Granddad, who was played by Lennard Pearce: after the actor sadly died, his role was taken up by Buster Merryfield as Uncle Albert. Which never quite seemed a fair swap – while the Granddad character had a bit of bite to him, Uncle Albert was just a bit annoying. This, however, was a minor quibble given that the writer John Sullivan (who also wrote *Dear John*) had come up with a couple of comic-gold characters: he'd even written and sung the theme tune himself, Chas and Dave being unavailable. And there was a wonderful group of supporting characters, such as Boycie and Marlene, Trigger, Mickey and Denzil, and a whole lexicon of memorable phrases: things like 'cushty', 'you plonker', and above all, 'lovely jubbly'.

As the show left the eighties and moved into the nineties, so Del Boy and Rodney got themselves into relationships (Raquel and Cassandra respectively). However, the programme had only managed to get to such a stage because the BBC had given it the time to find its feet in the first place. The early episodes of the show got low ratings, and it was only when the second series was repeated that the viewing figures finally started to pick up. These days, I'm not sure whether a similarly unpopular sitcom would be given so much leeway. By giving *Only Fools and Horses* a stay of execution, the BBC were rewarded with one of most successful sitcoms of all time – a reign that can best be shown by the fact that between 1983 and 1993 there was only one Christmas Day that didn't feature an *Only Fools and Horses* special.

'Mum! Dad! Come quick! *Blankety Blank* is starting, and you know who is on . . .'

It was always a red-letter evening in our house when, among the usual *Blankety Blank* celebrities such as Barbara Windsor or Willie Rushton, Su Pollard or Sandra Dickinson, there, in the middle of the bottom row, in the seat reserved for the comic star turn, was the impish, irreverent, irrepressible figure of Kenny Everett.

Kenny Everett's jousts with Terry Wogan were the game show's real 'supermatch game' (Supermatch Game!). The drill was that Terry would stride around the stage reading out his usual vaguely humorous question for the celebrities to fill in the gaps ('Scott of the Antarctic said, "We must be going entirely the wrong way. I just saw a polar bear wearing a blank . . . "'). Kenny Everett, the naughty schoolboy to Wogan's schoolmaster, would then entice the host over under the pretext of needing help. Then, once Wogan was within range, his real aim was revealed: Terry's pencil-thin microphone. Although the routine became more elaborate (on one occasion, Kenny attacked it with a pair of garden shears) my favourite was the first time I saw him go for it – the sheer cheek of him simply bending the microphone in two.

In a way, that single moment encapsulated what Kenny Everett was to the rest of mainstream comedy. *The Kenny Everett Television Show* was the bending of the microphone writ large: bold, surprising, playful and very, very funny. The show came with a range of memorable characters: Sid Snot, forever attempting and failing to flick cigarettes into his mouth; Gizzard Puke, the beer-swilling punk rocker; Brother Lee Love, the gospel priest with a pair of ridiculously sized hands; the American general whose calling card was 'Bomb the bastards!'; Marcel Love, the moustachioed Frenchman of leisure; Reg Prescott, the accident-prone DIY obsessive; and Cupid Stunt, the spooneristically named Hollywood actress with Parton-esque breasts and a penchant for criss-crossing her legs, 'all done in the best *possible* taste'. Cupid Stunt was the second choice of name for the character, after the BBC rejected the original moniker of Mary Hinge.

Then there were spoofing of pop stars and TV shows: the Bee Gees, complete with oversize teeth, chest hair and medallions; Rod Stewart, with a humungous rear-end beneath his leopard-skin trousers; *Dallasty*, a madcap merging of the two American soaps. As well as Kenny, many of the sketches contained a not-particularly over-dressed or undeveloped young actress called Cleo Rocos. Everett once suggested that people who found the flesh-bearing too much should write to the BBC – the camera then panned to reveal a miniaturized Everett reading out the address from inside Cleo's bra.

So many sketches stand out that I could go on all day about how brilliant they were. I remember laughing uncontrollably at the Spider-Man sketch, in which a desperate-to-pee Spider-Man found his way to the cubicles only to realize there was no way of getting out of his skin-tight costume. Another that firmly sticks in my mind was the one where Kenny's wife arrived home to find him in bed eating chocolates, and accuses him of having an affair. Triumphantly, she opened the cupboard door to reveal an inevitably semi-clad Cleo Rocos. 'I'm not seeing your husband,' Rocos protested, 'I'm waiting for a bus.'

'Waiting for a bus? In a wardrobe?' The wife shook her head in disbelief. Whereupon a bus drove through and demolished the bedroom wall.

That was the thing about Kenny Everett – you never quite knew what was going to happen next, except that it was probably going to be very funny. Not for nothing was he sometimes called Cuddly Ken: his was a sense of humour that was naughty rather than nasty, which allowed him to get on telly earlier in the evening (and to bigger audiences) than he might otherwise have been, and to get away with things that other comedians would have failed to get away with. Occasionally he went too far – he was banned from BBC radio for remarking that, 'When we were a kingdom we were ruled by a king . . . Now we are a country we are ruled by Margaret Thatcher.' But on the whole, the sheer cheek of his humour got him through – he was the sort of wonderful one-off comedian who comes along only once in a generation.

I was discovering meanwhile that my mother was a more complicated person than she seemed to be at first glance (the technical term, I believe, is a 'woman'). I would never have put money on her – as a literate, liberal individual – collapsing into hysterics at Kenny Everett's 'News for the Deaf' sketch. This short skit involved Kenny sitting behind a desk in newsreader mode, looking into the camera and shouting 'GOOD EVENING!' as loud as he could.

Perhaps the laughter was a release from the difficulty of having her eldest suffering from hearing problems. Perhaps. But the fact was that my mother laughed at my snotty deafness too. By now, my hearing problems had been passed up the NHS food chain to York District Hospital, where I had regular sessions with the optimistically named Mr Hope. I noted that it said 'Ear, Nose and Throat Specialist' on his door, and thought maybe my father was right after all.

Mr Hope's conclusion was that I had something called 'glue ear'. In the days when Wallace was little more than a ball of plasticine, a grommet was the remedy to this: an operation involving a hole being drilled in the ear drum, several years of Sid Snot being removed with a syringe and said grommet, a small plastic device, being stuck in to plug the gap. I don't remember much about the operation (the words 'general' and 'anaesthetic' spring to mind) but it was a success. My hearing was restored.

Of course I was pleased. But being able to hear everything again was not a complete panacea. For one thing, I no longer had the excuse to sit so near to the television and bask in the full close-up of Cleo Rocos. And for another, I'd lost my get-out-of-jail-free card to watch television well after my bedtime. When it came to sounding knowledgeable at school about the latest comedy programmes, this was to prove no laughing matter.

After the break, we head over to the capital of Texas, where one man gets shot and another comes back from the dead. Then it's on to Colorado to watch one woman have a fight with her identical double, and another have a close encounter of the shoulder-padded kind . . .

Ad Break

Yellow Pages

An old man is in a bookshop, asking whether they have a particular title in stock. They don't. He tries another bookshop: they don't either. And another. And another. Defeated, he returns home where he finds some soothing words of wisdom from his daughter. If this was 2010, the duffer's daughter would fire up what her father cutely calls 'your computer thing' and track the book down in seconds on Amazon Marketplace or eBay. But this is the eighties, so the most her computer's capable of is playing *PacMan* and thus she suggests using the *Yellow Pages* instead.

Success! One worries for a second that the old man might have a coronary on hearing that a bookshop has *Fly Fishing* by J. R. Hartley on their shelves. He asks them to put it aside for him. Under which name? By a remarkable coincidence, the old man is called J. R. Hartley too! I'm joking, of course – the old man is *the* J. R. Hartley, renowned writer and fisherman extraordinaire.

Before you start getting too sentimental over the teary-eyed old codger clasping the telephone receiver to his chest, let me tell you something: I used to work in a bookshop and these old people aren't cute, they're lethal. The guy isn't called 'J. R.' Hartley for nothing. Just as soon as he has put the phone down on the last bookshop, he'll be picking it up again and dialling his agent and editor with a long list of shops that aren't stocking his book, and demanding to know just what the hell is going on. And even the shop that *does* have *Fly Fishing* is not exactly immune: now J. R. knows it is there, he'll be popping in every other day to see how it's doing and rearranging the display on the front table to highlight his book.

Still, I guess I shouldn't be too harsh on the old guy. Because in fifty years' time there'll probably be another duffer doing the rounds, working his way through the phone book to a find a shop that stocks a particular out-of-print tome. *'What's that? You* do *have* All in the Best Possible Taste? *Yes, would you hold it for me . . .'*

Episode Four

'Nobody takes me to bed and to the cleaners in one night'

I was just about to be eight when John Lennon was shot dead in December 1980. I remember watching the report on *John Craven's Newsround* and my mother crying. None of it really made much sense. Sure, I knew that people got killed but they were normally soldiers fighting in a war, not musicians wandering down the street. And John Lennon was no ordinary musician at that – he dressed in white like an angel, had a beard like Jesus, wore glasses and sang about peace. As my young self, I couldn't imagine anyone less violent than John Lennon or why anyone would want to kill him.

I eventually came to the conclusion that being shot at must be part of the deal of being famous in the early eighties. Basically, if someone wasn't trying to take your head off, you couldn't really consider yourself an A-list star. As well as John Lennon, someone had tried to shoot the new American president, Ronald Reagan, apparently in a bid to impress the actress Jodie Foster (if only he'd known of her sexual preferences). The Queen was clip-clopping along The Mall as part of the Trooping the Colour when another gunman fired at her from the crowd: being terribly English, she just wobbled a bit on her horse and then carried on as though nothing had happened. Someone else thought, meanwhile, that when in Rome doing what the Romans do was taking a pot shot at the Pope. It was getting to the point where the list of famous people who hadn't got shot at was shorter than the one of those who had. By my reckoning, there was only a handful of prominent establishment figures left who might want to ring in for extra protection: Ron Greenwood, manager of the England football team, Roy Castle, host of *Record Breakers*, and Mrs McClusky, headmistress of Grange Hill Comprehensive.

There was another shot that rang round the world in the early eighties, this one fired from a fictional gun. In many ways it was history repeating itself (though the original incident, in the sixties, was real and was a tragedy, while the subsequent incident was simply farce): both shootings took place in the capital of the southern American state of Texas; both targets had the first name John, though were more commonly known by their initials; furthermore, the question of who actually carried out the shooting in either case was anything but clear cut, and became the subject of much heated debate. Just as my parents' generation could tell you exactly where they were when they heard the news that JFK had been killed, so my generation could pinpoint precisely the moment when they found out that JR had been shot: just before nine o'clock on the evening of 26 May 1980, sat in front of the telly, watching *Dallas* on BBC1.

Right from the opening credits, it was difficult not to be drawn in by the sheer scale and drama of *Dallas*. The intro began with that iconic shot of two ribbons of road leading to a horizon of skyscrapers against a brilliant blue sky: Shangri-La, if you will, but wearing a Stetson. As the opening shrill strings and brass gave way to that disco hi-hat and funky guitar, the visuals switched to a downtown of mirrored office blocks – a succession of buildings, each even taller than the last. They were so tall, in fact, that they were disappearing off the top of the screen, while the shadow of the cameraman's helicopter flew across the bottom.

At this point, the main refrain of the theme tune kicked in, and we were treated to a carousel of images showing what Dallas was all about. These included a row of jackhammer oil wells; a herd of cattle trudging through a mud-brown field; some more mirrored skyscrapers; and an overhead shot of Texas Stadium, then home of the American-football team the Dallas Cowboys. Overlaid here in large yellow capital letters was the show's title, *DALLAS*, with 'A Lorimar Production' written underneath.

Growing up in York, it was difficult not to be sucked in by such a sight. Compared to recession-hit Britain, Dallas just seemed bigger and better and brighter and more exciting. The only cowboys I knew were the ones who my dad had hired to plaster the bathroom, and the only people in York making any money out of oil were the owners of Friar Tuck's fish-and-chip shop. Indeed, had the series been relocated from Texas to Yorkshire, the opening shot would have been of the A64 ring road, the silhouette of York Minster just about visible in the grey overhanging rain clouds. With the city unable to rustle up its own orchestra-come-funk-group, a brass band would have accompanied the rolling group of images: Yorkie bars running off the Rowntree's conveyer belt; a tractor harvesting sugar beet; a delayed British Rail diesel train creaking out of York station; and Bootham Crescent, home of York City, both alphabetically and actually last in the football league.

Back on the intro to *Dallas*, meanwhile, the focus had switched again, this time to the characters, with each actor presented in fruit-machine format with three side-by-side head shots: Miss Ellie

(Barbara Bel Geddes) looked like the sort of innocent old lady who secretly wanted young offenders strung up and birched; Jock Ewing (Jim Davis) was hard-working and sweaty; Bobby (Patrick Duffy) was even sweatier, and had mislaid his shirt to boot; Sue Ellen Ewing, or 'Swellen' as she was properly known (Linda Grey), looked possibly wistful but probably just thirsty; JR (Larry Hagman) rubbed it in about his wife's alcoholism by cheerfully downing a glass of Scotch; Ray Krebbs (Steve Kanaly) wore his Stetson like a good ol' boy; Cliff Barnes (Kim Kercheval) was hatless and therefore not to be trusted; Pam Ewing (Victoria Principal) was for some reason – or possibly two reasons – brought on with a bouncy walk towards the camera; and Lucy Ewing (Charlene Tilton), just smiled vaguely and looked a bit vapid. As the music swept towards its final crescendo, there was an equally sweeping camera shot up the long tree-lined drive to the Ewing family home: Southfork, the Big Sod-Off House on the Prairie.

Big, indeed, was the word. Everything about Dallas reeked of size – the landscape, the characters' ambitions, their wad. As dazzling as the tower blocks were, there was no missing the programme's roots: the theme tune, the sprinkling of Stetsons and the name of the football team emblazoned across the end zone all hinted heavily that, for all the suits and fancy talk, the Ewings were cowboys for the late-twentieth century. Dallas 1980 was the Wild West all over again, just a little bit more oily.

So the Ewings did battle with the Barneses, and when JR wasn't arguing with them he was fighting with his brother, his wife and pretty much everybody else, to be honest – something that JR was certainly not. He regularly cheated on all his partners, business and otherwise. The business ones shook their fists and shouted, 'You won't get away with this!', while Sue Ellen just shook, on account of all the booze she'd just imbibed. Interestingly, for all that JR dominated *Dallas*, that hadn't been the producer's intention for the series. The original idea had been for a sort of *Romeo and Juliet* among the oil fields, with

Bobby and Pam the stars as young lovers from rival families. JR was 'just the brother', as Larry Hagman noted in his autobiography.

Before long, however, Hagman had taken centre stage. JR was a brilliant bad guy: he worked because he wasn't your classic villain who got what he wanted via brute force or physical threats, or played on his charm and a slithery line in seduction. Instead, with his Action Man looks and eagle eyes for an opportunity, his success was all down to low cunning and clever calculation – a type of malevolence that is guaranteed to get under an audience's skin. If that wasn't infuriating enough, his scheming was carried out behind a butter-wouldn't-melt way of calling his parents 'Mommy' and 'Daddy', and a pained expression like a three-year-old needing to go to the toilet. That masked the truth: JR was so daring in his double-crossing, you could never quite believe he was getting away with it – but you sure as hell wanted to be around when he finally got his comeuppance.

This moment finally arrived in an episode called 'A House Divided' – though it could equally have been called 'A City United in its Hatred for JR', because for a good hour or so there didn't seem to be anyone in the Deep South who didn't want JR dead. He'd used his insider knowledge to sucker his friends into buying shares from him, just as they were about to become worthless. Cliff Barnes triumphantly produced a document guaranteeing him part share in the Ewing company only for JR to order the relevant oil field to be shut down. Bobby, who'd had enough of JR, announced he was leaving Southfork for good. JR's lover, Sue Ellen's sister Kristin, tried to blackmail him but JR presented her partner with a trumped-up rape charge if he didn't leave town. Sue Ellen, meanwhile, also threatened JR if he tried to institutionalize her again.

All of which was the under-card to the main event. This took place late in the evening at Ewing Towers, where JR, dressed in a crisp white shirt, waistcoat and tie, was burning some of his ill-gotten midnight oil. Restlessly flicking between various memos, a cup of coffee and a glass of Scotch, he picked up a ringing phone only to hear a click at the other end of the line. As JR helped himself to a refill of coffee and looked moodily out over the Dallas skyline, it's just possible he was considering the dubious ethics of his business behaviour. It was more likely, however, that he was thinking, 'Where is all that creepy music coming from? Isn't that the sort that only gets played when someone is about to get shot?'

Sure enough, the next image was one of the wonky 'point of view' shots as the assassin wobbled their way through the darkened building towards him. As JR heard something – footsteps, or possibly just another one of the spooky violins – he called out 'Who's there?' and went to investigate. As he reached the doorway to his office, bam! The first shot rang out. JR fell forward, clutching the doorframe. Bam! A second shot sent him rolling over, flat on his back on the corridor floor. Cue close-up of his contorted face and the closing credits.

'Wow,' I said. 'Is he dead?'

'Well,' said Dad, giving his professional doctor's cough. 'It's a bit difficult to diagnose from this distance. But I have to say, it's not looking good.'

'I bet it was Sue Ellen,' Mum said. 'Getting revenge on an errant husband. Serves him right.'

Dad shifted a little uncomfortably in his seat. 'If she was that drunk, she'd have done extremely well to have driven over to JR's, tiptoed quietly up to his office and fired two perfect shots.'

'Why? What happens when you're drunk?' Joff asked.

'If it's your father,' said Mum, 'then you crawl round the floor doing an impression of a train before falling asleep on the sofa.'

The Bromleys weren't the only ones who were talking about JR and who might have shot him. Terry Wogan, whose Radio Two breakfast show my parents were big fans of, talked of nothing else. So much so that when the bookies decided to cash in on the series by taking bets on who had pulled the trigger, the DJ found himself in the running (albeit at odds of 1000–1). The serious front-runners, and I use the word 'serious' loosely here, were as follows: the favourite was Steven Farlow at 2–1, closely followed by Sue Ellen at 3–1; Kristin, meanwhile, was 4–1, with business rival Cliff Barnes at 7–1; bringing up the rear were various family members – Bobby at 10–1, Lucy, Pam and Miss Ellie at 12–1 and father Jock at 14–1. Steven 'Lusty Dusty' Farlow was a bit of a surprise favourite. Yes, he was a rodeo cowboy and Sue Ellen's former lover, but he was also presumed dead after an air crash. As a result, it was difficult to look at those odds without thinking that the bookies must know something we didn't.

For once, though, the bookies did not know anything. They couldn't have had any inside information for the simple reason that no one knew who shot JR. As the pinnacle scene in the series, you might have thought JR's shooting was the result of months of careful planning. But instead, buoyed by the success of the show, the American network had instead demanded a couple of extra episodes, so the original series cliffhanger had been buried within an earlier episode and this new climax tagged on. Indeed, not only was the infamous scene a last-minute addition, but also the producers hadn't even decided who had shot JR when they filmed it. To keep their options open, they recorded footage of all the major characters gunning JR down (even Miss Ellie – I told you to watch her).

Not just that, but no one was even sure whether JR was dead or not – though this was down to the ongoing haggling over Larry Hagman's contract. 'It was my turn to cash in,' Hagman explained in his autobiography. 'I had my agents tell Lorimar that I wanted to renegotiate my contract or else I was walking away from the show.' Hagman's agent ordered him to leave the country and to stay out of Lorimar's reach, but keep himself prominent in the news. So Hagman flew over to Britain, where he was interviewed by Terry Wogan, partied at Annabel's and went to Royal Ascot, where he was greeted with crowds chanting 'JR! JR! JR!' As the headlines rolled in, Hagman's agent asked for a cool

$100,000 an episode and a share of the merchandise (this included everything from JR cologne to dartboards to 'Private Stock' beer).

Even with Hagman's contract eventually settled, an actor's strike delayed the filming of the new series for a further three months. So it wasn't until the autumn that the next series finally began and we could finally find out who'd done it. Perhaps unsurprisingly, far from revealing that straight away, the producers decided to tease out the storyline for several further episodes. Not even royalty could winkle out the answer: in November 1980 Larry Hagman returned to Britain to sing at the Queen Mother's eightieth-birthday celebrations. Afterwards she demanded, 'Now I want you to tell me, young man, who shot JR?'

'Not even for you, Ma'am,' Hagman replied.

The episode where all was revealed was finally shown on American TV on Friday 21 November 1980, with the BBC showing it the following night. For the British broadcast, the tapes had been flown from LA under armed guard, and 21.5 million people settled down to watch: a then record audience for a soap opera. In America, meanwhile, more people watched the programme than had voted in that month's presidential election. Altogether, fifty-seven countries broadcast the show, and a total audience of 380 million tuned in to watch worldwide. It was the eighties equivalent of the 1977 *Morecambe and Wise Christmas Show* – except on a truly international scale.

To start with, it looked as though my mum was right: Sue Ellen's fingerprints were on the gun. But then maybe my dad had called it correctly, because Sue Ellen had been completely paralytic that evening – so much so that she couldn't remember whether she had shot JR or not. Once Sue Ellen's hangover had finally cleared, she began to work out what happened. On the night in question, Sue Ellen had been in possession of the gun, but had then been plied with alcohol by the actual shooter. The mystery person took the gun with Sue Ellen's fingerprints on it, shot JR, then 'hid' it back in Sue Ellen's wardrobe, ready to be discovered.

So who *had* done it? Sue Ellen revealed all to JR, recuperating at Southfork in a rather unflattering pale-blue dressing-gown. The answer, it turned out, was Sue Ellen's sister, Kristin. At first Kristin attempted to laugh off the accusation, but as JR reached for the phone and dialled the police she quickly cut short her sister's moment of triumph.

'I wouldn't do that if I were you,' she warned JR, 'not if you want your . . . child to be born in prison.'

Kristin, it turned out, was as pregnant as the pause halfway through her revelation. Sue Ellen's eyes went from wide-open disbelief to narrowed fury, and she switched her ire from her sister to her husband. Was JR about to conceal the truth in order to spare his unborn child? For a second, it looked as though Kristin had won and Sue Ellen was going down for a crime she did not commit. But then JR said, as only he could, 'I'll handle Kristin my own way.' The wobble in Kristin's victory smile said it all.

Larry Hagman's agent wasn't the only person to notice the huge success of *Dallas*. It wasn't long before another American network decided they wanted a slice of the action and set about making their own rival show. This series was called *Oil*, and was slated to star George Peppard as the chairman of another black-gold conglomerate and Sophia Loren as his devious, manipulative ex-wife. When George Peppard didn't get on with the original script, he was replaced by John Forsythe, the voice of Charlie in *Charlie's Angels*. Sophia Loren's involvement, meanwhile, went no further than the rumour mill, and her role went to the British actress Joan Collins. As for the name of the show, well, *Oil* was ditched in favour of something far more glamorous: *Dynasty*.

Set in Denver rather than Dallas, the dynamics of *Dynasty* revolved around the relationship between Blake Carrington (Forsythe) and Alexis Colby (Collins). Back in the day, Blake and Alexis had been married and had four children – Adam, Fallon, Steven and Amanda – some of which Blake knew more about than others. Following his divorce from Alexis, Blake had married his ever-so-slightly dreary secretary Krystle, who had thought she'd got her work cut out distracting Blake from his Denver-Carrington empire. Until, that is, his ex-wife turned up – depending on which day of the week it was, she wanted to destroy either Blake's business or his marriage, or have a hostile takeover of both. Her master plan included giving Blake's big business rival, Cecil Colby, a heart attack during a particularly energetic session of lovemaking. He married Alexis minutes before dying, and left her his ColbyCo oil company.

Alexis, who now had eyes for the walking piece of sandpaper that was Farnsworth 'Dex' Dexter, could only look on at the state of her children's lives: Fallon might have married Cecil Colby's son, Jeff, but like the Halifax advert remained easy like Sunday morning – her many infidelities almost included sleeping with her brother Adam (though she didn't know they were related); Steven, meanwhile, was struggling both with his sexuality and being married to Krystle's niece, Sammy Jo. Steven and Fallon would both go on to find themselves suffering from another sort of identity crisis, when their characters found themselves being played by different and not-that-similar-looking actors halfway through the series (Fallon, in particular, appeared to have been on the TV show *Ten Years Younger* as well as its associate programme, *Several Inches Shorter*).

If *Dallas* was all about the shots, then *Dynasty* was all about the shoulder pads. So wide and puffy did these get that had any of the actresses taken the wrong turning and ended up in the Denver Broncos American-football stadium by mistake, they wouldn't have needed much kitting up. Certainly British television screens hadn't seen this much concentrated glam since the 1974 Christmas episode of *Top of the Pops*. The clothes themselves were created by designer Nolan Miller, who released a Nolan Miller Dynasty Collection, based on the programme's outfits, for those who wished to be so attired.

Hand in hand with the catwalk clothes went the regular catfights between the female characters. These, for me, were the programme's party pieces, and usually involved a lot of expensively coiffured hair-pulling, much slapping of expensively made-up faces and some rolling around on the expensively carpeted floors. The slapping, of which Sammy Jo was something of a specialist, came accompanied by an over-the-top whip-crack noise, as though Indiana Jones had been hired to do the sound effects. In one famous scene, Sammy Jo fought tooth and manicured nail with sister-in-law Fallon; it started out with her punching her opponent backwards into a pool of water before the pair of them ended up grappling together in the mud.

For all JR's concerns about Kristin and Sue Ellen, the woman he really needed to keep an eye on was Alexis Colby. Because in Alexis he had a rival ready to wrest off his crown as public enemy number one: Joan Collins was both hot stuff and ice cold, with a tongue that could cut diamonds ('Nobody takes me to bed and to the cleaners in one night' was just one of many choice lines). *Dynasty* wasn't just glitzier and more glamorous than *Dallas*, it was Dy-nastier too. By the mid-eighties, investors were starting to switch their stock from Ewing Oil to Denver-Carrington and ColbyCo. In 1984 *Dynasty* won the Golden Globe for Best TV Drama series, and the following year overtook *Dallas* in the ratings to become the number-one show in America. The bitch, as Elton John might have put it, was back.

Meanwhile, with not quite so much glitz and a lot less success, the BBC decided to go one further from just buying in *Dallas* and *Dynasty* and dip their toe into the glamorous waters of soap opera. Unfortunately the water they chose was the North Sea, the setting for their ill-fated series *Triangle*. Rather than being a love triangle or something equally dramatic, the three-sided shape of the title in fact referred to the Felixstowe-Gothenburg-Rotterdam route of the ship on which all the show's action took place. I can only guess that some bright spark thought, 'What's British and glamorous? I know! Cruise ships!' I can also only speculate that this self-same person had never spent any time on a North Sea ferry. If they had, they would not have put Kate O'Mara in a bikini and made her attempt to 'sunbathe' under gloomy grey skies. (O'Mara not unreasonably jumped ship and joined *Dynasty* as Alexis' sister.) On top of that, filming the entire series on board a moving ship might have seemed a neat and innovative idea at the time but came with all sorts of problems, not least of which was the cast and crew's struggle to cope with the choppy waters. More often than not, their lunch went the same way as the ratings and the programme's supposed glamour.

If the JR shooting was the scene that got me hooked on *Dallas*, then the scene that got me off it was the climax of series nine. To the untrained eye it may have appeared to be a fairly innocuous picture. Victoria Principal, asleep in her double bed, woke up to the sound of a running shower. 'Funny,' she seemed to be thinking, 'I don't remember leaving that on.' For a split second, no doubt triggered by the spooky music that had started up, Pam considered the thought that there was an intruder in her bathroom. An intruder, it has to be said, with a thing about hygiene – I mean, he was taking a shower before attacking her. But then the creepy music became a big soppy string chorus as Pam, wearing a floor-length Sandra Dee-style satin sack, went to investigate. She glided into the bathroom, opened the shower door and there, soaping himself down, was long-time partner Bobby.

'Mornin',' he said, with a drawl and a twinkle.

All fairly harmless stuff then – except for one tiny, almost incidental detail: Bobby had actually died at the end of the previous series. As soap exits went, Bobby's was pretty conclusive: he was very, very dead. It wasn't as if he'd 'gone to Australia to start a new life', or had died in a plane crash 'without them ever finding the body'. *Dallas* viewers had not only watched him get knocked over – we'd also heard the 'bip bip bip beeeeeeeep' as he'd died in hospital, then we'd sat through his funeral and seen his coffin lowered into the ground. Now that, as John Cleese might have said in the classic Monty Python sketch, is what I call a dead Bobby.

Dallas' producers, though, had a problem. Since Patrick Duffy had left the show, ratings had gone down faster than a glass of bourbon in Sue Ellen's hand. Larry Hagman was unhappy with how the storylines were developing, complaining there was too much 'glitter' – a comment that echoed the criticisms of the programme's original producer, who said *Dallas* had become a 'woman's show'. All of these developments were, of course, in response to the success of *Dynasty*, but that wasn't the only programme that the American network were worried about: *Dallas* was now up against *Miami Vice* in the schedules, and the men not watching the 'woman's show' were switching over in droves. So the call went out to get Duffy back, and to get the scriptwriters to work out how to shoehorn him in.

In order to create maximum surprise value from Bobby's return, only a very select few were let in on the secret; not even Victoria Principal knew. You might think that was tricky, given that she is in the scene herself, but should you be so inclined to re-watch the footage you'll see that Pam and Bobby are never in the same shot. In fact, they recorded their parts completely separately: Victoria filmed the original series 'ending', in which Pam woke up to discover her post-Bobby husband, Mark, dead in the shower; Patrick, meanwhile, returned to the *Dallas* studios under the pretext of recording a soap commercial, and this footage was then dropped in at the last minute. Apparently, so well kept was the surprise that Victoria Principal only found out about it when she watched the episode at home along with everyone else.

So how do you create a storyline to bring back a character who is actually dead? The *Dallas* writers thought long and hard and came up with three possible scenarios. The first of these was that Bobby hadn't actually died at all: as his body was being wheeled away, a hospital orderly had noticed that his eyes were flicking; he was then secretly revived and spent a year recuperating in a private hospital, unbeknown to everyone. The second option was that Bobby wasn't Bobby at all, but was someone who had undergone plastic surgery to look uncannily like Bobby and thus carry out their dastardly plan of taking over Ewing Oil. Muhahahah.

What the producers decided to go with in the end was option three, the classic 'I woke up and it was all a dream' scenario. This quick-fix solution was one familiar to schoolchildren everywhere, particularly when there was a homework deadline and a story to finish. I can only guess that the *Dallas* writers had a more lenient English teacher than I did. One wonders how many other children got a D minus in the following weeks for coming up with such a weak storyline. Though perhaps not everyone was as stupid as me in defending their actions by revealing the source of their inspiration, thus losing an extra grade for plagiarism.

It was, frankly, a rubbish idea. It may have got Bobby back into the show, and yes, everyone was talking about *Dallas* again, but this time it was for all the wrong reasons. The cost of Bobby's return was that everything that had happened since his 'death' now turned out to be a minutely detailed and exceedingly long dream sequence. A dream sequence that lasted for thirty-one fifty-minute episodes, or, to put it another way, twenty-six hours of plot that the viewer needed to unravel in their heads. That's not a dream – that's a coma.

So Bobby's shower was the moment I fell out of love with *Dallas*. I felt cheated at having sat through so many storylines I was now being asked to forget. Also, I felt that if the previous series was really Pam's dream, then it wasn't a very realistic one. Where was the bit where she found herself falling through space? Or her father mutating into a giant ostrich? Or Pam turning up for an exam without any clothes on? As well as this, I couldn't help feeling sorry for the forgotten victim of the whole saga: Garry Ewing. Bobby's death had played big in *Knots Landing*, the spin-off show that starred the third Ewing brother. Not only had it caused Garry to undergo a complete reassessment of his life, but he'd also decided to name his son in memory of his dead brother. And while the clock went back in *Dallas* following Bobby's return, in *Knots Landing* it carried on as though he was still six foot under. The result was that Gary was now trapped in a dead-Bobby parallel universe, and unless Sylvester McCoy turned up in the TARDIS he was never going to see Southfork again.

Of course, anything that *Dallas* could do, *Dynasty* could go one better. Or one worse, depending on how you looked at it. Among its 'finest' plot moments was the Moldavian massacre, in which Amanda Carrington was lined up to marry the Prince of Moldavia (played by *Robin of Sherwood* heartthrob Michael Praed), only for armed men to burst in and machine-gun everyone to death. I say everyone . . . At the start of the following series all the important characters dusted themselves down and turned out to be not so badly hurt after all – maybe those shoulder pads weren't such a bad idea. Furthermore, who can forget the kidnapping of Krystle and her look-alike replacement called Rita, who managed to convince everyone she was the real Mrs Carrington? This culminated in the surreal scene of Krystle, played by Linda Evans, having the *de rigueur* catfight with Rita, also played by Linda Evans.

Even that, though, can be topped for sheer preposterousness by the *Dynasty* spin-off series *The Colbys*. This starred Charlton Heston and Stephanie Beacham as Jason and Sable Colby, but the star turn (quite literally) went to Fallon Carrington (the shorter, younger version). Fallon had transferred from the real *Dynasty*, no doubt expecting more of the big dresses and bitch slaps in the mud; what she got instead was a UFO landing in the desert in front of her, the door opening and an alien beckoning her in. As the spaceship whisked both Fallon and all sense of perspective away, the audience was left to wonder if the UFO got as far as the moon before Fallon started giving the alien the eye.

Dallas and *Dynasty* were a bit like the Blur and Oasis of eighties American soaps: *Dynasty* was Blur, the more fashionable and knowing one, while *Dallas* was Oasis, its strength deriving from its internal brotherly rivalry, and, in 'Who Shot JR?' enjoying that massive 'Wonderwall' moment. It has been suggested by better people than me that the success of the shows was because their motifs of greed and glamour chimed with the Thatcherite and Reaganite times – a capitalizing on capitalism, if you like. All of which might have some element of truth to it, but ignores the fact that people like my family loved the programmes and we certainly weren't so minded.

What I actually think was going on was something less to do with the political and more about the personal. As we watched these larger-than-life characters be corrupted by their riches, *Dallas* and *Dynasty* actually served to reinforce our own sense of values. The Bromleys might never be as wealthy as the Carringtons or the Ewings, but we were the ones sitting down to watch the telly together and enjoying each other's company like a proper family. And, at the end of the day, I think I know what is more important.

After the break, we watch a spaceship that doesn't want to take off, meet a plant that wants to eat you, and consider the philosophical undertones to Mark King's slap bass.

Ad Break

Prestige Pans

In a suitably MFI MDF eighties kitchen, an apron-wearing vet turned doctor Peter Davison is going off on one about saucepans. Picking up one that, with prescient timing, falls apart in his hands, he makes it clear why he doesn't like wasting money on such shoddy goods. Fortunately for Peter, Prestige saucepans are at hand with their copper bottoms and real teak handles: these 'lifetime' pans are guaranteed to last for, well, ten years actually. But before you have time to say, 'Hang on a minute! What sort of lifetime is that?' events have fast-forwarded to a space-age kitchen, and a Bacofoil-clad Davison is receiving a call on his digital watch from his good lady, Sandra Dickinson.

'You can put the dinner on,' she squeaks, 'I'll be home in twenty minutes.'

Davison and Dickinson were a match made if not in heaven then certainly in outer space. With their respective roles in *Doctor Who* and *The Hitchhiker's Guide to the Galaxy*, they were sort of a low-rent, pre-*Heat*, small-screen, early-eighties, science-fiction version of Brad and Jen (a status confirmed by their singing of the theme tune to *Button Moon*). With no *OK!* magazine around to show round their house, they did what celebrities had to do in those days: they sat on the *TV-am* sofa and did adverts for copper-bottomed saucepans.

To be fair to Prestige, I've got one of their saucepans from the eighties, and you know what? It's still in pretty good nick. Unlike their copper-bottomed pans, however, relationships do not come with a lifetime guarantee. That aroma wafting across from the kitchen is not Peter Davison's cooking, but the bouquet garnis of a couple breaking up. Things between Peter and Sandra, for want of a better phrase, did not pan out. By the time Sandra Dickinson was telling Peter Davison to put the supper on ten years into the future, the two stars were no longer in each other's orbit.

Episode Five

'Mostly harmless'

One warm April day in 1981, the headmaster of my primary school called everyone into the sports hall for a special assembly. Mr Bradley was a tall and upstanding sort of teacher, with a booming Bradford voice and shoes that went up at the end like a clown (one notices these things sat on the floor). Among the many words of wisdom he saw fit to pass down to his young students, the phrase of his that sticks in the mind is: 'Sweat doesn't smell. It's only stale sweat that smells.' I presume it's about the virtues of hard graft, though it might just have been that some of his pupils were in need of a good bath.

On this particular day, as we sat there cross-legged in rows, Mr Bradley told us that we were about to witness something historic: the launch of *Columbia*, the first space shuttle. At which point the school's TV set was wheeled in, sitting atop one of those special television trolleys that you get only in schools. Mr Bradley opened the trolley shutters, stretched out the top canopy, and there, live from Cape Canaveral in Florida, sat the space shuttle on its launch pad, pointing towards the sky. It was stuck, Velcro-like, on the back of its fuel container, a huge dirty orange cylinder reminiscent of the brand-free washing-up bottle *Blue Peter* would use to make one of their models. On each side, like a pair of bicycle pumps, were further booster cylinders.

Mr Bradley had been headmaster of the school before I'd even been born, and had been in charge when Neil Armstrong landed on the moon in July 1969. Years later, I watched the original footage as television celebrated the mission's fortieth anniversary, and it remains an astonishing spectacle. There is that iconic image of the earth as seen from above the moon – a solitary blue gem sewn into the black curtains of space. There are Neil Armstrong and Buzz Aldrin planting flags and bouncing around among the craters. There is President Nixon, talking on the phone to people *on the moon*. And all done with a computer with less memory than my mobile phone, all held together with string and sticky-backed plastic.

Back in 1981, by contrast, the space shuttle was still sat firmly on its launch pad: 'like the Taj Mahal minus the ornamental lake', as Clive James noted in the *Observer*. With less than twenty minutes to take-off there was a technical problem and the countdown was paused. As the sun beat down into the sports hall, Mr Bradley was beginning to realize that, history in the making or not, one of teaching's golden rules still holds: it's only for so long that small children will sit cross-legged without fidgeting. With the sci-fi test card holding firm on the screen, my classmates were beginning to space shuffle about.

Mr Bradley announced with a sigh that anyone who didn't want to wait could go and play outside instead. After a hesitant start – no one wanting the disapproving look for going first – the lure of a sunny playground proved too much for many. Pretty soon, the hall audience had thinned down to a select band of us watchers, still glued to the image of the not-taking-off space shuttle. We listened as the commentator tried to explain what the problem was: a bit like a pair of sulky teenagers, two of the computers were refusing to talk to each other.

Time ticked on. T minus became T plus. Even I, with my interest in both space and television, was beginning to get restless. Mr Bradley did his best to do the fill-in act, keeping us entertained while listening to the television, trying to glean when the countdown might restart again. But Kieran Prendiville from *Tomorrow's World*, who the BBC had flown out to cover the event, had about as much idea as the rest of us. I can't honestly remember who gave up first – NASA, Kieran or Mr Bradley – but after several hours of will-they-won't-they, 'That's enough, IBM, or you'll go to your room', the launch was called off.

It wasn't until Sunday lunchtime that Mr Bradley's hoped-for history was finally made. The shuttle was sat under another crystal-clear blue sky, but this time the T-Minus countdown wasn't interrupted. I watched as huge clouds of smoke billowed out like the dry ice you got on *Top of the Pops* when Alison Moyet or Bonnie Tyler were on. Slowly at first, and then quicker and quicker, the shuttle sped upwards, leaving behind its highlighter pen of molten fumes. It was an impressive sight, though the TV pictures were brought back to earth by the man from mission control.

'The shuttle has cleared the tower,' he announced, as if this was some sort of achievement. One hoped it was going to do slightly more than that.

'The altitude's too high for ejector-seat use,' he added, just in case any of the astronauts were having second thoughts.

The shuttle continued upwards, like someone was drawing a line in cloud on the sky. To cheers from the onlookers on the ground, the side rockets split off in symmetrical union, peeling away like a pair of pacesetters. On the space shuttle went, piggybacking on its rusty Fairy Liquid bottle out of view of the cameras, its vapour trail fading slowly into blue.

*   *   *

ALL IN THE BEST *POSSIBLE* TASTE

The launch was an impressive sight, but in television terms it was that Friday-morning failure that really summed up space in the 1980s. This was the decade in which intergalactic viewing just never quite got off the ground. The sixties, as was the case with most things, had got there first, with all the hope and excitement such imagery entailed. The seventies counteracted this with disaster and disappointment. Following on from all that, the eighties was never quite sure which way to turn. The decade was less about giant leaps and more to with small bunny-hops. Not so much 'Houston, we have a problem' as 'Houston, we have a minor computer fault that is going to take twenty-four hours to rectify'.

For all Mr Bradley's attempts to excite us about the space shuttle, the problem was that it didn't look much like a rocket or a spaceship – it looked a bit like a plane, and not even one that could manage to take off on its own accord. Rather than fly to the moon or land on Mars or anywhere exciting, all it did was go round and round for a bit and then come back to earth again. The fact that it was the world's first reusable spacecraft may have excited the bean-counters at mission control, but it did little to grip my own excitement.

All of which was a shame, because as a young boy I was very much space obsessed. Where this interest in space came from, and what both the shuttle and eighties science-fiction struggled against, could be summed up in two words: 'Star' and 'Wars'. In those formative years I was just the right age to be sucked in, like the *Millennium Falcon* on a *Death Star* tractor beam. Though I was too young to see the film when it originally came out in 1977, I more than made up for it as it was re-shown every school holidays at the local cinema. *The Empire Strikes Back* I first watched on video with a bucket in my hand, as I was off school with some sort of virus – I still don't know if it was that or the revelations about Luke Skywalker's father that left me feeling more queasy.

I spent quite a lot of my early-childhood years playing *Star Wars*. In the playground we'd take turns to be Luke Skywalker, fighting for the hand of Princess Leia – this was before the brother-sister revelations of *Return of the Jedi*. One friend had a pair of knock-off lightsabers, which were essentially plastic tubes with a bulb in. They were at their most impressive when swished around in the dark, but also at their most lethal – particularly for the ornaments on the mantelpiece. Then there were the *Star Wars* figures. My brother and I spent much of our pocket money on these and between us built up the sort of sizeable collection that in retrospect we shouldn't have allowed Dad to flog off in order to make some room in the attic. Our *Star Wars* collection was light in the spacecraft department; and, though I attempted to make a *Millennium Falcon* out of blue and red Lego bricks, it was never quite the same. So imagine my delight one Christmas Day when I ripped through the wrapping paper to discover I was finally the owner of my very own . . .

'. . . Rebel Transporter?' I said, a little confused.

You might not instantly remember the pivotal role that the Rebel Transporter played in the *Stars Wars* film. To be honest, you wouldn't be alone. I knew the films pretty well, but even I was struggling to remember just when this large beige turd-craft had turned up, particularly as I was being distracted by the sight of my brother gleefully opening his own Christmas present, the very *Millennium Falcon* I'd been dreaming of.

Perhaps Luke Skywalker's X-Wing Fighter would have made for a better alternative as a spaceship Christmas present: it might not have been the *Millennium Falcon*, but at least it had blown up the *Death Star*. The Rebel Transporter, however, doubled up as a carry-case and somewhere to store your figures. To a practical man like my father, it was too good a combination to resist.

It didn't take long for television to follow George Lucas in cashing in on the success of *Star Wars*. The small screen was quick to copy his formula of dashing heroes, intergalactic princesses and comedy robots – though the results were quite often light, rather than light-speed.

Buck Rogers in the 25th Century had plenty of money thrown at its effects, if not its scripts. The show's eponymous hero had actually been launched into space in 1987; but, thanks to a freak accident, his spacecraft was 'blown out of his trajectory, into an orbit which freezes his life-support systems'. No, I'm still not completely sure what that means either, but the result was that Buck ended up back on earth in 2491. Fortunately for him, the planet appeared to be going through one of its late-twentieth-century fashion revivals, complete with big hair, mini-skirts and seventies disco dancing. I can't say it ever quite did it for me – it may have looked good but one could never shake the thought that in a shootout of space cowboys Han Solo would get more bang on his Buck every time.

What did work better, and which joined *Star Wars* in the hallowed ranks of being re-enacted in the playground, was *Gatchaman*. This early-1970s Japanese cartoon was re-dubbed into *Star Wars* lingo and given the American once-over. I wasn't at the meeting when the cartoon was retitled, but it probably went something like this:

'OK, guys, we need a name for this cartoon that sounds as close to *Star Wars* as we can legally get without being sued.'

'What about *War of the Stars*?'

'No – too similar. What's another word for stars?'

'I've got it! Worlds! We'll call it *War of the Worlds*.'

'It's nice, but hasn't Jeff Wayne just written a prog-rock album called that?'

'All right, then. Why don't we swap 'Worlds' for 'Planets'? We could call it *War of the Planets*?'

'Even better, what about *Battle of the Planets* . . . ?'

Just in case young boys like me hadn't quite picked up the association, the title sequence had *Battle of the Planets* shrinking into space in exactly the same way as the *Star Wars* lettering did. And it may have been pure coincidence (the Japanese cartoon predated the American film) but the cast list of characters mirrored that of *Star Wars*. Rather than Luke and Han, there was Mark and Jason vying to be in charge; instead of Princess Leia, there was a not-unattractive leading female called simply Princess. Chewbacca's role was given to Tiny, a rotund character who was anything but. There were even the annoying comedy characters – Keyop and 7-Zark-7 instead of C3P0 and R2D2. As for the main spaceship, it was called the *Phoenix* rather than the *Falcon*; and there might not have been 'the Force' but the group were collectively called G-Force, which is close enough.

Thus, in terms of lunchtime in the playground, *Battle of the Planets* became all but interchangeable with *Star Wars*. Many a lunch hour was spent with my classmates imitating G-Force's mission to thwart surprise attacks from 'galaxies beyond space', wherever that is meant to be. Note the detail '*my classmates* imitating G-Force's mission', by the way. For much as I would have loved to have been one of the 'five incredible young people with superpowers', once again my parents put the skids on my sci-fi dreams. Basically, the law of our playground was that anyone with a parka coat could do the top button up but leave the zip undone, thus creating a *Battle of the Planets*-style G-Force cape. Anyone who didn't got to play Zoltar and one of his sidekicks. Of course, once I realized this, I asked my parents to buy me a parka immediately. Surely they could understand that without such a coat I simply couldn't compete effectively with my classmates to be one of G-Force? Out came the usual middle-class practical excuses – difficult to wash, not very warm, poorly made, working class (OK, so they didn't say the last one, but they might as well have done).

'If you want to wear a coat as a cape, we could always get you a duffel coat,' my mother suggested.

This might sound like a generous offer, but we both knew it was a double bluff. Clothkits was bad enough, but even I was smart enough not to turn up at school looking like Paddington Bear.

*　　*　　*

ALL IN THE BEST *POSSIBLE* TASTE

Not everyone jumped on the *Star Wars* bandwagon. At the BBC it was as though the film and its advances in special effects had never happened. At the start of the 1980s the BBC's main sci-fi programmes were *Doctor Who* and *Blake's 7*. Tom Baker, with his scarf that went on forever, was a great Doctor, but by 1981 had been regenerated into Peter Davison, fresh from *All Creatures Great and Small* (fresh apart from the hand that had gone up the cow). Davison, for reasons I was never completely certain of, was dressed for a game of cricket in 1926 and had a stick of celery in his jacket pocket. That wasn't great, but from here the Doctor degenerated even further into Colin Baker, who looked a cross between Willy Wonka and Christopher Lillicrap.

One might think it couldn't have got any worse, but then came Sylvester McCoy. Setting his stall as a sort of Johnny Ball meets Jimmy Cricket, he was several planets away from the booming air of menace that Tom Baker had brought to the role. Baker had the better of the assistants, too – I had huge crushes on the likes of Leela (Louise Jameson) and Romana (Lalla Ward, the future Mrs Richard Dawkins), and would while away school assemblies by imagining them turning up in the TARDIS to whisk me away. They never did – which, given that I wasn't even ten years old at the time, was probably just as well. By contrast, Sylvester McCoy had to make do with Bonnie Langford. I don't remember her tap dancing around the TARDIS, but I can't say I was watching too closely by that point. I wasn't the only one: the viewing figures by then were so low (down from 16 million in 1979 to 3 million by 1989) that the show was put into suspended animation.

Tom Baker's *Doctor Who* was cut from the same cloth as Paul Darrow's Avon in *Blake's 7*. I always saw *Blake's 7* as the polar opposite of *Buck Rogers*: while that had bad scripts and good effects, *Blake's 7* had decent lines and appalling attempts at action. Clearly some bean-counter at the BBC had looked at the costs of special effects and thought, 'Why spend a fortune on creating a spaceship that looks as if it's under attack, when you can flick a light switch on and off and shake the camera a bit from side to side?' By contrast, the character of Avon, who headed a group of renegades on the run from some Intergalactic Federation, was superbly done: charismatic, ruthless, self-serving and arrogant, he was a British army officer to Buck Roger's cowboy in outer space.

Unlike *Doctor Who*, *Blake's 7* avoided the sad eighties slide towards cancellation with a clearout of the main characters in a brutal final episode in 1981. This bleak Blake ending, which saw every major character bar Avon shot in a shootout (and Avon himself surrounded by space soldiers ready to fire) was reported to have led to a spike in the national suicide rate. As much as a life without wonky special effects might seem empty and futile, I suspect that's a bit of an intergalactic urban myth.

Another BBC science-fiction programme without a huge budget was the *The Day of the Triffids*, an adaptation of John Wyndham's novel. It began with a freak meteor shower blinding pretty much the entire population of earth and causing the swift breakdown of society. Only a few people survived with their sight intact – among them a guy called Bill Masen, recovering in hospital at the time of the meteor shower.

And who saw this as the perfect opportunity for world domination? Why, a bunch of flowers of course . . .

The Triffid plants were the mutant result of a Russian experiment that went wrong. They had a venomous sting that could melt flesh, and they could wander around and chatter in a dolphin-style 'clk-clk-clk' dialect. The meteor shower was their chance to take over, and take over they did. As the humans struggled to cope with bumping into lampposts, the Triffids did their best Leylandii impression and became the hard perennial of choice.

I found *The Day of the Triffids* properly scary, unlike *Doctor Who*. I'd never been one to do the clichéd *Doctor Who* thing of watching it from behind the back of the sofa. Firstly, it always seemed a little bit too silly to be scary, and secondly, the back of our sofa was against the wall.

The Day of the Triffids, however, gave me the horticultural heebie-jeebies right from the title sequence. This involved close-ups of various people, their faces lit up in a blue-green 'night vision' wash, looking up to the sky while an eerie-sounding choir hummed in the background. Then, as the music built to a crescendo, there was a glimpse of the meteor shower, before a Triffid tongue flicked out and lashed a woman's face. I don't know if Gloria Gaynor was watching the opening credits, but from the first I was certainly afraid and worried that I might end up similarly petrified.

Of course, the Triffids themselves were, with the benefit of hindsight, a bit naff. Each moving flower had a person inside, sat on a go-kart seat in the base, with a fan hidden in the neck to keep them cool. That was about as hi-tech as the show got. But someone worked out that the secret was not to overuse the Triffids, or indeed to overuse anything at all – the programme's strength lay in its space and silence and atmosphere. A forerunner of *28 Days Later*, twenty-something years away.

What happened to the Triffids? With Alan Titchmarsh and his *Ground Force* team not yet in existence, the characters had to take matters into their own hands. Bill Masen (the one who looked a bit like Badly Drawn Boy) and Josella Peyton (who looked a bit like Peaches Geldof) escaped to the countryside and eventually joined their fellow survivors on the Isle of Wight. I'm not sure whether moving to the Isle of Wight was considered a happy or a downbeat ending, but after the *Blake's 7* finale I wasn't going to be too choosy.

What science fiction did do well in the 1980s was to get itself a sense of humour. Towards the end of the decade, *Spitting Image* stalwarts Rob Grant and Doug Naylor launched their sci-fi sitcom *Red Dwarf* into space. For me, the success of this stood firmly on the shoulders of *The Hitchhiker's Guide to the Galaxy*, the TV show of the book of the radio show of the extraordinary mind of the man who had read too many physics books. Douglas Adams, who died in 2001, came from the cerebral end of the comedy spectrum, providing a heady cocktail of philosophical knowledge and extreme silliness that Monty Python had previously made their own.

The series opened on planet earth, with our hero Arthur Dent (resplendent in an M&S dressing-gown, a sort of counter-culture Noël Coward) waking up to find that his house was about to be knocked down in order for a bypass to be built. This concern was then superseded by a slightly bigger one when Arthur's friend Ford Prefect revealed that the earth itself was about to be blown up to make way for an intergalactic highway. The pair escaped by hitching a ride on a passing spaceship, and so began their adventures.

Ford Prefect was helping to write an updated edition of the inter-galactic bestseller *The Hitchhiker's Guide to the Galaxy*, described as 'a sort of electronic book' (his description of earth was 'Mostly harmless'). Thirty years on, as electronic books struggle to get off the ground, perhaps they could do with emulating *The Hitchhiker's* USP of having 'Don't Panic!' written in big letters on the front. (Given the current vogue for the wartime poster 'Keep Calm and Carry On', it could really work . . .)

The programme followed Arthur and Ford on their philosophical tour of the universe, hooking up with the two-headed Zaphod Beeblebrox, his girlfriend Trillian (played by the squeaky-voiced Sandra Dickinson) and Marvin, their depressed robot. When they ate at The Restaurant at the End of the Universe, they discovered that the world was actually a long-standing experiment to find out what the Great Question was. The answer to life, the universe and everything, as worked out by the computer Deep Thought, was '42'. Arthur and Ford ended up back on a prehistoric planet earth, where they walked off into the sunset to the tune of Louis Armstrong's 'What a Wonderful World'.

ALL IN THE BEST *POSSIBLE* TASTE

The original radio show was a much-loved thing and the BBC did well to avoid the wrath of sci-fi fans in making the transition to TV. Adams originally wanted to film the show in Iceland, but the timing wasn't right and they ended up in Cornwall: a lot of the planetary scenes were shot in a clay pit near St Austell, not a million miles away from where the Eden Project now stands. There's probably something symbolic in that somewhere. Zaphod Beeblebrox's second head, meanwhile, was moved by remote control, the mechanics of which excited *Tomorrow's World* no end. At the actor's insistence Zaphod also had two penises, the length of which was reduced by the BBC costume department from nine to seven inches. These dangled down, one on each leg, though you'd be hard pressed to spot them, even when repeatedly pausing the action and zooming in to check. You're right: I really should get out more.

The biggest challenge was getting the electronic graphics of the book to work: the Terry Gilliam bits of the programme, if you will. Rather than risk fledgling computer technology, good old-fashioned animation was used instead. Perhaps this is one of the reasons why the programme holds up so well – the computer graphics resemble what you *think* early-eighties graphics should be, rather than actually *being* early-eighties computer graphics. In fact, the only part of the programme that has aged is the moment when Arthur and Ford sank six pints of beer in preparation for space travel. Ford handed the landlord a fiver and told him to keep the change, and the landlord looked astonished. He'd still look astonished at being handed a fiver now, but only in a slightly different way because it wouldn't cover two pints never mind six with change.

Up in space, the preferred tipple was not a pint of best but a Pan Galactic Gargle Blaster, whose intoxicating effects were shown in a cameo appearance from an alienated Cleo Rocos. Hers wasn't the only famous 'blink and you'll miss it' moment in the series: when an actor turned up late to one scene, Douglas Adams stepped up to take his place – stripping naked and running into the sea Reggie Perrin-style. And at The Restaurant at the End of the Universe, the dish of the day (an extraterrestrial cow suggesting parts of his body for the diners to eat) was played by Peter Davison.

The Hitchhiker's Guide left many legacies, some of which were musical. Without wishing to nail the watching demographic as 'thoughtful but slightly angst-ridden middle-class boys', it presumably included a young Thom Yorke of Radiohead and Coldplay's Chris Martin, whose respective 'Paranoid Android' and '42' both reference *The Guide*. More queer is the fact that *The Hitchhiker's Guide to the Galaxy* was also where eighties Brit-funk foursome Level 42 got their name. I may be wrong, but that low thwacking noise on 'Lessons in Love' is perhaps not so much the sound of existential undertones as it is Mark King's trademark slap bass.

The headmaster of my primary school was not the only teacher who was keen to try to inspire his pupils about space. In January 1986 an American schoolteacher, Christa McAuliffe, went T minus one better than Mr Bradley: there was no wheeling out the school television for her – not when she had bagged herself a seat on the *Challenger* space shuttle. In schools across the United States children did what I'd done five years earlier and gathered round the TV set to watch the shuttle launch.

I didn't see the *Challenger* launch live, but I saw it later, again and again, on the TV news. To begin with, the launch followed the familiar pattern of previous successful take-offs – the whoops from the crowd, the banal comments about clearing the tower, the shifting through the gears into orbit. But this time, about a minute in, the space shuttle did something darkly different: like a pantomime villain, in a puffball of smoke, it disappeared. For a few seconds, the side rockets raced on, like horses at the Grand National after their jockeys have been dislodged. Then they too joined the ticker-tape rain of debris cascading from the sky.

ALL IN THE BEST *POSSIBLE* TASTE

I pretended to be cool when the bad-taste jokes did the rounds at school: 'What's an astronaut's favourite drink? 7-Up!'; 'Where do astronauts take their holidays? All over Florida!' But my laughter was the same false giggle I'd learned to give when anyone told a rude joke that I didn't understand. I'd like to say that I felt terrible about the astronauts and for their families, but that wasn't what I was really gutted about. For me, the *Challenger* disaster was the moment when the romance of science fiction was no longer strong enough to deal with the reality of science fact. It wasn't just the astronauts who died when the shuttle exploded – my childhood fascination for space went with it too.

After the break, dust down your hat, because we've been invited to the wedding of the decade! And bring your raincoat too, because we're also going to a soggy day out at Alton Towers . . .

Ad Break

Heineken

Welcome to the School of Street Credibility, where an 'Enry 'Iggins type is teaching people how to speak propahh rather than proper, and turning my fair ladies into loose women. His well-to-do student today is an Eliza Doolittle only in the sense that Daddy is so absolutely minted she doesn't need to work. Eliza can talk precisely about the rain in Spain falling mainly on the plain and hurricanes not happening in Hampshire, but is having a little more difficulty with today's lesson: the water in Majorca don't taste like what it ought to.

'Majorca,' our 'Enry pronounces, with a 'j'.

'Mayorca?' Eliza tries, with a 'y'.

'Majorca,' he corrects.

'Mayorca!' She smiles both brightly and dimly at the same time.

When 'what it ought to' has been translated to 'quite how it should?', 'Enry calls his assistant for some 'elp. 'Elp, it transpires, is a can of

'Eineken for Eliza to get her laughing gear around. Opening it with a 'Golly' and taking a swig of lager, Eliza's language is transformed. Suddenly all her Sloane Ranger trappings have slipped away and she's talking street; another sip and she could be in the queue outside the kebab shop on a Saturday night.

It's possible that Heineken are using the advert to make a sophisticated linguistic point about the declining influence of received pronunciation and the unstoppable rise of the more everyman estuary English, glottal stops and all. It's more likely, though, that they're taking the piss out of posh people in order to shift some beer. And while I don't want to cast aspersions on the educational standards of the School of Street Credibility, I do feel it my duty to refresh the facts that parts of the advert don't reach. Yes, as it has been for many holiday resorts, water shortage has been an issue for the island of Majorca in recent years, and, yes, there have been instances of the Spanish government having to tank the stuff in. But in terms of the *quality* of the stuff, the water in Majorca is very much up to EU standards; and, having been on holiday there myself, I can tell you it tastes just fine.

Episode Six

'Here is the stuff of which fairy tales are made'

My brother might have got the *Millennium Falcon*, but he didn't get to watch the royal wedding. The marriage of Prince Charles and Lady Diana took place during the school holidays, on Wednesday 29 July 1981, and my brother was busy on a course. School holidays for my brother and I meant getting packed off on a selection of holiday clubs, run by sports groups, churches and anyone else who would keep us out of my mother's hair for six weeks. As a parenting plan it was simple but effective: as long as one of us was out of the house, we couldn't spend all day fighting with each other.

That particular week, it was my turn to be at home while Joff was at Gym Club. Quite where my parents had got the idea that Joff was into gymnastics, I am not entirely sure. Quite where my parents had got the idea that Gym Club was into gymnastics, I am equally uncertain.

The entire session, as far as I could gather, involved farting about in the foam pit, a discipline that I don't think has yet graduated to Olympic status.

'I can't go today,' Joff had argued in vain over his bowl of Ricicles at breakfast. 'What about the royal wedding?'

Mum shook her head. 'We've paid. You're going. That's it.'

My mother's rejection of my brother's pleas was based on a number of middle-class maxims. Firstly, the notion of not turning up to something was pure anathema to our parents. If the Bromleys said they were going to be somewhere, then they would be there and on time (if not ten minutes early). Secondly, hard cash had been handed over: that was not going to waste under any circumstances. But perhaps most crucially of all, like any left-leaning liberal parents, my parents did not buy into the royal family one little bit. Being middle class, they were far too well-mannered to suggest that the royals would be first against the wall when the revolution came. Instead, their attitude echoed that taken by the *Independent* when it launched in 1986. That paper reasoned that the royals weren't proper news and thus had an editorial policy of ignoring their existence. My parents also turned the other way: the Queen's speech at Christmas has never once graced the Bromley television set. And on royal-wedding day my dad went off to work as usual, my brother was packaged off to Gym Club and my mother got on with her daily routine as though nothing out of the ordinary was happening.

Someone else not watching the royal wedding was Ken Livingstone, then leader of the GLC, who had declined his invitation to the service and headed for the office instead. He would have got some work done, too, if he hadn't had to answer the telephone every couple of minutes to journalists wanting to know what he was doing. Ken's no-show to the wedding was matched by the King of Spain: he refused to attend because he was cross that Charles and Diana were visiting Gibraltar on their honeymoon.

The socialist Mayor of Boulogne, meanwhile, had offered a day trip to France for anyone who wanted to get out of Britain for the day. Among the scores of left-leaning leavers who caught the ferry were the young Labourites Peter Mandelson and Harriet Harman. Less politically motivated but equally anti-royal were the mass of coach trips to the Lake District, with each visitor enjoying the countryside while wearing an 'I hate Prince Charles' T-shirt. Missing the ceremony too were the street cleaners in Liverpool, who spent the day clearing up the bricks and burned-out cars after another night's rioting in Toxteth. And should you have been tuning in to Russian television for a glimpse of the royal wedding, you'd also have been disappointed: the Soviet authorities celebrated the ceremony with a special programme about Britain on the brink.

But apart from my brother, my parents, Ken Livingstone, Peter Mandelson, Harriet Harman, the 'I hate Prince Charles' day-trippers, the King of Spain, the Liverpool street cleaners and the Soviet Union, the only other person in the world not to watch the royal wedding was the woman running Gym Club. When we turned up at the sports hall to drop Joff off, it is fair to say that she was not overly thrilled to see him. I think the giveaway clue was the fact that she was standing in the doorway, bag in hand, about to make a run for it.

'Oh,' she said, with a welcome not quite as warm as the Mayor of Boulogne's. 'Hi.' She put her bag back down dejectedly on the floor. 'I didn't think that anyone would be coming today.' She pushed the door to the gym open forlornly to prove her point. It was completely empty.

'Do I really have to go?' Joff looked at the woman, who looked at my mother with the sort of look that said, 'Yes, Mrs Bromley – do you really have to leave your son with me today, when what I really want to be doing is heading back home to watch Charles and Diana get married?'

'It's not a bank holiday,' Mum said, which technically was true. 'It's just a normal *working* day.' Before the woman could come back with a response, Mum pushed my brother through the doorway and looked at her as if to say, 'He's in your hands now.'

Almost 28.5 million people in the UK watched the royal wedding, and 750 million tuned in worldwide. It was, I think I'm right in saying, the biggest television audience of the eighties in Britain, and the then fifth-biggest audience of all time: if there hadn't been 2 million people not watching because they were lining the London streets, it would surely have been bigger still. As it was, it was beaten only by the 1966 World Cup final (32 million), the 1969 *Royal Family* documentary (30 million), the 1970 splashdown of *Apollo 13* (28.6 million) and the 1970 FA Cup replay between Leeds and Chelsea (28.49 million). The *EastEnders* Christmas special of 1986, which we'll come to later, is regularly cited as getting just over 30 million viewers. However, that was the number for both the Christmas Day showing and the Sunday omnibus combined, so as figures go is arguably a bit of a fiddle. In fact, there has probably only been one occasion since 1981 when more people watched television in the UK at the same time. That event also starred Princess Diana, though not in quite as happy circumstances.

I was one of the millions, not because I was an ardent royalist or showing my parents some sort of reverse rebellion, but because school holidays meant sitting in front of the box for as long as I could get away with. If the wedding hadn't been happening, I'd have been happily tucking into the regular summer schedule of the *Wombles*, *Jackanory*, *Cheggers Plays Pop* and even the ubiquitous *Why Don't You?* In the latter, a group of irritating stage-school children put socks over their hands and pretended they were puppets, told a succession of terrible jokes and suggested that its viewers should 'switch off your television set and go and do something less boring instead'. This do-good philosophy left the viewer in no doubt that they were watching a programme being made by the sort of people who didn't think that small children should be wasting their lives watching television in the first place.

Which begged the question why they were wasting their lives *making* programmes for small children, when they could be doing something they actually considered worthwhile – I don't know, brass-rubbing or polishing their arseholes or something – and leaving the rest of us in peace with a double helping of *Scooby Doo*.

On this particular Wednesday, not even the BBC were telling us to switch off our sets. Far from it – their coverage of the big day started at 7.45 in the morning: an unheard-of hour for television to start in the days before breakfast TV. ITV started even earlier, with their cameras rolling from 7.30. By 9.45 BBC2 had got through its rather bizarre morning-schedule mix of *Open University*, *Play School* and the comedy Western *Son of Paleface* (their average viewer presumably being a Stetson-wearing scientist juggling a two-year-old and a Bunsen burner). They were now showing exactly the same coverage as BBC1, except with subtitles for the hard of hearing. So that was it: every channel in Britain was showing exactly the same thing. It was either watch the royal wedding or dig out the passport and hope that Peter Mandelson still had space in his car to give you a lift to the ferry port.

No expense was spared in the royal-wedding coverage. It was the biggest outside broadcast the BBC had ever attempted, with more than sixty cameras positioned at various vantage points. As well as the ones lining the route, they had one on board Prince Charles' old ship, HMS *Bronington*, and also at Caernarvon Castle and Balmoral – where, so anchorwoman Angela Rippon informed us, 'all thoughts of salmon fishing have been put aside'. Angela Rippon had not come cheap for the BBC: her fee reputedly ran into tens of thousands of pounds. She was helped on the presenting front by a cream-crackered-looking John Craven, who'd got the short straw of hitting the streets at 4.30 a.m. to talk to the gathering crowds. Back in the studio, Angela was joined by Eve Pollard (or Claudia Winkleman's mum) to wax lyrical about 'the dress' and Michael Wood to look at the day's 'funnier moments'.

With the BBC between Dimblebys, the plum job of commentator was given to Tom Fleming. Despite remaining off camera throughout the broadcast, Tom chose to do the entire commentary in full morning dress. This was purportedly to help him get into the right mood, though I can't help wondering whether he had plans to gatecrash the reception later on.

The BBC were not alone in splashing out on their coverage. The United States, being both staunchly republican and royalty mad at the same time, went on something of a land grab: their television networks were waving around cheques for £2000 per camera spot and in one case paid £8000 for the use of someone's balcony. ITV, not to be outdone, hired the Goodyear airship *Europa* for some panoramic shots, and stuck the somewhat unlucky Alastair Stewart in it for the day. Among their bulging roster of heavyweight reporters were Alastair Burnett, Sandy Gall, Jon Snow, Peter Sissons and Judith Chalmers. But perhaps the best example of the lengths to which television was prepared to go for the coverage was the hiring of a young ferret who went by the name of Nipper. Egged on by bits of streaky bacon tied to a piece of string, Nipper threaded the all important electrical cables through an underground duct between Buckingham Palace and the television-commentary box on the Victoria Memorial. Only in Britain.

Having dropped Joff off at Gym Club, back at home Helen and I sat down on the beanbag to watch the build-up. This mainly consisted of John Craven asking the crowd how long they'd been there (ages) and several hours of speculation about what Diana was going to be wearing. Guesses about dresses included that it was going to be 'romantic' and 'white' with 'lots and lots of lace'. These stunning insights were interspersed with Tom Fleming trying to remember who all the famous people were who were beginning to turn up at St Paul's Cathedral: 'Oh look! There's Harold Macmillan! Isn't that the King of Liechtenstein? And here's Nancy Reagan, swishing up the aisle like she was Alexis Colby's mother . . .'

Those are my words, by the way, rather than Tom Fleming's. His commentary was far more reserved and reverential, all spoken in his lovely honey-coloured actor's tone.

'There, the unmistakable figure of King Olaf,' he soothed with the authority of someone who knew what the King of Norway looked like. Or maybe it was just with the authority of someone who knew the rest of us hadn't a clue what King Olaf looked like.

Eventually, after what seemed like a marriage-worth of waiting (to the point where I was beginning to consider that maybe *Why Don't You?* wasn't so bad after all) there was a clip-clop of horses from Buckingham Palace, a rendition of 'God Save the Queen', and there, in an open-topped, horse-drawn carriage were the Queen and Prince Philip.

'Have you ever heard such cheers?' grovelled Tom Fleming, as the Queen waved at the wealth of Union flags waving back at her. The Queen was dressed in the sort of toothpaste-green outfit that looked out of fashion even when it was in fashion. Or maybe she'd brushed her teeth that morning with vigorous fury at the thought of what Charles was about to get his family into. In the carriage behind the Queen came the Queen Mother, also in toothpaste-green (that must have been an embarrassing moment at breakfast), who was travelling with Prince Edward ('Such a tall young man now,' Fleming cringingly observed). Behind them came Princess Anne and, well, all the other ones – the minor royals who are about as regal as a packet of cigarettes, and who even the Queen can put a name to only when she thinks really hard about it.

Meanwhile, five minutes back up the road, appeared Prince Charles and Prince Andrew, travelling in the 1902 state landau.

'A lovely carriage this,' Tom enthused, not remotely struggling for something to say. 'Slightly lighter in its coach paint than the others.'

A pale-looking Prince Charles, meanwhile, was also slightly lighter in his 'coach paint' than the other members of his family, and as the carriage headed for St Paul's was doing his very best hedgehog-in-the-headlights expression.

'Going through his lines, perhaps,' Tom offered, just a little diplomatically.

So far, so Silver Jubilee. But, as the cameras switched to Clarence House, the event transformed from a royal occasion to one out of a storybook. Waiting outside Clarence House was the glass coach, with Lady Diana and her father, Earl Spencer, inside. That's right. The glass coach. The only way this could have been more like the stuff of fairytales was if it had magicked into existence from a pumpkin. I don't know if the TV cameras had been told not to show Diana until she was inside the coach, but knowing she was there and that we couldn't see her only heightened the sense of drama and expectation. Finally, the coach pulled away and clip-clopped past the camera, and there was the nation's first flash of the bride to be: head to foot in ivory silk and taffeta, hidden behind her veil like a ghost of a girl.

'A wonderful fairytale sight,' Tom Fleming declared. 'Perhaps like all royal brides, the veil will be thrown back and we'll see that lovely face.' But the veil stayed firmly in place. Tom thought about this, and quickly turned it round to commend Diana on her 'air of mystery'.

'So it's all very exciting,' he continued, 'we now have three processions on the hoof.' The sprinkling of fairytale fairy dust spread forward from Diana's coach all the way along the route. The Strand, on any other day a traffic jam of red buses and black cabs, was transformed. 'This street used to be a country road along the banks of the River Thames,' Tom sighed wistfully, as though he was old enough to remember this himself. Up ahead at St Paul's, meanwhile, the bridesmaids had arrived and they too were 'straight out of a fairy story'.

The fact that all three processions were horse-drawn certainly helped create a sense of timelessness: it probably wouldn't have been as romantic if they'd been driven to the church with a phalanx of motorbike outriders. Diana's 'air of mystery' helped too. Before the service, she had actually been seen speaking on television on only two occasions – once briefly when the engagement was announced, and once in a joint ITV/BBC interview. For most of the time, then, she was a face not a voice: a silent-movie star for modern times. This made her effortlessly enigmatic, and put all the attention on her looks. All of which made it easier for people to romanticize her, and to see her as the two-dimensional princess of a fairytale rather than the fragile and complicated mix of a real person. Certainly, when Diana arrived at St Paul's and stepped out of the glass coach, she looked every bit the fictional princess. The train of her dress was twenty-five-feet long and, as she slowly made her way up the aisle, her unwell father clinging on to her as much as she clung on to him, it stretched out behind her like a single elongated teardrop.

The wedding itself, I'm sure you are familiar with. It was quite reserved from a television point of view, with Tom Fleming interrupting only to say who was who or which hymn was which. Like in a modern-day home-movie recording, the vicar (in this case the Archbishop of Canterbury) seemed to get in the way of all the key moments. Just as Tom Fleming had opened his commentary by saying, 'Once upon a time', so the Archbishop, Robert Runcie, began his sermon by saying, 'Here is the stuff of which fairytales are made.' He then tried to be a bit more grown up about events, but singularly failed to do so. Then, once the ceremony was over, nervous mistakes and all, there was a rendition of 'God Save the Queen', just in case anyone forgot who was really in charge.

Later, back at Buckingham Palace, the crowds poured down The Mall in their hundreds of thousands, demanding another view of the bride.

'It is not just the size of the crowds,' Tom Fleming said, the headiness of the day's events beginning to get to him, 'it is the happiness of the crowds. It is as though a whole nation is gathering in front of Buckingham Palace saying, "Yes we do respect law and order, yes we can be happy, yes we do like each other and, yes, we do like being British."'

To huge cheers, the royals came out on to the balcony, with Princess Diana (a 'commoner' no more), understanding exactly what they and the media were after.

'Kiss me,' she said to her new husband.

'I'm not getting into that caper,' was his touching reply. He then doubled the romance of the moment by asking his mother if it would be OK to do so. With the Queen allowing Charles' stiff upper and lower lips to relax, the crowd had their kiss and the papers their photo. The front page of the *Daily Mail* the next day, for example, consisted solely of the image and the one-word headline 'Perfect!'

The fact that Prince Charles asked his mother's permission before kissing his wife might seem faintly ridiculous now, but back in 1981 public displays of affection were simply not part of royal protocol. There had been no kiss in the church; Prince Charles held his ceremonial sword rather than his wife's hand as they sat side by side during the service. Despite what the song says, a kiss can be more than just a kiss. Here, it was the moment when the modern world came up against centuries of tradition – and the modern world won.

A year earlier, ITV had controversially shown a programme about another modern-day princess torn between the present and the past. The princess in this case was Princess Masha'il of Saudi Arabia. In the 1970s Masha'il had been sent to school in Lebanon, where she met and fell in love with the son of the Saudi ambassador. Their love affair continued back in Saudi Arabia and was subsequently discovered. Adultery is a crime under Sharia law, though someone can be convicted only if either there were four male witnesses to the adultery or the accused states three times in court, 'I have committed adultery'. Despite being unmarried, and rather than giving up her lover, Masha'il confessed to her affair the requisite three times and, in 1977, when Masha'il was aged just nineteen, both she and her lover were publicly executed.

That, at least, is one version of events: how much of it is true remains open to debate but certainly this was what was told and retold throughout the Middle East over the following years – the heart-breaking story of a beautiful young princess who died for love, whose modern mores and lifestyle did not sit with the traditional teachings of Arabic culture. It was a story whose potency was spotted by British journalist Anthony Thomas. 'Whoever I spoke to,' he recalled in a later interview, 'whether they were Palestinians, whether they were conservative Saudis, whether they were radicals, they attached themselves to this princess. She'd become a myth. And they identified with her, and they kind of co-opted her to their cause.'

Thomas decided to make a documentary about Masha'il, *Death of a Princess*. The problem was that, although everyone in the Middle East was familiar with some version of the story, no one was willing to talk to him about it on camera. To get round this, the documentary became a drama-documentary, mixing interviews with scenes played out by actors. This 'factional' way of telling a story is commonplace on television now, but it was both unusual and controversial back at the start of the 1980s – particularly given the programme's subject matter. The documentary depicted a loosely fictional country called 'Arabia', in which traditional Islamic teachings were flouted for a more extravagant lifestyle: rich wives, for example, were shown driving out into the desert to pick up men for sex.

The documentary quickly escalated into a major diplomatic concern. The Saudi Arabian government were furious and attempted to stop the programme being shown. They appealed to both ITV and the British government, the latter of whom offered regret for any offence caused but made it clear that they had no power to interfere in editorial content. It was undoubtedly a difficult position for the British government to find themselves in – 16 per cent of the UK's oil came from Saudi Arabia, and business links between the two countries had been booming. There were ongoing construction contracts with British firms worth just short of £300 million; British Aerospace, meanwhile, were supplying equipment to the Saudi Air Force to the tune of almost £1 billion. The previous year, Britain had sold $2 billion of exports to Saudi Arabia, the eleventh-largest market for British goods.

With their pleas ignored, the Saudis were quick to make clear their displeasure. *Death of a Princess* was 'an unprincipled attack on the religion of Islam and its 600 million people and the way of life of Saudi Arabia, which is at the heart of the world of Islam'. They criticized the British government's 'negative attitude' towards this 'shameful film' and immediately expelled the British Ambassador. There were economic responses too: visas for British workers were withheld; various firms were told not to work with British businesses; and Concorde was banned from flying supersonically in Saudi airspace, effectively cancelling its regular flight to Singapore.

To begin with, the British government maintained their stance that it was nothing to do with them. 'It is most unfortunate,' the Foreign Office said, 'that Anglo-Saudi relations should have been damaged by a film that the British government was in no way responsible for and which it could not prevent from being shown on British TV.' But a month on, and with no sign of the stand-off ending, they changed their tune to bring the crisis to an end. The Foreign Secretary Lord Carrington now decided that the programme had been 'deeply offensive' and 'wished it had never been shown'. Or, as *Not the Nine O'Clock News* put it, 'Lord Carrington . . . says he offers the Saudis the hand of friendship, which had previously belonged to the producer of the programme.'

Both *Death of a Princess* and the royal wedding showed the romantic pull of a contemporary fairy story and the power of the moving image to deliver it. They weren't the only ones to realize this: George Lucas had understood something similar when he was making *Star Wars*. Much of his plotting had its origins in Joseph Campbell's work on classic stories and mythologies – and, for all the spaceships and science fiction, his film was the timeless telling of a princess (Leia) being rescued from a castle (the *Death Star*).

The houses of Saud and Windsor, too, were ultimately in the business of selling stories. Princess Diana looked like an old-fashioned princess, and that was why she tugged so many heartstrings. Princess Masha'il had not behaved like a princess should, which was why the Saudi family were so keen to suppress the documentary about her. They were different sorts of fairytales but came from the same point – that respect for and strength of a royal family came from their being different to the 'commoners', as a pre-wedding Diana was described. Once that distance began to erode, then so did the justification for their existence.

Some members of the Windsors understood this better than others. In 1987 all the acclaim that the royal family had achieved with Charles and Diana's wedding was dissipated in a single television programme. The couple weren't involved with the show, but you could argue that it was the logical extension of their kiss on the Buckingham Palace balcony several years before. It was fine to add a dash of modernity to proceedings if you were a Princess Diana, skilled enough to do the touchy-feely thing and still maintain your air of mystery. But if you were a Prince Edward, then a similar attempt to be at one with the people was always going to be a more tricky affair.

Poor Prince Edward. His eldest brother had married the fairytale princess. His other brother mixed flying helicopters in the Falklands War with regular rumours about a more earthy form of chopper action. Edward, for all Tom Fleming's adulation at the wedding about his height, spent the 1980s failing to cut it in the marines and suffering the inevitable tabloid insinuations about his lack of both masculinity and girlfriends. An insinuation, it has to be said, that wasn't helped by a switch of careers into the theatre.

Then, in 1987, Prince Edward came up with a plan. Following on from the success of Band Aid, Live Aid and Comic Relief, Edward hit upon the idea of putting together a charity event himself. What if he dusted down the old television chestnut *It's a Knockout* for charity? He could pull in a selection of celebrities from music, sport, film and television to do the running-about bit and get various members of the royal family to captain each team. At a stroke, he could show how in tune the royals were with the modern world, he'd have a calling card to launch his career in television and, because it was for charity, he was guaranteed to get a good press.

On 15 June 1987 the great, the good and Su Pollard gathered at a somewhat sodden Alton Towers for the unnecessarily titled *The Grand Knockout Tournament* – what was wrong with *It's a Royal Knockout*, as everyone else was calling it? The Queen, Charles and Diana were not there, having had the foresight to keep out of it (actually, in a rare lapse of media judgment, Diana had wanted to go but was overruled by her husband). One wonders in retrospect why, if *they*'d had the sense not to get involved, the rest of the royal family weren't banned from turning up as well.

The contestants were divided in four teams, each led by a different royal: Princess Anne's team included Jenny Agutter, Sheena Easton, Emlyn Hughes and Cliff Richard; Prince Andrew bagged George Lazenby, Gary Lineker, Anneka Rice and Nigel Mansell; Sarah Ferguson's team, meanwhile, boasted Michael 'Dempsey' Brandon, Chris de Burgh, Viv Richards and Meatloaf; and, bringing up the rear, Prince Edward had snared Duncan Goodhew, Eddy Grant, Tessa Sanderson and Toyah Wilcox. To this list of contestants, we must add Rowan Atkinson, as the Blackadder-ish host Lord Knock of Alton, and his Lady wife for the day, Barbara Windsor. Then there was the main host, Stuart Hall, incidental commentator Les Dawson, sidekick Su Pollard, and official scorer Paul

Daniels. No, I'm not sure why a magician got to do the adding up rather than, say, Carol Vorderman, either. Maybe Edward saw Paul counting up every second on his quiz show or something.

With a few notable exceptions, a bit like the royals on show themselves, this was a B-list collection of eighties stars. No one from the *Comic Strip* generation of comedians was there, not even a Dawn French or a Lenny Henry. Similarly, none of the music stars rounded up had ever found a message on their answer phone from Bob Geldof. There was no Andrew Ridgeley, let alone a George Michael or a Simon Le Bon; no one who had sung on Band Aid or performed at Live Aid was present.

When it comes to branding, association is everything. Which is why putting Princess Anne in the same show as Su Pollard was never going to be a good idea. The fact that you had real royals alongside pretend lords and ladies didn't help matters either. It blurred the lines between what was real and what wasn't, and the net effect was that it was difficult to take any of them seriously. Which doesn't matter so much if your day job is to be a comic actor, but makes quite a big difference if you're in line to the throne. The carefully cultivated fairytale of the royal wedding had been replaced by a royal comic book and Diana's 'air of mystery' swapped for the whiff of silliness.

On top of this, Prince Edward decided that the various games, such as 'Knock a Knight' or 'The Joust' would be sponsored. Which would have been fine if they'd got some high-end companies to blue-chip in. Instead, though, the cash came from people like McDonald's and Asda. Even then, it might all have been worthwhile if the event had pulled in some serious cash; but, while Bob Geldof's efforts raised £150 million, Prince Edward's managed just a solitary million pounds (couldn't his mum just have written him a cheque?). Bob was a man who played the media to perfection, with callers jumping to the phone when he shouted for contributions on screen. Prince Edward, by contrast, erred considerably by keeping all the media stuck in a tent without access to the stars. By the time he turned up for the end-of-day press conference, expecting adulation and applause, he was greeted instead by a room of severely hacked-off hacks.

'Well, thanks for sounding so bloody enthusiastic,' Edward snapped, storming off. The papers got their revenge by christening him 'Sir Prat-a-lot'. And the royal image, which had once been so powerful, was never quite the same again.

Prince Edward's efforts may have been farcical, but at least they weren't fake. Sitting here on the sofa of hindsight, we now know that the apparently fairytale wedding of Charles and Diana was anything *but* a fairytale. One of the very few members of the St Paul's congregation that Tom Fleming did not mention was in fact the most significant of all: Camilla Parker Bowles. Goodness only knows what she, and Charles and Diana were going through during the service – the only thing the wedding had in common with a fairytale was that it too was make-believe.

In a strange kind of way, I don't think this diminishes the meaning of the day's events – I think it heightens them. Whatever you might think about Camilla, it's clear that she and Charles were in love and meant to be together, and ultimately there was nothing that was going to get in the way – not the fact that Camilla was already married, nor that Charles was saying 'I will' to one of the most famous and beautiful women in the world. Real love, the proper, grown-up, adult kind, can be awkward, messy, confusing and complicated, but all the richer an experience as a result. The royal wedding was proof of that: an iconic ceremony that had everything to do with romance – just not the one we thought we were watching, and not of the sort you get in fairytales.

After the break, we shout 'Gotcha!' as we head south to liberate a load of sheep. We watch a geography teacher give the Prime Minister a lesson and meet a here-today and (if we may say so) gone-tomorrow politician . . .

Ad Break

Carling Black Label

Germany, the Ruhr Valley, the Second World War. Or rather, if we're feeling accurate, the 1955 black-and-white film version of the 1940s Ruhr Valley mission. Or, if one wants to get particularly specific about things, a 1980s pastiche of the 1955 film of the Second World War mission, when a squadron of Lancaster Bombers flew in dangerously low to drop their bouncing bombs and bust the Germans' dams.

As this particular Lancaster Bomber flies in, with its two co-pilots speaking through their masks in the spit and crackle of radio communication, a lone German guard looks out from his watchtower and rushes out to defend his dam. He watches carefully as the bomb bounces along the surface of the water like a particularly well-thrown skimming stone. It should be mission accomplished but, just as it is about to burst through the wall behind him, the guard reaches up and catches the bomb.

The Lancaster Bomber comes back round for another drop, unleashing a full set of five bombs. The German guard, who has now taken off his coat and rolled up his sleeves, stops each one with the skill of a world-class goalkeeper: catching some, tipping others over the bar. Like the Polish 'clown' who kept England out of the 1974 World Cup, nothing is going to get past this guy. Admitting defeat, the British pilots head for home; one of them says he'd put money on the fact that the guard drinks Carling Black Label.

If one wanted to be picky, one might point out that it is highly unlikely that this bestselling beer was on sale in Nazi Germany. Which is probably just as well: if it had been, and it had this sort of effect, we might never have won the war.

The British pilots might have been disappointed not to score, but at least they hadn't found Harald Schumacher in goal that night. Schumacher was the German national goalkeeper in the early 1980s, complete with the compulsory bubble-perm and moustache, and is best known for his Carling black-mark performance in the 1982 World Cup semi-final against France. As the French player Patrick Battiston chased down the pitch after a long ball, Schumacher came racing out of his goal to meet him. The charitable description of what happened next is that he collided extremely heavily with his opponent. Battiston was stretchered off the pitch with an oxygen mask, and was exceedingly fortunate not to have broken his neck: as it turned out, Schumacher's 'tackle' had 'only' broken several vertebrae and knocked out a number of teeth.

The British bombers, then, could count themselves lucky. If that's what Schumacher could do to a footballer, one can only shudder at what he might have done to their plane.

Episode Seven

'I counted them all out and I counted them all back'

In 1962 my father was one of the earliest people to take part in Voluntary Services Overseas, or VSO as it is more commonly known. This involves doing good deeds in a faraway land, using your skills learned in Britain for the benefit of those abroad. Not for my father the route of most VSO volunteers, with a journey to somewhere exciting, exotic and scorching hot. Instead, he caught a plane to Buenos Aires, hopped over the River Plate to Montevideo and boarded a boat sailing for a small group of islands 200 miles away in the South Atlantic.

I'm not sure whether Dad chose the Falklands or the Falklands chose him. But what I do know in intimate detail is what he did during his year there. If only I had a pound for every time in my childhood my father started a story with the words 'When I was in the Falklands . . .' My dad isn't a bad storyteller, but it's fair to say that the material he had to work with here was somewhat limited. His year was spent mainly travelling from farm to farm, teaching children and generally helping out with whatever needed doing. Consequently, the anecdotes involved one or more of the following: penguins, sheep, bareback horseriding, eating steak for breakfast, and more penguins. I wouldn't say that the Falklands were cut off from the rest of the world, but Dad only found out about the Cuban Missile Crisis about two months after it happened.

The Falklands weren't the only part of the South Atlantic about which Dad regaled us with stories. He was also fascinated with turn-of-the-century Antarctic explorers, such as Scott and Shackleton, and their various doomed attempts to make it to the South Pole. Shackleton in particular was a hero of his, not least because of his infamous journey across the South Atlantic seas in a lifeboat. With his ship, *Endurance*, crushed by ice, Shackleton and the remains of his men travelled several hundred miles across violent seas to another nearby British island, South Georgia. The story is all the more impressive if you ever get to see the boat, which is now at Dulwich College (Shackleton was a pupil there) where my father took me to see it.

To be honest, all this talk of the Falklands Islands, South Georgia and the vicious South Atlantic seas all seemed quite distant to my nine-year-old self. They weren't so much tales from the Magic Faraway Tree as Tales from the Not-That-Magic Faraway Sheep Island. But then, overnight, my father's anecdotes transformed from Jack-a-snorey to twenty-four-carat playground gold. On 2 April 1982, taking pretty much everyone by surprise, Argentina invaded the Falklands. And, while no one else at school even knew where the islands were ('Aren't they off the coast of Scotland, Brommers?'), I was suddenly a world expert on the coming war, proudly holding forth about 'When *my* dad was in the Falklands . . .'

The Falklands War began as yet another big British cock-up. In the late 1970s Argentina had been taken over by the military and made various tub-thumping noises about regaining the Falkland Islands – or Las Malvinas, as they called them. The question of who owned them depended really on how far back in history you wanted to go. The British had been there since the mid-nineteenth century. At the same time, the Spanish had also claimed them when they took over the New World and bequeathed them to the fledgling Argentine people when they became independent in 1820.

The Argentinean junta continued making noise, while the British Foreign Office did their polite bit – 'We really *must* sit down and chat about all this' – while finding no space in the diary to do anything. At the same time, the British Navy were undergoing a round of cost-cutting, including plans to withdraw the longstanding 'Antarctic protection vessel', the *Endurance*. The junta, now led by the not entirely pleasant General Leopoldo Galtieri, took this as a sign that the British weren't that bothered about the islands. They'd already tested the waters a couple of years earlier by landing in another British territory, the South Sandwich Islands, and had found that not much happened as a result. So in March 1982 an Argentinean ship turned up at South Georgia on the pretext of demolishing an old whaling station – and their demolition experts just so happened to raise another Argentinean flag on British soil in the process. This time, the British sounded slightly more cross, and Argentina, who had been waiting for the *Endurance* to leave in June before invading the Falklands, decided to speed things up and launch their attack straightaway.

Just as in the Monty Python sketch where nobody expects the Spanish Inquisition, so nobody in the British government expected the Argentinean invasion. While the Argentinean media were declaring the military raid a success, the PR officer at the Ministry of Defence was happily telling journalists throughout the night that there had been no such attack. The following day, the same line of denial was continued by various ministers in the House of Commons. 'We were in touch with the governor half an hour ago and he assured us that no such invasion had taken place,' MPs were told. It was only by early evening that the government grudgingly admitted what had happened.

So far, so seventies. But all this ineptitude was quickly forgotten in the shock at what had happened, and by the sheer speed of Margaret Thatcher's response. The Argentineans were somewhat surprised to discover that the British were now way beyond diarizing a chat about things, and were in fact assembling a task force to recapture the islands. Despite a United Nations resolution, urging Argentina to withdraw and to work with Britain to find a diplomatic solution to the crisis, the British government were gearing up to do anything but talk.

All of which was, to my young self, incredibly exciting. We were going to war! From the suburbs of York, I could see there wasn't a huge amount I could do to make a difference, but I was determined to do my bit. Firstly, my youthful dalliance with supporting Tottenham Hotspur, which had largely come about because of Ricky Villa's mazy run in the 1981 FA Cup final replay, was going to have to come to an end. Ricky Villa seemed a nice guy, as did Ossie Ardiles, but it just didn't seem right to cheer for them in a time of crisis. I was going to have to return to my first love, the slightly less glamorous York City, instead. Secondly, to show the level of personal sacrifice I was willing to make to support our troops, I informed my mother that I would no longer be eating Fray Bentos corned beef.

'Isn't Fray Bentos in Uruguay?' Mum said, as I passed my supper back across to her. 'I don't think we're at war with them.'

After a careful look at the family atlas, I had to concede that she was right, as usual. 'But it's on the border with Argentina,' I pointed out, 'and that's where all the beef comes from. My friend Paul's dad's friend's wife is a dinner lady, and she says we shouldn't eat it because it might be contaminated.'

There was a slight frisson in the air between my parents, which was largely because of a difference in opinion about the war. My father was slightly more gung-ho, particularly as he'd lived there, and was very much of the impression that we should go and get the islands back. My mother was more a pacifist by nature. She also instinctively took the alternative viewpoint to Margaret Thatcher by default.

'What is it you're always telling the children, John?' she asked. 'The importance of compromise? And learning to share?'

'Well, yes,' said my father, 'but . . .'

'And settling arguments by talking about things, not by fighting.'

'Well, yes,' my father continued to concede. 'But this is, well, different.'

'If you ask me,' Mum continued, 'it's just a piece of windswept rock thousands of miles away in the middle of the sea. Is it really worth killing lots of people to get them back?'

'But what about the islanders?' Dad asked.

'And the sheep?' I added. 'And the cows.' I pointed at my plate to show the sort of outlook that British cattle could expect under Argentinean rule.

'And the penguins,' Joff added. 'The Argentineans might be horrible to them.'

'Well, it's hardly a paradise for them at the moment, is it, John?' My mother fixed my father with a glare. 'Strange that out of all your Falklands stories, you never tell the children about the "kick a penguin" competitions.'

'Well, I don't think we need to bring that up now . . .' Now it was my dad who was being all diplomatic while my mother seemed all battle-hardened.

'I can't quite remember how it worked . . .' Mum feigned confusion. 'Didn't you used to sneak up behind them and . . .'

'Who is for more corned beef, then?' my father asked, knowing when he was beaten.

Despite my mother's best efforts, I remained almost bed-wettingly excited about the Falklands War. That's almost, please note. I was nine at the time of the war, and as such was still at the 'snips and snails and puppy dogs' tails' stage of growing up. Although my parents had always balked at buying me plastic guns I was very much into Action Men, complete with their *de rigueur* eagle eyes. I was particularly fascinated by Harrier Jump Jets – a plane that could take off and land on a sixpence? How ace was that? I would draw pictures of them at every given opportunity, taking off and shooting one of Argentina's Super Étendards in a dogfight before landing back precisely on the deck of the aircraft carrier.

'I don't think you'd be drawing pictures if there was a *real* war,' Mum once said when I showed her one of my many efforts.

She was right, as usual. The Falklands War wasn't a 'real' war like the Second World War. It also wasn't a real war in the way it was shown on television. As I watched the task force (a good hard name, that) leave Portsmouth to cheering crowds and Rod Stewart's 'Sailing' wafting out over the Tannoy, little did I know that this would be the last time I would see any proper television pictures for several weeks. The Falklands War was not going to be like when the SAS stormed the Iranian Embassy live on television: everything we watched of the war was going to sanitized, censored and, like a British Rail train, very, very delayed.

As well as the troops, the departing ships contained a small contingent of British journalists and TV crews. The three days between the invasion and the task force setting sail were spent with the government and the media haggling over who was going to go – a sort of Willy Wonka's golden ticket, except with fewer chocolate bars and more Exocet missiles. This squabbling summed up the inherent conflict that exists between the armed forces and journalists at times of war: the latter instinctively want to tell everything that is happening; the former want to keep it all hush-hush and secret.

The British military had Vietnam in their minds when dealing with the media. It was commonly thought that uncensored television footage had been a huge factor in turning public opinion against the war in the United States, and the Ministry of Defence were determined not to let the same thing happen with the Falklands. The uniqueness of the conflict allowed them a rare opportunity for complete control of the coverage. Because the Argentinean attack had been such a surprise, there were no reporters on the ground in the Falklands: the only way a journalist was going to get to cover the war was to hitch a ride on one of the British ships. The only way they were then going to send a report back was with the navy's help, and that would have to go via the Ministry of Defence.

The navy's natural instinct was to have as few members of the media on board as possible. After pressure from Bernard Ingham, Margaret Thatcher's bluff, no-nonsense PR chief, they reluctantly found fifteen spaces. Five of these were given to the BBC and ITN on board the fleet's flagship, the aircraft carrier HMS *Hermes*. The two organizations agreed to share a cameraman, sound recordist and engineer, and to send one correspondent each.

The correspondent chosen by the BBC was Brian Hanrahan.

'You've just been on a sailing holiday,' his editor cheerfully said on the phone, 'how do you fancy another one?'

He was told at one o'clock on the Sunday afternoon, and needed to be in Portsmouth by eight in order to get on board. The ITN correspondent Michael Nicholson, meanwhile, was walking in the Lake District when his clearance came through. He was finally tracked down in the early afternoon, and was told to head straight to Carlisle, where a light aircraft was waiting to take him down to the south coast.

As the ships began the long 8000-mile trip to the South Atlantic, it soon became apparent to Hanrahan and Nicholson how difficult their task was going to be. Accompanying them were a group of Ministry of Defence minders, whose attitude to the media was described as 'lazy', 'unhelpful' and even 'dishonest'. Then there was the crew themselves.

Captain Middleton on board HMS *Hermes* 'did not like the press', according to Michael Nicholson. 'He said from the very start that we were an embarrassment to him.' This was not an atypical view – later on, after Nicholson watched the British attack on Pebble Island, he wasn't allowed to get back to file his report: 'You bastards are the lowest-priority rating,' said the lieutenant in charge of assigning helicopters, 'and that's where you'll remain.'

There were huge practical problems in getting reports back to Britain as well. Sending television pictures back directly from the ships was all but impossible: the moving ships and size of the files made any satellite link-up all but untenable; and the navy were worried it might give away their position, so they were unwilling to try too hard to see if it was possible. Consequently all television pictures made their way back to the UK via a combination of ship and plane, and took weeks to arrive. The average delay between footage being shot and being shown on television during the Falklands War was seventeen days. In some cases, reports were shown more than three weeks after they'd been filmed – a delay longer than the coverage of the Charge of the Light Brigade during the Crimean War.

The result, of course, was that when the footage did arrive (the 'Dead Sea Scrolls' as one ITN producer described them) events had moved on and thus the impact of the reports was minimized. This was particularly true for bad-news stories, such as the sinking of HMS *Sheffield*, which appeared to take longer to arrive than reports of British success. For much of the war, then, television coverage consisted of promotional footage of British weaponry and drawings of events done by that guy who usually sits in court with his paintbrush. All of which meant that on TV the war looked a bit like one of those old war comic books – *Battle* or *Commando* – which served only to fuel my youthful interest even further.

The best that Brian Hanrahan and Michael Nicholson could do was to send back audio reports, which were broadcast on TV accompanied by a still photograph of the correspondent. Even getting the audio material through was no straightforward task, though. With HMS *Hermes* under radio silence, Hanrahan and Nicholson had to hitch a helicopter ride to another ship: the auxiliary vessel *Olmeda*. Often travelling through thick fog, the journalists were then winched down on to the ship, where they would wait for a secure line to be set up to send the report back to London before hitching another ride back to HMS *Hermes*. This process, to send reports that were at most a couple of minutes long, would take hours – and on several occasions no return helicopter could be found so they had to stay on *Olmeda* overnight.

The coverage was further compromised by the fact that it was controlled by the military – we were therefore being given the impression that the British were winning easily, and doing so with minimal casualties. One early example of this was the recapture of South Georgia. Margaret Thatcher announced the news herself, telling reporters to 'Rejoice!' A photo of the British troops re-raising the Union Jack was somehow immediately available, having avoided the usual media delays. Continuing the good-news feel, Admiral Woodward told journalists that it had been a 'walkover'. In fact, the episode had been close to a complete disaster: 100mph winds had made conditions near impossible and two helicopters had crashed; it was only the heroics of the other crew that meant no lives were lost. It was weeks until the true story emerged – by which point both the war and the viewer's interest had moved on.

Some censorship of footage was understandable and the TV correspondents were happy to go along with this. So references to fog were removed, because such might have allowed the Argentineans to pinpoint where the fleet was. Also omitted was the fact that Argentinean bombs were failing to go off: again, had they known this they could have made readjustments and with deadly consequences. Even the number of planes flying on a particular mission was classified, leading

Brian Hanrahan to come up with the vague but victorious phrase, 'I counted them all out and I counted them all back.'

However, there were also many instances of the military hiding behind the notion of 'classified information' in order to hold back details that may have been awkward to acknowledge but that did not *need* to be secret. The MOD asked for footage of body-bags to be removed, for example. When the ship *Sir Galahad* was hit, with many soldiers trapped by the fire that broke out, Brian Hanrahan found his report of 'badly burned' troops and survivors 'shaken and hysterical' stopped by the censors, while Michael Nicholson's more positive account of 'a day of extraordinary heroism' was allowed through. At one point, so frustrated was Nicholson with the Ministry of Defence that he suggested that the very fact that his reports were being censored should be flagged up, as reports from places such as Poland and Israel were: ironically the use of the word 'censored' in his report was itself censored.

Nicholson recalled afterwards one discussion with his MOD minder, Graham Hammond, who told him, 'You must have known you couldn't report bad news before you left. You knew when you came you were expected to do a 1940s-propaganda job.' Certainly, the recapture of South Georgia wasn't the only piece of media manipulation. The navy suggested quite strongly that the submarine HMS *Superb* was on patrol in the area to alarm the Argentineans, when it was actually back in Scotland being repaired. Journalists were also briefed that there would be no D-Day-style landings in the Falklands – the day before D-Day-style landings took place.

The ultimate frustration for Nicholson and Hanrahan came after they were finally allowed off the ship and on to the Falkland Islands (this was ten days after the initial landings; up until then it had been argued that they would have been a liability), where they watched the white flags being raised over Port Stanley. After a hair-raising journey back to ship to report this, they were told there was a news blackout on the information . . . only to hear Margaret Thatcher on the radio triumphantly announcing the white flags herself.

As well as fighting the Argentineans in the Falklands, the British government spent the conflict waging a second war closer to home. Margaret Thatcher had never been a particularly huge fan of the BBC – the fact that a Monty Python sketch in the early seventies described her pea-sized brain being found in her foot probably didn't help matters. More seriously, in 1979 her close friend and one-time campaign manager Airey Neave was killed by the Irish terrorist group the INLA. The BBC ran an interview with the terrorist group afterwards, a fact that Thatcher considered unforgivable and never quite forgot. It was perhaps no surprise, then, that her husband Denis referred to the BBC as the 'British Bastard Corporation'.

Thatcher felt that the BBC should be as supportive of the war effort as many of the British newspapers were being. At the more thoughtful end of proceedings, *The Times* ran a huge editorial declaring: 'We are all Falklanders now'. The *Sun*, meanwhile, quickly declared itself 'The paper that supports our boys' and firmly nailed its jingoistic colours to the mast. Declaring 'Stick it up your junta!' the newspaper 'sponsored' the first missile to be fired at the Argentineans, with the *Sun* reporter on ship painting on 'Up yours, Galtieri' on its side in case he didn't get the message. Most notoriously, the newspaper responded to one of the most controversial episodes of the war, the sinking of the *Belgrano*, with the single-word headline 'Gotcha' (this was changed in later editions to 'Did 1200 Argies drown?').

The BBC, meanwhile, took the view that as the country wasn't at 'total war' (indeed, no actual declaration of war was ever made by either side), its public duty was to be more objective about proceedings. Rankling Thatcher hugely, the BBC employed what she called 'the chilling use of the third person', referring to 'British' rather than 'our' troops (BBC policy was that 'our' was only used for its own correspondents). Asked about the issue at Prime Minister's Questions, Thatcher said, 'it seems that we and the Argentines are being treated almost as equals', an attitude that 'gives offence and causes great irritation among many people'.

As the war went on, the limited information and footage coming back from the British ships contrasted sharply with what was being offered by the Argentine media. While most of their coverage was propaganda, it became clear that, despite the denials from the Ministry of Defence, there was an element of truth to some of what they were reporting. Armed with a large pinch of salt, reporters like Peter Snow, then *Newsnight*'s defence correspondent, began to factor in Argentine reports to piece together what was actually going on. Snow described himself as 'a citizen of the world, a detached journalist' and said, 'I don't think it is right to twist things so that you have put the British case over in the most favourable light.' One Tory MP described Snow's attitude as 'unacceptably even-handed' and 'almost treasonable'. Viewers, however, did not appear to agree with this – audiences for *Newsnight* quadrupled during the war, and that can't all have been people staying up to write letters of complaint.

Infuriating the government still further, as the task force headed south, the BBC ran a special edition of *Panorama* entitled 'Can We Avoid War?'. The programme included an interview with one of the Argentine diplomats at the United Nations, who was allowed to put forward his country's case for sovereignty of the islands. It also featured contributions from the small number of MPs (both Labour and Conservative) who opposed going to war, and reported rumours about 'reservations' about the campaign from high up in the military. All of which was meant to be presented as the minority view, but this got mangled in the introduction – as it was, it looked as though these opinions were representative of what the country was really thinking.

Margaret Thatcher was described as being 'transfixed' by what she saw. Others were less frozen in their response – the phone lines to the

BBC complaints department went into meltdown, with the hundreds who did get through being only a fraction of those who tried. One former minister described the programme as 'odious'; another as 'despicable'. Mary Whitehouse labelled it 'arrogant and disloyal' while defence secretary John Nott described the BBC as 'the propaganda wing of the Argentineans'. The *Panorama* presenter Robert Kee, meanwhile, furious that some of the editorial cuts he had asked for had not been made, disassociated himself from the programme and resigned. Matters came to a head when the director general, Alasdair Milne, and BBC chairman, George Howard, were subsequently called before the backbench Conservative media committee to explain themselves. One hundred and fifty Tory MPs turned up to let off steam and lambaste them. In very heated exchanges, the two were accused of being 'traitors'; refusing to be cowed, the BBC chairman's response was 'stuff you'.

Even after the Falklands had been regained, the tension between the BBC and the government continued. At a dinner event in 10 Downing Street, Thatcher took Milne to task over the BBC's announcement during the war that British troops had landed from the *Queen Elizabeth*. 'I was astonished,' she told him, 'you are taking risks with people's lives.' When Milne pointed out that the only people in a position to give the BBC such information were the government, Thatcher said that the BBC must have got it from their satellites. She remained unmoved when Milne told her they didn't have any: 'I don't care,' she replied, 'it is true.'

The next skirmish occurred in an interview between John Nott and Robin Day. Robin Day had an interviewing style that was as arresting as his glasses and as flamboyant as his bow-ties. Grilling the defence secretary about possible cuts to the navy budget, Day asked Nott (who had announced his retirement from politics at the next election), 'Why should the British public . . . believe you, a transient here-today and, if I may say so, gone-tomorrow politician?' You could tell by the way Day was raising his eyebrows and trying not to smile as he said 'if I may say so' that he knew he was being naughty. You also didn't need to be a mind-reader to tell that the defence secretary was Nott happy at being questioned like this.

'I'm sorry, I'm fed up with this interview,' he announced, taking off his microphone and walking out.

'Thank you, Mr Nott,' Day cheerfully called after him.

All this, though, was mere hors d'oeuvres to the main course of Thatcher's beef. What everyone remembers more than anything about the Falklands War on TV was not the ships or the Harrier Jump Jets or the Union Jack flying proudly again over Port Stanley, but an exchange between Margaret Thatcher and a geography teacher from Cirencester the following year. It took place in the run-up to the 1983 general election, when Thatcher was taking questions from the public on a BBC programme hosted by Sue Lawley. The programme should have been a stroll for the prime minister – the Falklands had transformed her poll ratings, and she was odds-on to return to power with a thumping majority. Mrs Thatcher was sat with Sue Lawley behind a desk in a London studio, while members of the public asked questions from other studios around the country. One such person was Diana Gould, an innocent-looking middle-aged woman in a pink tartan jacket, who was asking her question from the Bristol studio.

'Mrs Thatcher,' Mrs Gould politely began, 'why when the *Belgrano*, the Argentinean battleship, was outside the exclusion zone and actually sailing away from the Falklands, why did you give the order to sink it?'

The right answer to this question was probably as follows. As in a game of battleships, a British submarine, HMS *Conqueror*, had chanced upon the location of the ship. There was a small window of opportunity in which to attack it before the ship went out of range. It was a difficult decision to take politically in that not only was the

Belgrano outside the agreed 200-mile exclusion zone and sailing away from the Falklands, but attacking it would also simultaneously torpedo the peace negotiations that were going on at the time. The navy, though, thought it was too good an opportunity to miss, and Margaret Thatcher agreed. The *Belgrano*, which in a previous life had survived Pearl Harbor as an American warship, was holed with the loss of 323 lives.

Mrs Thatcher chose a different tack in answering the question. 'But it was not sailing away from the Falklands,' she incorrectly corrected. 'It was in an area which was a danger to our ships,' she continued, another statement that could also be described as disputable.

And that, she presumed, was that. She was Mrs Thatcher, and no one contradicted her. Mrs Gould, however, came back.

'It was on a bearing two eight zero, and it was already west of the Falklands,' she said, resisting the opportunity to add: 'I'm a geography teacher, so I know about these things.' 'I'm sorry,' she continued, not sounding the remotest bit sorry, 'I cannot see how you can say it was not sailing away from the Falklands.'

At this point, I suspect that Margaret Thatcher must have realized she was in a bit of a hole. Mrs Gould was right: the *Belgrano* was indeed sailing away from the Falklands – and Mrs Thatcher had made the mistake of denying this. Now, she could either correct her original answer, which would mean admitting an error, or she could repeat the assertion, which would mean that her response was in danger of becoming a lie. Margaret Thatcher was too smart a politician to do the latter, and too proud to do the former. Instead, she tried to brazen it out.

'When it was sunk it was a danger to our ships,' she replied, completely dodging Mrs Gould's point. Mrs Gould, though, wasn't going to be put off that easily. She was on to a winner, and she knew it.

'Nobody with any imagination could say it was anything other than sailing away from the Falklands,' she said.

At this point, I checked our television to see if there were any icicles on it, so frosty was the exchange becoming.

'I'm sorry,' Mrs Thatcher smiled back falsely, 'I forgot your name.' She continued to say nothing about sailing away, and attempted to corral Mrs Gould into agreeing that the *Belgrano* was a danger to British ships. 'You accept that, do you?' she finished, in a tone that suggested this was a more of a statement than a question.

'Well, no, I don't,' said Mrs Gould.

'Well, I'm sorry, it was.' Mrs Thatcher tried again: 'You *must* accept . . .' she continued. 'I must ask you to accept . . .'

Mrs Gould, however, just sat there looking nonplussed. As it happened, this was because in the Bristol studio there were no pictures, only an audio feed from London. So, as much as Mrs Thatcher was using body language to try to get her point across – tilting her head to show she was listening, smiling in varying degrees of warmth – none of it was making any impression because Mrs Gould couldn't see it. On the TV screen, her apparent lack of reaction perhaps made her look harder and more unforgiving than she actually was.

The prime minister tried again to close the conversation down: 'One day, in about thirty years' time, all the facts will be published.'

'That is not good enough, Mrs Thatcher,' Mrs Gould came back. Which was fair enough. It wasn't really good enough, was it?

By now Mrs Thatcher's eyes were boring a hole through the screen, the sort of death-at-twenty-paces stare that had led the French president François Mitterrand to describe her as having 'the eyes of Caligula'. 'I think it could only be in Britain,' her voice now dripping with contempt, 'that a prime minister could be accused of sinking an enemy ship that was a danger to our navy.'

In the grand scheme of things the exchange didn't change much, gripping and memorable television though it was. The Conservatives still romped home at the general election; and, being already at odds with the BBC, their white fury about the incident made little impact there. Mrs Thatcher felt that Sue Lawley should have intervened and cut Diana Gould off, and she refused to ever be interviewed by Lawley again; Denis Thatcher, meanwhile, gave the producer a piece of his mind after the show, castigating the BBC as a 'a bunch of pinkoes'. The BBC, though, stuck to their position: if the government of the day was complaining, the BBC were probably doing something right – after all, Labour had been equally critical of the BBC when Harold Wilson was in power, and would be so again over the second Iraq war. In other words, whoever was in power, the BBC got it in the neck.

What the exchange also showed was that, as much as a government and the military might like to manage the media during a war, the truth always finds a way of seeping out. And the truth is that war is a messy and complicated business. For a while, the fiction that the Falklands Conflict was an emphatic and fairly pain-free success continued: in the autumn following the war, 300,000 people turned out to watch a victory parade through the streets of London – Margaret Thatcher, rather than the uninvited royal family, taking the soldiers' salute. Even here, though, the official line was not all it seemed – soldiers who had been injured in the war were not invited to take part in the parade, for fear that their presence would spoil the celebratory mood.

Slowly, a different account of the war emerged. The British victory, far from being a foregone conclusion, had in fact been a touch-and-go thing, and the number of soldiers who'd died or been injured was substantial: there were 255 deaths and 777 'non-fatal casualties' on the British side; 649 Argentineans were killed and a further 1118 injured. To put this into some sort of perspective, the total number of soldiers killed and injured in the war was greater than the actual population of the islands they were fighting over.

As I grew up and began to learn more about the world, I made that 180-degree switch from boyhood warmonger to teenage pacifist. One of the prods in that direction came from the children's author

Raymond Briggs' book about the Falklands War, *The Tin-Pot Foreign General and the Old Iron Woman*. It depicted a childish squabble between the two characters over ownership of the islands, both claiming they'd 'baggsied' them first. Halfway through the book, the style of Briggs' pictures changed from brightly coloured cartoon to black-and-white pencil drawings: images of soldiers being shot, drowned and burned alive; some in wheelchairs and with limbs missing – 'real men, made of flesh and blood . . . not made of Tin or Iron'. As in the real world, they 'were not invited to take part in the Grand Parade, in case the sight of them spoiled the rejoicing'. The final picture was a simple sketch of a father, a mother and a young boy tending a grave. I can't say I drew many pictures of Harrier Jump Jets after that.

After the break, we witness a little piece of television history as a new television station is born, ask for 'a consonant please, Carol', and enjoy lashings of ginger beer . . .

Ad Break

Foster's

To a wine-tasting now, in a London wine cellar. Paul Hogan, half crocodile, half Dundee, has entered into the spirit of the occasion by bringing along a pint of Foster's lager. Given that he is not a big wine fan, one has to wonder why he has bothered to turn up to a wine-tasting event in the first place. Anyway, Hogan is glad for his lager, the wine being to his mind about as popular 'as a rattlesnake in a lucky dip'. Cut to various stuffed shirts sipping and swilling the wine before spitting it out.

'Strewth,' says Hogan, 'that stuff is worse than I thought.'

This is just one of various 'Paul Hogan taking the piss out of Britain' ads for Foster's, during the course of which he sees some Morris dancing ('Which one's Morris?'), visits the Bloody Tower ('All right, sport, I only asked'), and takes a trip to the ballet ('There's a bloke down there with no strides on!'). Then there's the one where he about-turns at a cocktail bar when the bloke in front asks for a Harvey Wallbanger, a Dickie Dickie and a Kiss in the Dark (he's sort of right to do so actually – so far as I can ascertain, there is no such cocktail as a Dickie Dickie).

All of which is nice knockabout stuff, though I'm still not completely convinced by the wine-tasting advert because, this being the early 1980s, having the British as the wine experts and the Australian as the beer drinker is getting things the wrong way round. At this moment in time the British wine market is dominated by sickly sweet things such as Blue Nun, Liebfraumilch and (if you're lucky) Le Piat d'Or. By contrast, the Australian wine industry is beginning to crank into life, and producing what will become recognizable and reliable brand names like Jacob's Creek, Nottage Hill and Wolf Blass. So perhaps the advert would be more accurate if it was set in Sydney and featured Jim Bowen supping on a pint of best – though admittedly it might not shift quite as much Foster's that way.

Episode Eight

'As the countdown to a brand-new channel ends, a brand-new *Countdown* begins'

The first I knew about Channel 4 was when an announcement from the IBA (the Independent Broadcasting Authority) came on the television screen. Against a backdrop of a sky full of fireworks, a large number four was lit up in the centre of the screen, and a female announcer with a posh voice was telling me the sort of news I couldn't quite believe.

'The new Channel 4 TV service will be launched early in November, the first brand-new television service for nearly twenty years . . .'

Joff and I looked at each other.

'Did she just say we were getting another TV channel?' I needed to double-check what I'd just heard (it could have just been my hearing).

Joff nodded.

'Mint!' I exclaimed. ('Mint' being early-eighties Yorkshire primary-school slang for 'great', rather than a request for a Polo.)

'Will you be tuned in for it?' the posh lady asked.

Are you kidding me? I thought. What time does it start?

'Try tuning a spare button on your set before eight p.m.,' the posh lady continued, showing us a picture of a test card that looked a bit like a game of Pong on acid. *'If you can get this clearly then you're all set.'*

I looked at my watch. It was ten minutes to eight. My initial joy at the news of a new Channel 4 was beginning to drain as a nightmare scenario ran through my head. If I couldn't get our television tuned in the next ten minutes, my chances of watching this new channel might be gone forever.

'DAAAAAAD!' I shouted.

'. . . if you can't it may be you're not in range of a Channel 4 transmitter just yet . . .'

The television showed a picture of a Channel 4 transmitter, which appeared to be a large white stick sat on top of a hillside. I racked my brains to try to remember seeing something like that near York. Tell me we're not out of range, I thought.

'. . . we're bringing more on just as fast as we can,' the announcer tried to reassure. *'But perhaps all that you need is expert advice: ask your dealer or rental company.'* The advert cut to another number four, this time made up of blocks of different bright colours, like a children's jigsaw puzzle, against a black background. With a flourish, the announcer finished by saying excitedly, *'Channel 4 is on its way!'*

Dad appeared in the doorway, looking anxiously for the serious injury my cry must surely have been about. 'Are you all right?'

'We need to tune this television in the next few minutes,' I explained, 'or we may never get Channel 4.'

'Presuming we're in range,' Joff added, authoritatively.

As luck had it, the eight o'clock deadline wasn't date sensitive, and the next day we were the proud owners of our very own new test card.

'Wow,' I drooled.

'Ooh,' agreed Joff.

'I hope it's going to get a bit more exciting than that,' said Dad. Over where it said 'IBA 2' by the side of the fourth button, he had stuck a small piece of masking tape with 'Ch. 4' written on it, just in case we got confused by the vast array of television stations shortly to be available. Quite why it had taken so long for Channel 4 to come into existence is probably down to a number of things, mainly to do with (as Ben Elton would say) a little bit of politics and some boring technical stuff about bandwidth. I could explain in detail, but then I'd have to kill you (presuming you hadn't taken your own life to escape the boredom).

In a bad-science nutshell, there is only so much 'width' of 'band' to go around, and hence only so many TV and radio stations that can be broadcast in this manner. The result is that governments and politicians can thus be a bit choosy about what is allowed to go ahead. The general assumption was that a second commercial channel would follow quickly on the heels of the launch of BBC2 in 1964, and transmitters were sorted and readied in anticipation. The Labour government of Harold Wilson, however, had a natural leaning towards more public-service broadcasting, and so decided to put its time and effort into getting colour television off the ground instead. By the time Edward Heath and the Conservatives came into power in the early 1970s, they were also less interested in another television channel and more into setting up a network of commercial radio stations to compete with the BBC.

It was only in the late 1970s that the idea of an 'ITV2' channel came back on the agenda. Perhaps unsurprisingly, the main political parties had quite different ideas as to what this new channel should look like. In their manifesto for the 1979 general election, Labour suggested that the new station should be a third force, separate from both BBC and ITV, with its programmes focused very much on marginalized interests such as women and ethnic minorities. The Conservatives, who were a bit more interested in how the new channel would be funded, suggested that it should be owned by ITV: in return for subsidizing it and sorting out the advertising, ITV could shift some of its programming obligations on to the new channel, thus allowing it to make more money by putting more populist programmes on. At the same time, the Plaid Cymru party in Wales were pushing hard for a Welsh-language station, with their president Gwynfor Evans threatening to go on hunger strike if this didn't happen.

The result was a classic British fudge, with a hotchpotch of the above ideas going into the new station's make-up. The new channel was to be commercial, as the Conservatives wanted, but there was to be a strict remit as to what sort of programmes the channel should be showing. The programmes should 'appeal to tastes and interests not generally catered for by ITV', a good proportion should be 'educational', and there should be 'innovation and experiment within the form and content of programmes'. As well as this, a minimum amount of time each week had to be allocated to certain types of programming – including 'high-quality news', current affairs, educational and schools programmes and a sort-of optional one hour of religious broadcasting.

This underlying tension between on one hand being commercial and maximizing audiences and on the other having a programming remit wasn't really an issue while Channel 4 was finding its feet. It wasn't until the early 1990s, when Channel 4 became its own company and separated completely from ITV, that questions began to arise about what Channel 4 was, well, *for*. Particularly from ITV, who found that the young upstart to whom it used to give pocket money was now paying its way by helping itself to a nice chunk of ITV's audience. Like Luke Skywalker and the ways of the Force, this tension was something that Channel 4 was born with but that would become significant only later.

It seemed to take an age for the launch date of Tuesday 2 November 1982 to come round, and my brother and I would periodically flick

over to the new channel just to check that the test card was working. For reasons I was not quite sure about, Channel 4 had decided
to launch the station at 4.45 in the afternoon. It seemed then – and
still does – a slightly arbitrary time to begin a channel. Apart from
anything else, it missed by precisely a minute the glaring open goal of
beginning Channel 4 at precisely 4.44.

When we got back from school that day, I didn't even bother watching children's TV on BBC1, but turned straight over to the new channel.
To my huge excitement the test card had gone and in its place was that
big multicoloured number four again, with 'Channel 4 Television' written underneath. In a red strip across the right-hand corner, like it was a
sale at Allied Carpets, were the words 'Starting at 4.45 Today'. If all that
wasn't thrilling enough, there was a man speaking too!

'This is Channel 4,' he said, in another one of those posh-announcer
voices, 'the new national television service broadcasting through the
transmitters of the Independent Broadcasting Authority. Channel 4
starts today at 4.45,' he continued, just in case anyone had missed that
information, 'offering a variety of new and interesting programmes,
seven days a week.' Then some vaguely funky lift music started playing, sort of Haircut 100 jamming with Matt Bianco. To my ears, it
sounded cool. It sounded like the future.

New and interesting programmes? Seven days a week? This was so
crush-a-grape exciting I could barely contain myself. I ran round the
house, gathering everyone up to witness this historic moment.

'It's only ten to four,' my mum said, looking at her watch. 'No, I'm
not watching that test card for another hour.'

'Aren't you excited?' I asked. 'This is television history we're about
to witness.' I told her about the new and interesting programmes they
were going to show seven days a week.

'I'll believe that when I see it,' Mum replied.

By four-forty my persistent nagging had gathered everyone up in
the sitting room, to watch the unmoving '4'. Helen wandered up to

the television with interest, staring thoughtfully at the digit on the screen.

'Three,' she declared proudly.

'What was it like watching when television started?' I asked.

'We're not *that* old,' Mum said, a little huffily. 'I do remember when Radio One started, though, back in the sixties. Now that was *exciting*. Tony Blackburn played "Flowers in the Rain" by the Move.'

'Great song that,' Dad continued. 'A proper tune you could . . .'

'. . . whistle in the bath,' I finished his sentence for him.

Before Dad could attempt to demonstrate what great songwriters the Move were, something thrilling happened on the by-now black screen. Blocks of flying red, blue, yellow, green and purple were flying in from all sides, forming the number four to the sound of four notes: '*Daah, Daaarrh, Di Daaaaaah.*'

'Good afternoon. It's a pleasure to be able to say to you: welcome to Channel 4,' said the first voice to be heard on Channel 4 (apart from that of the bloke talking about new and interesting programmes a bit earlier). Urban legend tends to forget this announcer, but the honour of being the first person to speak on Channel 4 actually belongs to Paul Coia – a man, you'll note, whose Christian and surnames were both four letters long. Coincidence? I don't think so. No ordinary announcer, Coia was to go on to have an eighties television career himself, firstly on *Pebble Mill at One* and then, slightly more memorably, as host of the daytime BBC2 quiz *Catchword*. *Catchword*, it has to be said, was always flawed as a quiz-show concept. Contestants would be given three letters and asked to come up with the longest word they could think of that contained them, which more often than not turned out to be 'floccinaucinihilipilification'. I don't suppose Paul minded too much, though: after a hard day's quizzing, he got to go home for a bit of floccinaucinihilipilification with one of my top teenage crushes: Debbie Greenwood, the host of *First Class*.

Paul Coia's 'welcome to Channel 4' was just the beginning of our introduction to the new channel. Rather than launching into the first programme straight away, Channel 4 played the full-length version of their four-note signature tune (called, appropriately enough, 'Four Score', which lasted for precisely four minutes and was subsequently, if unsuccessfully, released as a single). As the tune was playing out, the nation was treated to a montage of clips that showed what the new channel was all about. Like a technological *Generation Game* without the cuddly toy, the conveyer belt of images included the following: a man popping a bottle of champagne, a computer, a statue, an airport departures board, a deer, another statue, a fairground ride, some people running through some doors, another fairground ride, someone jumping with an umbrella, a line of Can-Can dancers, a bear splashing in some water, some fireworks going off in the night sky, and a seventeenth-century aristocratic couple kissing, with the woman looking at the camera and using her thumb and index finger to make the universally recognizable hand gesture for 'OK'.

Back in York, the Bromleys were staring at the television in a somewhat dazed, stupefied manner.

'Woah,' said Joff.

'Amazing,' I agreed.

'Three,' said Helen again, pointing proudly at the screen.

So this was why they only launched a channel every twenty years, I thought, my eyeballs aching from the visual onslaught: any more frequently and our brains wouldn't be able to take it. This wasn't just the launch of a television channel, I concluded – this was the beginning of the future. And, from what I could gather here, the future was going to be about dancing, deer and fireworks.

And that was just the prelude. What was Channel 4 going to give us for their first programme proper? It was going to have to be pretty spectacular to top all that. Surely they weren't going all out for an eyeball-burning beginning and were about to pull out a chorus of dancing frogs who would suddenly be launched into the air, exploding into sparkling fragments across the sky? I sat back further in my chair, just to be on the safe side, in case my eyes and ears weren't up to the imminent high-tech bombardment.

'And now our first programme,' Paul Coia announced. '*Countdown*.'

I didn't want to come across as churlish, given that I had a whole new television station starting in front of me, but I couldn't help feeling that Channel 4 was not quite living up to its pre-launch promise of 'new and exciting programmes'. To pick up on a couple of things: one, this programme was not actually new. I'd watched it before, when it had been shown on ITV in Yorkshire under the title *Calendar Countdown*. Even then, the programme was only 'new' to Yorkshire viewers – it was an adaptation of a long-running French quiz called, with typical Gallic bluntness, *Des chiffres et des lettres* (*The Numbers and the Letters*), which had been knocking around since the late 1960s. The only difference was that the French were a little more philosophical about the whole quiz thing and gave contestants forty-five seconds rather than thirty to come up with some really good words. (That's why the *Countdown* clock has a whole minute on it: when it was built the plan was to follow the French – if you'll excuse the pun – to the letter.)

Secondly, while there are any number of nice things that one could say about the host Richard Whiteley, 'exciting' is not one of them. Looking ever so slightly nervous, Whiteley began the show with the sort of trademark half-joke that Yorkshire viewers were used to: 'As the countdown to a brand-new channel ends, a brand-new *Countdown* begins'. He then proceeded to litter his presentation with similarly wonky one-liners. For example, he said that *Countdown* 'is to word games what Cyril Smith is to hang-gliding'; and the programme was, apparently, a bit like the post office, in that you have a jumbled-up group of letters and then work out what to do with them. On learning that one of the contestants had lived in Liverpool, he congratulated him for having 'the nous to buy a Scouse house'.

To help him through the show, Richard Whiteley was given a succession of lady lovelies. Rather than the multi-tasking role she was later to embrace, Carol Vorderman, the show's 'vital statistician', was limited to showing up the contestants in working out the sums in the numbers game (which she managed to do both times in this opening programme). To add a touch of glamour, two Brucie-style hostesses in the curvaceous shapes of Beverley Isherwood and Cathy Hytner were on hand to pick out the vowels and consonants and numbers. This glitz was balanced with a bit of grit from Dictionary Corner guest Ted Moult. Moult was a down-to-earth farmer type turned quiz-show celebrity, whose CV ranged from inventing 'pick-your-own' strawberries to advertising double glazing on TV. 'If you're going to fit double glazing,' he'd regularly advise, shutting out a gale and letting a handy feather float effortlessly down, 'fit the best: Everest.'

The two contestants both shared Whiteley's first-night nerves, looking a little more like they were doing an exam than taking part in a quiz show. This nervy uncertainty extended through to the first-ever Countdown Conundrum (LIGHHGIHT) when the out-buzzed contestant claimed to have got the answer (HIGHLIGHT) but had forgotten he needed to press his bell. To commemorate being the show's first loser, he was given a *Countdown* board game to relive what perhaps was not the LIGHHGIHT of his life. Baring just a small flash of Yorkshire teeth, Whiteley told him the game would help pass 'the long dark nights ahead in Rochdale'.

As another countdown ended, so the rest of Channel 4's opening night began. After a fifteen-minute preview of programmes, next up was *The Body Show*, keeping fit to music in a 'Let's Get Physical' sort of a way. Barely an hour in and Channel 4 had its first American import in the shape of *People's Court*, consisting of 'real-life Californian cases' in a slightly less real television court room. I'm afraid I cannot recall what Judge Wapner decided in 'the case of the one hot rollerskate'. Nor indeed why there was only one rollerskate. Or even in what sense this particular rollerskate was 'hot'. I think I must have been eating my Alphabetti spaghetti at this point, and similarly when *Book Four* aired at 6.30, featuring Fay Weldon, William Boyd and Len Deighton. I wasn't the only one: 3.7 million people had tuned in to *Countdown*, and by now only 1 million were still watching.

After the first-ever *Channel 4 News* at 7 p.m., hosted by Peter Sissons and Trevor McDonald, the viewing public got their first-ever sighting of Brookside Close. Originally going to be called *Meadowcroft, Brookside* was very much the brainchild of Phil Redmond, who was also the creative force behind *Grange Hill*. In a way, it was a bit like *Grange Hill* for grown ups, with a similarly uncompromising attitude to 'real' life and 'real' issues. In keeping with keeping it real, Redmond bought a Liverpool cul-de-sac with a loan from the Department of Trade to film the programme: the 'real' rather than studio setting helping to realize the realistic feel. Coupled with this was a succession of thick Scouse accents and a liberal sprinkling of swearing, all of which was a world away from the Oxford English of traditional television and brought Mary Whitehouse out in hives. Which, when you think about it, was probably half the point.

After *Brookside* came what Channel 4 considered to be one of its ratings bankers: the imported Australian television comedy vehicle *The Paul Hogan Show*. Paul Hogan was hot property in the early 1980s, with both his forthcoming films and adverts for Foster's. As well as this, with Australia about to win the America's Cup and Men at Work shortly to have a global number one with 'Down Under' (not to mention the magnanimity of letting Rolf Harris back into the country for the Commonwealth Games) there was a definite sense that this was a nation coming of age. Yet, despite all that, *The Paul Hogan Show*, with such subtle characters as Leo Wanker, Inspector Donger and 'no-poofters' man-about-town Hoges, always felt a bit too broad for British tastes, and not especially Channel 4.

Following this was Ian McKellen's star turn in the drama *Walter*, in which he played a mentally handicapped man institutionalized after the death of his parents (to help prepare for the role before filming began, McKellen had tried out his character in Marks and Spencer). The schedule then returned to comedy with *Five Go Mad in Dorset*, the first television outing for the Comic Strip (of which more later), which starred, among others, Jennifer Saunders, Dawn French and Adrian Edmondson in an edgy-yet-affectionate send-up of Enid Blyton. The show so successfully lampooned Blyton that certain phrases made up for the programme, such as requests for 'lashings of ginger beer', are now common if erroneous shorthand for the author's style.

After that, closing the evening was *The Raving Beauties' in the Pink*, a 'witty provocative revue celebrating women's lives'. As it turned out, it was neither particularly witty nor provocative – perhaps not totally surprising given that it starred Anna Carteret, who was about to take the lead role in the equally un-witty and un-provocative BBC police drama series *Juliet Bravo*. By the time the beauties had finished raving at 11.45 p.m., most of the Channel 4 audience had already gone to bed.

The birth of Channel 4 was not without its hitches. On the day of the launch the newspapers were full of the first of the station's many controversies: a documentary about animal rights called *The Animal Farm*. The IBA were concerned about an interview with masked members of the Animal Liberation Front, and wanted twelve minutes cut from the programme. Channel 4, however, needed permission from the programme's producer to make the cuts, and he was digging in his heels. At the same time as this stand-off was going on, the senior director of *Brookside* was handing in his resignation, saying it was full of bad language and 'unacceptable levels of physical violence'. There were even problems with the bits between programmes: Equity were still arguing about the rates for actors appearing in commercials on the new station, and in some parts of the country stills and music were shown instead of ad breaks.

In the grand scheme of things, however, these were minor issues. If anything, the controversy over *The Animal Farm* and *Brookside* actually helped the station, both giving it publicity and helping create its slightly edgy image. And among its opening-night programmes were a substantial number of successes: *Countdown* and the hour-long *Channel 4 News* have remained a constant on the station ever since; *Brookside*, after a slow beginning, quickly became the most watched show on the channel; *Walter* was heaped with critical praise, with one reviewer calling it 'one of the most successful television films of recent years'; and *Five Go Mad in Dorset* established the station as the cutting edge of British comedy (pipping *The Young Ones* to the post by just seven days).

The start of Channel 4 was the first time that the launch of a television station had been a national event: both BBC1 (1936) and ITV (1955) had been London-only affairs to begin with; when BBC2 launched in 1964, a power failure at Battersea Power Station led to the launch night being cancelled, and *Play School* the following morning being the opening programme. At the same time, the start of Channel 4 was also the last time a television launch was a national event. With the number of available stations set to multiply thanks to satellite and cable, the significance of each new one was inevitably diminished (and often watched by viewing figures to match those of the 1936 audience). By the time the Spice Girls launched the next terrestrial station, Channel 5, in 1997, it hardly seemed worth the bother of retuning your video recorder to watch it.

The day after the Channel 4 launch Peter Ackroyd wrote in *The Times*: 'It is of course impossible to discern at once the personality of this new-born infant . . . The limbs seem to be in the right places and it made all the appropriate noises.' He did, however, note that, as demonstrated by many babies, 'there was a tendency . . . to excessive wind.' His analogy echoed the words of Paul Coia, the station's 'first voice', who had appeared on screen to thank the nation for watching when the curtain went down at the end of Channel 4's first evening. 'As with any new baby,' he'd said, 'I hope you'll stay with us and watch us grow.'

Indeed Channel 4, like a newborn, spent a lot of time asleep in its early life – for the first few years it would only come on air each day at the start of *Countdown*. Then, as it got older, its schedule began to start earlier and finish later. Also like a newborn, even when it *was* awake it didn't always appear to be doing much. Audience figures in the first few years started small (a 4.4 per cent share in its first full year) and it wasn't until the early 1990s that viewing figures hit the 10 per cent or so mark it has held on to ever since. And, like any baby, while there were undoubtedly high points in the early years there was also a lot of shit. For every adaptation of *The Snowman* there was a programme like *Mini-Pops* (to which I'll return later).

But all that was for the future. As Paul Coia wished the nation a cheerful goodnight (his chirpiness perhaps or perhaps not being to do with Debbie Greenwood waiting for him at home) the screen cut to a candle in the shape of a number four, the sort you might get on a child's birthday cake. Its orange flame flickered brightly for a few seconds against the black background, before being blown out.

After the break, we visit the most squalid house on eighties TV, we hear something that – ooer – sounds a bit rude, and is that a canoe in our pocket or are we just pleased to see you?

Ad Break

Toshiba

An animated advert now, with something like a crash-test dummy wandering across the screen to ask the immortal eighties question, 'Hello Tosh, gotta Toshiba?' The Toshiba he is talking about is something called an FST television: FST, our friendly dummy tells us, stands for 'Flattest Squarest Tube' (or 'Futuristic-Sounding Television', if you're watching it on the sort of shed-sized box that resides in the Bromley household). The dummy (voiced by the late, great Ian Dury) goes on to explain that the Toshiba FST 'ain't half built well' and is 'stronger to last longer — know what I mean?' Then, just in case the catchphrase hasn't already jammed in your head for the fortnight, he asks, 'Hello Tosh, gotta Toshiba?' a few further times.

As catchy as the catchphrase is, it does bear more than a passing relation to its original inspiration: the Alexei Sayle single 'Ullo John! Gotta New Motor?' During the course of which Sayle not only enquires of John about his latest set of wheels, but also ponders whether or not there is life in Peckham, claims to keep tropical fish in his underpants, and – if you have the twelve-inch version – gets very sweary indeed. (The single, which eventually charted in 1984, was Alexei's second stab at the pop charts: his first attempt being with the wonderfully named Alexei's Midnight Runners.)

Of course, this being the eighties, and given the high levels of unemployment and rioting that Thatcher's economic policies have unleashed, the chances are that if Tosh *does* have a Toshiba it's probably because he's nicked it.

Episode Nine

'Permission to wobble bottom lip, sir'

Bedtime was, inevitably, a childhood battleground. It was First World War-style trench warfare in our house, with my parents drawing their line at 9 p.m., and refusing to cede their ground for several long years, no matter what Joff and I threw at them.

Nine o'clock was no arbitrary line in the sand, however. It coincided with the watershed, that switchover moment where television stopped being sweet and family-friendly and became sweary and offensive, vulgar and violent, torrid and titillating. Or at least that was the impression my parents gave us. The more I thought about it, the more my parents' stance didn't quite make sense with their philosophy. I thought they were meant to be liberal, but here they were taking parenting tips from that woman who blew up horses' noses.

'That's Barbara Woodhouse,' my dad would no doubt have said. 'I think you mean Mary Whitehouse.'

The thing was, my parents were quite happy for Joff and I to come across post-watershed material as long as it took place pre-watershed. They had a number of cassette tapes of comedy programmes, such as *Not the Nine O'Clock News*, which we were allowed to listen to. So how did that square with the Mary Whitehouse moralism? The answer was simple – the watershed was a smokescreen for my parents to hide their real motive. They weren't illiberal at all: they just wanted to get shot of us for the rest of the evening and have a couple of hours' peace and quiet to themselves.

Apart from the fact that I was sent to bed without actually being remotely tired, the nine o'clock bedtime created difficulties in the school playground because other, less resolutely middle-class parents allowed their children to stay up and watch hour after hour of Mary Whitehouse-disapproved filth. In those days, the BBC1 evening news went out at nine o'clock, which was usually balanced out by BBC2 by means of a comedy programme. That was where *Not the Nine O' Clock News* got its name from.

It tended to be these programmes that were discussed at length at school – and such conversations were fraught with difficulty if you hadn't actually been allowed to stay up to see the show. This was never more true than in the case of one of the most influential comedies of the decade.

'Great programme last night, wasn't it, Brommers?'

'Oh yeah, er, brilliant. Really funny.'

'Which was your favourite joke, then?'

'Oh well, you know. All of them really.'

'What about that song at the end?'

'Oh yeah, that was special.'

'It certainly was, because there wasn't a song in the programme. Oh my God, you weren't allowed to stay up and watch it, were you? Hey, everyone, Bromley didn't see *The Young Ones* because it was past his bedtime. What a girl . . .'

*　　*　　*

ALL IN THE BEST *POSSIBLE* TASTE

Two hundred miles south, in London, in venues such as The Comedy Store and under the Comic Strip banner, a whole new generation of young 'alternative' comedians were finding their feet. These comedians were considered 'alternative' in the sense that they were a) sweary, b) aggressive, c) political, d) not always graduates of Cambridge Footlights or the Oxford Revue, and e) actually funny. Leading lights included the Dangerous Brothers, Adrian Edmondson and Rik Mayall, the Outer Limits, featuring Nigel Planer, and the Comedy Store compère Alexei Sayle.

Perhaps nothing would have happened if Channel 4 hadn't turned up. Alternative comedy fitted their bill and so it signed up the leading lights of the movement in *The Comic Strip Presents . . .* The BBC responded by signing up Rik Mayall, his then girlfriend Lise Mayer and another burgeoning comedian, Ben Elton, to write a sitcom about students, *The Young Ones*. The choice of name was appropriate – the writers were barely out of university and only just into their twenties. They were closer in age to me than they were to my parents, as our responses to the programme bore out.

The Young Ones was loosely set around the lives of four students who lived together in the sort of grotty house I would come to know myself about a decade later. There was Rik, played by Rik Mayall, a spotty anarchist-come-Cliff Richard fan, whose typical pose was hands on hips, nose in the air and a snort of laughter at his own hilariously unfunny joke. There was Vyvyan, played by Adrian Edmondson, a chemistry student-come-punk, with four stars studded to his forehead and a penchant for shouting, swearing and blowing things up. Nigel Planer played Neil, the long-haired hippy in need of a bottle of Timotei, who said 'heavy' and 'oh wow' and ate a lot of lentils. And there was Mike, who was meant to be cool but was actually a bit dull.

The plots of the programmes were more free range than the traditional British sitcom fare – sometimes they'd go off on a tangent, sometimes they'd end up totally random and unresolved. Bands like

Motörhead would appear and thrash out the 'Ace of Spades' or whatever for no discernable reason. One of my favourite episodes was 'Bambi', in which the Scumbag College four ended up on *University Challenge* against Footlights College, Oxbridge (played by Ben Elton and real-life Footlighters Hugh Laurie, Emma Thompson and Stephen Fry). After blowing up the other team, the Young Ones were about to romp their way to victory when they were squashed by a giant éclair.

Following the rule that all great sitcoms should only be two series long (see also *Fawlty Towers* and *The Office*), the final episode saw the four robbing a bank and making a getaway on a *Summer Holiday*-style double-decker bus. This crashed through a billboard poster of Cliff Richard, then smashed its way down to the bottom of a quarry. 'Phew, that was a close one,' someone said, only for the bus to explode. These sorts of things just didn't happen on *Terry and June*.

The scene that best sums up the impact of *The Young Ones* came in the episode where the opening credits for *The Good Life* appeared. The cartoon bird had barely time to flap its wings around the cartoon flower before Vyvyan burst through the screen, tearing it down and swearily denouncing Felicity 'Treacle' Kendal and Richard 'Sugar-Flavoured Snot' Briers for being 'so bloody nice'. 'They're just a couple of reactionary stereotypes,' Vyvyan ranted on, 'confirming the myth that everyone in Britain is a lovable, middle-class eccentric, and I hate them!'

That short scene said everything you needed to know about *The Young Ones*. Yes, it was aggressive and sweary. But as well as all that it was clever and articulate and wasn't taking any prisoners. *The Young Ones*, in denouncing what was already on the box, had what every comedy show really wanted: the ring of truth. It was heady. It was thrilling. And it was on past my bedtime.

My parents were tucking up my chances of having any credibility at school. Not only wouldn't they let me stay up to watch *The Young*

Ones but they also made matters worse by watching it themselves then feeding me titbits that best demonstrated its total unsuitability for me. Which of course served only to make me even more desperate to watch it.

'Last night, the punk person was travelling on a train, and he saw a sign saying "Do not lean out of the window". So he leaned out of the window and his head got knocked off.' My mother shook her head. 'Is that meant to be funny? It was completely gratuitous.'

'Of course, *The Young Ones* was originally a Cliff Richard film,' my father said, in that 'trying to be hip but failing' sort of a way. 'Now that was properly funny.'

'Cliff Richard. Now there's a real rebel,' my mother continued. 'When he first came on the scene he was very controversial.'

'Was he the one who split his trousers?' I asked, mixing up my parents' various sixties anecdotes.

'That was P. J. Proby,' my father said, a little irritably because I hadn't been listening closely enough to his stories. 'They were very tight trousers,' he added, wincing at the thought.

'Cliff did this hip thing,' Mum said, going a little misty-eyed. 'The way he danced was so shocking it was considered too rude for television, you know. So all this supposed rebellious thing with *The Young Ones*, you might think it is exciting, but it's nothing compared to what we got up to in the sixties.'

The Young Ones was a pivotal programme in our household for a number of reasons. It was probably the first show that had something generational going on – essentially my brother and I 'got' it, and Mum and Dad didn't. In that lay the first twinges of teenage rebellion, which I think my parents must have subconsciously realized. Their response was to stop us watching it and hope that it would go away. But battening down the hatches had the opposite effect.

As well as the age gap starting to open up there was an ages gap too. My parents were very much still in love with the sixties – for

143

them, the sixties had been the golden decade in which they'd left home, gone to university and fallen in love, all to a soundtrack of the Beatles, the Beach Boys, Simon and Garfunkel and the Rolling Stones. To look at their record collection you'd think the music industry had decided to shut up shop once the Fab Four went their separate ways. My parents had a box set of cassettes called *The Swinging Sixties*, which was dusted down for any long car journey and featured such lesser lights as Dave Dee, Dozy, Beaky, Mick and Tich and Herman's Hermits. They'd also recorded a radio series called the *Rock and Roll Years*, which mixed the music of the sixties with news reports of the time. My parents would listen to the shooting of JFK with something verging on a warm glow.

'And you'll never guess what happened next,' Dad would say cheerily, turning up the sound as Lee Harvey Oswald was mown down. 'Jack Ruby,' he smiled at mother as Manfred Mann started 'doo wah diddying'. He didn't actually sigh and say, 'Ah, happy days . . .' but he wasn't far off.

The cliché about the sixties was that if you could remember it you weren't there. I don't know where my parents were then, because unfortunately they could remember the era in minute and reverential detail. Everything about the decade was the best: the Beatles were the biggest band in the world; England were World Cup champions; *That Was the Week that Was* was the funniest thing on the telly; Labour were in power; Twiggy was on the catwalk; and Michael Caine was on the big screen. So amazingly wonderful were the sixties that, as far as I could make out, the whole country spent the entire decade swinging their pants down Carnaby Street in celebration.

My parents' knowledge of sixties culture was not, however, foolproof. One of my mother's earlier boyfriends, prior to her stepping out with my father, had left after she'd given him an ultimatum over a particular weekend: it was her or the concert he'd got a ticket for, Cream at the Royal Albert Hall. Thankfully this guy had a modicum of musical taste and chose Eric Clapton over my mother. Which is probably just as well, otherwise my mother would never have been in a position to meet my father and I'd never have been born. So, in a roundabout way, you could say that I owe my life to Eric Clapton. Thanks, Eric.

The Young Ones did for comedy what the Sex Pistols did to music – it shook things up, and it shocked. In the same way that my parents would see the Sex Pistols as tuneless, so they considered *The Young Ones* unfunny. In the place of craft and talent they saw only gratuitous violence and rudeness. If mocking the mighty Cliff wasn't bad enough in my parents' eyes, the use of bad language was even worse in my parents' ears. Swearing simply wasn't tolerated in our house, so a programme with a character called Vyvyan Basterd was always going to be on a sticky wicket. 'Bastard' and 'bloody' were liberally sprinkled throughout the show's script, at times gratuitously so ('Bloody bloody bloody!') which appalled my parent's sensibilities.

So much was swearing disapproved of that the Bromleys had come up with their own alternative system of child-friendly taboo words to compensate. The most popular of these was 'sugarooney', which was the Bromley-approved alternative to 'shit'. While sugarooney might have had pride of place in the *Laura Ashley Book of Swearwords*, it didn't cut much ice in the playground. It was, and I think I can use the word correctly, a shit swearword. In terms of offensiveness, it was up there with the sort of phrase that *Crackerjack* presenter Stu Francis came out with: 'Ooh, I could crush a grape!'; 'Oh, I could test drive a Tonka Truck!'; 'Grrr, I could arm-wrestle an Action Man!'

At school, such words and phrases quickly had their heads flushed down the toilet by a spikier set of invented profanities and terms of abuse: 'Slaphead', which involved having your forehead slapped, had been upgraded to 'Tefal' after a television advert for saucepans that featured a particularly high-foreheaded professor; then there was 'Jimmy Hill', after the football pundit, which was a scratching of the chin to denote lack of belief in what was being said; and, most of all, the deeply incorrect 'Joey Deacon'.

The latter was all *Blue Peter*'s fault: 1981 was International Year of the Disabled and the programme did its bit by showing the story of Joey Deacon, a man who had suffered from cerebral palsy throughout his life. *Blue Peter*'s intentions were well meaning enough – to show children that, despite his disabilities and difficulties, Joey was a warm and perfectly bright individual underneath. What children took away from the programme, however, was a whole range of new terms of abuse – 'spaz', 'spazmo' and 'Joey', the latter accompanied by the facial expression of pushing the tongue below the bottom lip, to imitate Joey Deacon's speech patterns. It was nasty and shocking, which is probably why it ripped through playground lexicon like a dose of headlice.

'Spaz' turned up in *The Young Ones* too. I don't know if that was the writers making a point about the infantile nature of their characters or whether it was one of those things, like drink driving, that didn't seem so much of a big deal back then. Either way my parents, Canute-like, were attempting to protect my ears from *The Young Ones'* waves of bad language. The show had an endless stream of rude words, like 'stiffy', 'whiffy', 'bloody', 'ruddy', 'heck', 'hell', 'crap', 'bum', 'pooh-faced git', 'Rick with a silent P', 'ploppy pants', 'knob-end' and 'bogey-bum'. Nobody actually called anyone a 'silly canute' (this was the BBC after all), but in a spoof sketch of *Grange Hill* one of the characters pointed out that they were, 'The only kids in Britain who don't say f . . .' (They didn't actually say 'fuck', of course, but did that clever cut-away thing just after the first syllable.)

My parents won the battle but lost the war on *The Young Ones*. I couldn't watch the programme but I did at least learn how to spin out their titbits into playground survival. I remained in awe of my friends who had actually watched the programme, and via their and my parents' comments tied together the whole thing with my imagination so it became in my mind the funniest thing ever. When I finally saw the show myself, on one of its endless repeats, it didn't quite live up to the billing my brain had given it. But it was pretty funny nonetheless.

And I didn't just stop at the show. This was the 1980s and comedians, alternative or not, were not immune to making a bit of money on the side. I bought Alexei Sayle's single 'Ullo John! Gotta New Motor?' and Neil's *Heavy Concept Album* (which among others featured covers of 'Hole in My Shoe' and Donovan's 'Hurdy Gurdy Man'). I'd been given some book tokens as a Christmas present (I can't remember what I'd actually asked for), and told Mum that there was a new book that I wanted to buy.

'At last,' Mum smiled. 'You've seen sense and have got yourself into reading. Which particular writer did you want to buy? Jane Austen? Charles Dickens?'

'Adrian Edmondson.'

'I don't think I know his work.' Mum looked half chastened by this gap in her literary knowledge. 'And what's his book called?'

'*How to Be a Complete Bastard.*'

Which just further reinforced my parents' opinions of the show. As with Neil's album and Alexei's single, Adrian's comedy book was not quite as funny as the real thing but at the time I still thought it was hilarious. There were 'bastard' versions of Janet and John ('See John's chainsaw . . . run Spot run!'), a bastard's guide to alternative contraception (including a Toblerone wrapper and Leon Brittan), bastard toys (My Little Pony Abattoir and Action Leper) and bastard Trivial Pursuit ('What sort of people play Trivial Pursuit? Stupid nerdy virgins who should be either getting pissed or showing some girlie a good time').

There was one final outing for the Young Ones, and that was when they teamed up with my parents' beloved Cliff Richard to record 'Living Doll' for charity – the original Comic Relief single. Yes, it raised lots of money, but if it had flopped we'd never have had to hear Hale and Pace's 'The Stonk', so it wasn't all good. The original Comic Relief was a one-off show at the Shaftesbury Theatre, and the Young Ones dominated. Neil attempted to introduce Ben Elton ('Give us a B . . .') but spelled his name wrong and ended up shouting out 'Ladies and gentlemen . . . Benetton!' The Young Ones' performance was the finale and the audience was led to believe that, with Cliff unavailable, they would be singing the song with John Craven. But then Cliff turned up after all.

It was, I have to say, something of a relief that 'Living Doll' was funny, because the immediate post-*Young Ones* output was something of a disappointment. First up from Ben Elton was *Happy Families*, a sort of pastiche comedy drama in which Jennifer Saunders played an elderly dying woman and Adrian Edmondson her son, charged with rounding up her four daughters (all played by Jennifer Saunders). The show had big ideas and a big budget, but none of the sparkle of *The Young Ones*. Maybe my parents were right – without the swearing and the violence, there wasn't much to laugh at.

Ben Elton's next show, co-written with Rik Mayall, was *Filthy, Rich and Catflap*. Back on post-watershed BBC2, this was billed (again) as the successor to *The Young Ones*, and (again) it wasn't quite as funny. The violence and the swearing were back, along with a new catchphrase – 'Ooer . . . sounds a bit rude!' – but it was a load of, well, catflap.

'Is this what passes for humour these days?' my dad asked, not unreasonably.

One of punk history's famous scenes was when Johnny Rotten went on Capital Radio to reveal the tracks that inspired him. To Malcolm

McClaren's disgust, Rotten picked out what his manager considered to be 'hippy music' – Captain Beefheart and Neil Young. It went against everything punk was meant to be about, that the lead singer of its main band secretly liked the 'dinosaur' bands they were slagging off in public.

Ben Elton wasn't Johnny Rotten (apart from *Happy Families*) but, unlike some of his peers on the alternative-comedy scene, he did have a place in his heart for the programmes they were meant to be taking on. He was a huge fan of Morecambe and Wise and his nineties show *The Man from Auntie* found Ronnie Corbett dusting down his big black chair and hilarious shaggy-dog stories. Elton wanted prime-time mainstream success – and, though *Happy Families* didn't achieve this, he got a second chance in the shape of another failing show.

I must confess that *The Black Adder* didn't really cross my radar when it was on in 1983. Written by Rowan Atkinson and Richard Curtis, it told the story of the Dark Ages ancestor of the Blackadder dynasty. Despite boasting a big-name cast (Peter Cook as Richard III, Brian Blessed as Richard IV), it failed to win over critics or audiences alike. On top of that, in the words of Rowan Atkinson, it 'looked a million dollars and cost a million pounds': much of the filming had been expensively shot on location at Alnwick Castle in Northumberland. It cannot have been a huge surprise, then, when one of the first acts of Michael Grade as the newly appointed controller of BBC1 was to try to cancel the show.

Fortunately, as with *Only Fools and Horses*, the series somehow managed to survive. And then some. Out went the costly outdoor scenes and in came a cheaper, studio version of the show. Out went Rowan Atkinson as writer and in came Ben Elton to accompany Richard Curtis. And out went the original, weasel-like version of Edmund Blackadder and in came his dry, cynical, knowing descendant. *Blackadder II* was set in the time of Elizabeth I, and found our eponymous hero treating his servant Baldrick (Tony Robinson) and friend Lord Percy (Tim McInnerny) with utter disdain, while doing battle in court with Lord Melchett (Stephen Fry) for the favour of the Queen. Elizabeth was played brilliantly by Miranda Richardson as a sort of spoiled teenage girl with the ability to execute people.

Blackadder II was the funniest thing I'd ever seen. I could sit here all day quoting many of the programme's wonderful lines, and if it weren't for copyright reasons (and not wanting to show up my own attempts at humour) would be more than happy to do so. I loved the episode where Blackadder took charge at the tower, and rearranged the executions so he could take half the week off only for Baldrick to chop off the wrong person's head. Similarly, the one where Blackadder fell for his manservant 'Bob' then discovered to his relief that 'Bob' wasn't a 'Bob' after all – only for his old friend Lord Flashheart (Rik Mayall) to thrust into town and steal both his girl and the episode.

In *Blackadder the Third* things had moved forwards to Georgian times, with Blackadder now the butler to Hugh Laurie's Prince Regent. It was still extremely funny, though for me not quite as much as the previous series – Hugh Laurie's inclusion did not quite compensate for the lack of Stephen Fry, and Tim McInnerny and Miranda Richardson made only minor contributions. Also, the show was a little bit literary, from the titles of the programmes (called spoof-Austen things like 'Ink and Incapability') to the episode in which Baldrick made a fire out of the only version of Dr Johnson's dictionary: cue Blackadder attempting to stay up all night to try to rewrite it, with the 'help' of Baldrick and Prince George; cue the discovery that Baldrick hadn't put the dictionary on the fire at all, but the only copy of the novel that Blackadder had spent years writing. (Even this plotline had literary origins: the manuscript of Thomas Carlyle's history of the French Revolution was similarly put on the fire by an unsuspecting maid.)

Back up to the standards of *Blackadder II*, to my mind, was the final series: *Blackadder Goes Forth*. The setting was the First World War, with the Blackadder-Baldrick-George dynamic now moved to the mud and squalor of the trenches. Stephen Fry and Tim McInnerny were back – much further back, behind enemy lines – as General Hogmanay Melchett and Captain Darling; and there were guest appearances from Rik Mayall (his Lord Flashheart now a flying ace) and Adrian Edmondson (Flashheart's Red Baronesque rival, Baron Von Richtoven).

Blackadder Goes Forth wasn't war as comedy in the *'Allo 'Allo* sense: if the humour of the previous series had focused on the 'adder' of the lead character's cunning, here the emphasis was on the black part of his name. All wars have a streak of stupidity to them, and the First World War particularly so – a whole generation of heroic young Englishmen found themselves putting their lives on the line over a patch of mud, for a bunch of reasons that no one was ever completely sure about. Lions, as the phrase has it, led by donkeys. *Blackadder Goes Forth* pulled off the difficult trick of finding humour in the futility of the situation, while laying bare the honour and sacrifice of those who had fought in the war.

Nowhere was this point more poignantly made than at the end of the final episode, 'Goodbyeee'. Having made every effort to escape General Melchett's 'big push' and its inevitable consequences, Blackadder, George, Baldrick and even Captain Darling found themselves grimly waiting for the whistle to go over the top. 'Permission to wobble bottom lip, sir,' was George's poignant request. As the signal sounded, the four characters were up and out of their trench, charging into no-man's land and straight into German gunfire. At which point the action was slowed right down, with the characters moving and reacting in a fraction of real time. As the explosions and gun flashes continued, the familiar Blackadder theme tune was played out on a single piano. The characters were slowly faded out, first to an empty shot of no-man's land and then to a field of poppies.

Like many great moments in popular culture, this final scene fell into place almost by accident: the action was slowed down because the original real-time footage of the characters charging and dying was not particularly convincing. The poppy field and accompanying birdsong were last-minute additions. The result, though, was incredibly moving – particularly as this final episode went out just before Remembrance Sunday.

From the arrival of *The Young Ones* to the end of *Blackadder*, Ben Elton and his strand of comedy had travelled a long way in the eighties. By the close of the decade, alternative comedy had grown to the point that it was no longer the alternative and, in moments such as these, could be far more than just comedy as well.

After the break, set your alarm clock because we have a very early start. Prepare to get hit on the head by a giant mallet and consider whether it is possible for a rat to mate with a guinea pig . . .

Ad Break

Kellogg's Start

A warehouse-conversion flat, about breakfast time. A single man is having a shower, while listening to 'Let's Stick Together' by Bryan Ferry at full volume. Actually, I don't know for definite that the guy is single; but, put it this way, having been out for a run or something he's just left his sweaty clothes and trainers in a heap on the floor. And, as I say, he's listening to 'Let's Stick Together' by Bryan Ferry at full volume.

There's something wrong with time in this man's flat, because before the song's introduction has finished the man has got out of the shower, dried his floppy-fringed hair and got dressed (if one can call wearing black tracksuit trousers and a white vest being dressed). Clearly hungry after his exercise, the man has helped himself to a large bowl of Kellogg's Start — a cereal that I presume is aimed at sporty types but to my addled eyes always looked a bit like Monster Munch, except not quite as much fun. (Certainly, the cereal's not around in my local Morrison's today, so I guess it was at some point Kellogg's Stopped.)

Back in the eighties, our man is feeling good about life and about his cereal. Look! He's flicking his spoon in the air and catching it! Listen! His record has got stuck but so delicious is his breakfast cereal, he doesn't care! Only once his bowl is clean does the man climb on to the back of a chair, leaping skywards as it crashes to the floor and jumping the record forwards in the process.

All of which probably explains why the man's records are sticking in the first place. While I don't want to come across as completely anal about looking after your vinyl, should you find that your album is getting stuck you should really be lifting the needle off and checking it for fluff, then getting out a cloth and giving your record a bit of a clean. Sure, it's not as sexy a technique as the 'chair slam', but in the long run it won't leave your entire record collection sounding like it's been remixed by Grandmaster Flash and the Furious Five.

Not that this man cares – no doubt he saw Kieran Prendiville play with one of those newfangled compact-disc things on *Tomorrow's World*, and he's ready to replace all his scratched-up albums as soon as they become available. One can only hope he doesn't copy *Tomorrow's World*'s experiment of covering CDs with strawberry jam to prove their indestructibility: if he does that, it won't just be his Bryan Ferry records that end up sticking.

Episode Ten

'Hello, good morning and welcome . . .'

I don't think there can be much doubt that the arrival of breakfast television was responsible for the dumbing-down of an entire generation of British children. Before it began, the only thing that was on TV at that time of the morning were the delights of the Open University. Without wanting to stereotype every Open University presenter as a long-haired, kipper-tied, NHS-spectacled, wizard-bearded scientist, the programmes would normally be hosted by long-haired, kipper-tied, NHS-spectacled, wizard-bearded scientists. And that was just the women. The presenters would then proceed to entertain the nation's children with a mixture of degree-level mathematics and physics, complete with hieroglyphic-style squiggles on a blackboard. Admittedly it was slightly over the head of someone like me, still trying to memorize my times tables, but it was better than watching *Pages from Ceefax* (and I say that as someone who has watched *Pages from Ceefax*). What's more, it was educational, and so my parents would waver before telling me to switch it off.

At the start of 1983, with my head still spinning from the launch of Channel 4, came the stunning news that the bearded professors were going to have to make way for an exciting new televisual concept: breakfast television. Having grown up in northern Britain in the early 1980s, I'm not ashamed to say that I found this prospect positively space age. A new channel I could just about get my head round: first we had three of them; now we had four. But Breakfast Television – a form of programming that deserved capital letters in my book – was something new. I liked breakfast, especially when it was Ricicles or Frosties. I liked television too. But the thought of combining these two previous separate entities had never entered my head. It must have taken some kind of genius, I decided, to put these two things together.

As brilliant as the idea was, I could also see an immediate mountain-Mohammed problem with this new form of television. In the Bromley household, breakfast was eaten, naturally enough, in the breakfast room. The chances of being able to take my bowl of cereal through and eat it on the sofa were about as likely as Del Boy becoming a millionaire. Equally, the idea that the television might be brought through to the breakfast room to take advantage of this technological breakthrough was similarly unlikely. Dad liked to read his copy of the *Guardian* in peace before going to work.

As far as I could see, there were only three choices open to me. The first was to get up before Breakfast Television started broadcasting, and eat my breakfast then. Not a bad idea in theory, but it would mean setting my alarm clock for about ten to six, and I wasn't sure I liked the sound of that. The second option was to not have any breakfast at all. I didn't like that idea much either, to be honest. Which left option three – to wolf my breakfast down as quickly as possible, thus missing the bare minimum of the show. It wasn't perfect as plans went, but given the visual riches that were about to unfurl before my eyes, chronic indigestion seemed a small price to pay.

Breakfast Television might have been a new concept in Britain in the early 1980s, but in America, it had been going since the early 1950s. The original breakfast show, *Today,* broadcast on NBC, featured a heady mix of hard-hitting news, pouting 'Today girls', and J. Fred Muggs, the show's resident chimpanzee. In the 1970s, its breakfast crown (if one can have a breakfast crown, I'm imagining something with cornflakes stuck all over it) was wrestled from it by *Good Morning America* on ABC, who served up a slightly more sugary cereal concoction of sofas, showbiz and celebrity.

Britain, by contrast, was very much a newspapers and radio nation. Breakfast television had only ever been tried once before, and once again (rubs chest proudly) it was Yorkshire that found itself ahead of the curve. *Good Morning Calendar* was shown across the region in spring 1977, but nobody watched it (myself included) and the experiment was dropped after a couple of months. By the early 1980s, the main choices for those who didn't want to eat their breakfast in silence were the Radio One Breakfast Show (the baton having just been passed from Dave Lee Travis, the 'Hairy Cornflake', to Cliff Richard-a-like Mike Read), Terry Wogan holding forth about *Dallas* on Radio Two, or the *Today* programme on Radio Four. The latter was hosted by one of the Conservatives' least favourite presenters, the suitably named Brian Redhead (Redhead, once accused by then Chancellor Nigel Lawson of political bias, famously responded, 'Do you think we should have a one-minute silence now in this interview . . . for you to apologize for daring to suggest that you know how I vote?')

Although there wasn't any particular government plan to wean the nation off the *Today* programme, Margaret Thatcher can't have been disappointed when the IBA (Independent Broadcasting Authority) announced it would take bids to run a new national breakfast station on ITV. There were eight bids in all: ITN proposed something called 'computerized news' (given this was 1983, this presumably would have been hosted by a sort of Jeremy PacMan figure); while at the other end of the spectrum was *Good Morning TV*, put together by, among others, Tim Rice and Ned Sherrin. I don't know exactly what they proposed, and can only guess that it was a hilarious mix of cutting-edge journalism, theatrical anecdotes and such adapted songs as *Any Jam Will Do*, and *Don't Fry for Me, I'll Have Those Eggs Poached, Please*.

Somewhere between these two bids, but slightly closer to the former, was the one put together by Peter Jay and David Frost. Peter Jay, who had been both economics editor of *The Times* and British Ambassador to America, had exactly the right establishment credentials to impress the powers that be. David Frost, meanwhile, sprinkled his celebrity stardust to pull in a stellar list of presenters to host the show: he would be joined on the sofas by Michael Parkinson, Anna Ford, Angela Rippon, Esther Rantzen and Robert Kee (Kee, for those of you not paying attention, was the *Panorama* presenter who resigned over that Falklands programme). When Esther Rantzen discovered she was pregnant – that's life – she pulled out, leaving the remaining present-ers to be dubbed the 'Famous Five'.

With their auction bid accepted, all was set for *TV-am* to make television history. No expense was spared on their studios, a reno-vated building at Camden Lock that cost £5 million plus to develop, complete with larger-than-life boiled-egg statues on the roof. The show's introduction was equally impressive: a couple of skydiv-ers holding a sign that said 'Good'; the pigeons in Trafalgar Square spelling out the word 'Morning'; sailors on the aircraft carrier HMS *Hermes* making the word 'Britain'; and just in case you'd missed it, 5000 people on Bristol Downs standing together to form the words 'Good', 'Morning', and 'Britain'. All that was left was for David Frost to tweak his famous catchphrase, greet viewers with the words 'Hello,

good morning and welcome,' and the Golden Grahams era of breakfast television in Britain was launched.

Except.

If I can just interrupt you for a minute, David.

What's that happening over on BBC1 . . . ?

Two weeks before *TV-am* were set to make historic television history,
the BBC snuck in first and launched *Breakfast Time*. Unshackled by
the complicated auctioning system that ITV needed to set up *TV-am*,
the BBC simply had a meeting and decided that they were going to
have a go at breakfast TV themselves. With no Egg Cup Towers needing to be built, nor complicated advertising systems to negotiate, it
wasn't going to be too expensive to set up a rival programme. It also
made ratings sense, too: in this pre-remote-control age, there was a
chunk of the population that seldom bothered to switch channels. If
these people could be hooked in to BBC1 first thing in the morning,
then they may well stay tuned for the rest of the day.

After much thought, the BBC came to the conclusion that what the
British wanted for breakfast was a Fruit & Fibre approach to television.
The fruity element came in the form of Selina Scott, a fringe-heavy, honey-
voiced former ITN newsreader, all topped off with a dash of Diana good
looks. The fibre was Frank Bough – a man for who the phrase 'avuncu-
lar' never seemed far away. Bough was one of those BBC stalwarts, best
known for presenting Saturday-afternoon sportathon *Grandstand* and
inane early-evening news 'magazine' *Nationwide*. It was a background
that lacked in terms of hard-hitting news coverage but came with buck-
ets of experience of live television. Frank and Selina didn't make for an
immediately obvious television couple, but they worked well in what
Selina described as a 'second-wife syndrome' sort of a way: the older man
having traded in his wife for a younger and more glamorous model.

The Fruit & Fibre adverts from the eighties (one of which featured
a younger but no-greater-follicled Ross Kemp) boasted of the cereal's

sheer variety of ingredients: 'apples, hazelnuts, bananas, raisins, coconuts, sultanas'. *Breakfast Time*, too, offered viewers a similar variety pack of ingredients: there were horoscopes from Russell Grant, a man as frothy and full of beans as a cappuccino; cookery from chef Glynn Christian; weather with Francis Wilson and his computerized weather map (no sticking rain clouds on a map for him); sport was presented by a pre-turquoise-tracksuited David Icke; pop music by DJ Mike 'Smitty' Smith; and aerobics came from the leotarded Diana Moran, better known as the 'Green Goddess'.

All of which was served up in a studio kitted out with comfy red sofas and bubbling coffee pots. The result had the feel of a slightly upmarket bed and breakfast, if that isn't a contradiction in terms: Frank the proprietor buzzing around, asking you if you'd slept well and chatting about stories in the paper; Selina the wife catching your eye and refilling your coffee. The B&B feel wasn't especially BBC, but the associations were all good – it reminded you of being on holiday, lingering over a slightly larger breakfast than you probably should be eating. This relaxed atmosphere was undoubtedly complemented by Frank's selection of chunky knitwear, worn in favour of the presenter's usual suit and tie. As with so many things in TV, this happened completely by accident: Frank turned up to one of the pre-show rehearsals in a pullover and some bright spark decided that was the dress code.

A fortnight after Frank Bough had welcomed the nation to breakfast television, *TV-am* finally had their 'relatively historic occasion', as John Cleese put it when interviewed on the first programme in his pyjamas. That interview, along with Loyd Grossman going 'through the keyhole' into Stirling Moss' house, was about as lively as the ITV launch got. If the BBC's approach was like Fruit & Fibre, *TV-am* appeared to have taken their inspiration from the period's adverts for rival cereal Weetabix.

In these, the Weetabix biscuits had been brought to life in cartoon form, and turned into what is best described as a gang of wheaty skinheads, complete with braces and bovver boots. The gang was led by Dunk, a no-nonsense chap who had it in for 'titchy' breakfasts that were only 'fit for sparrows'; he was backed by Brains, perhaps unsurprisingly the brains of the outfit (he wore glasses, so he must have been intelligent); then there was Crunch, the resident hard man; Bixie, the resident female; and Brian, the resident annoying one, who squeaked 'Ok!' at any given opportunity. The basic philosophy behind the adverts seemed to be that all other breakfasts were a load of sugar puffs and only Weetabix was hard enough to fill you up until lunch-time. This slightly unpleasant bout of breakfast bullying was summed up in the accompanying shoutline – 'If you know what's good for you'.

TV-am had a similar sort of philosophy to their programming. Their mantra was a 'mission to explain': to give viewers the sort of in-depth news coverage and detailed analysis that was missing on TV. In breakfast terms, this was all fibre and no fruit: intellectual roughage to stimulate the mind in the same way that Mr Kellogg's cereals were meant to do for the bowels. An ideal early-*TV-am* guest would be a cabinet minister, who would dutifully turn up to be lightly grilled. If Frost thought the conversation was interesting he'd simply continue firing questions, even if it was time for the news or the adverts: one interview with Norman Tebbit went on for seventeen minutes. Meanwhile Nick Owen, the young sports reporter, found himself with a battle to read out the football results: 'the programme editor . . . just wanted natty little film pieces about curling or grouse-shooting'. The 'if you know what's good for you' approach even extended to the weather: a somewhat barking former naval commander called David Philpott barked out the forecast as though he was calling the nation into battle rather than telling them to bring an umbrella.

The press gave the breakfast battle all but unanimously to *TV-am*: 'the Top of the Morning show', declared the *Daily Express*. By contrast, BBC's *Breakfast Time* was 'the end of civilized life as we know it', according to the *Sunday Express*, while the *Telegraph* sat firmly on the fence by declaring it 'the most fatuous, mind-eroding, nerve-jangling and, above all, the most completely superfluous and unwanted innovation television has inflicted on the people of this country so far'. But, and not for the last time, the view of the press did not chime with what the public really thought. For all their sneering, the BBC had actually got it about right: having the television on in the morning felt a little bit decadent, in a low-rent sort of a way, and a little bit dirty; the B&B feel of their programme reflected that. By contrast, the *TV-am* approach was akin to someone topping your porridge off with prunes and not allowing you to get down from the table until you'd finished every last worthy mouthful. (Except that with all the politicians being interviewed, it wasn't so much porridge that needed to be eaten up but a large plate of waffles.)

It wasn't long before viewers gave *TV-am*'s cold-shower approach the cold shoulder. In its first week of broadcasting, 2 million people tuned in to BBC's *Breakfast Time*; by contrast, *TV-am*'s audience was just 800,000. And, while the BBC's viewing figures settled down at about 1.8 million, *TV-am*'s numbers were hurtling downhill like Eddie 'the Eagle' Edwards attempting a ski-jump: 500,000 in the second week; 300,000 after four weeks. Achieving well below the break-even numbers needed to stay in business, *TV-am* was looking very much like toast.

The recriminations were swift and brutal. Behind the scenes, investors Jonathan Aitken MP (him of the simple sword of truth) and his cousin Timothy took control. Their immediate 'mission to explain' was to tell Peter Jay that his services were no longer required. This did not go down well with either Angela Rippon or Anna Ford, who both criticized his removal on air, and joined the 'JAY MUST STAY' protests outside the building. Both were promptly fired – though later Ford famously got her revenge by throwing a glass of red wine over Jonathan Aitken at a party.

The job of overhauling the station was given to a young Greg Dyke. Dyke, who'd go on to be Director General of the BBC, was then best known for *The Six O'Clock Show*, a breezy London show that mixed news and popular culture under the auspices of presenters Michael Aspel, Danny Baker and Janet Street-Porter. Dyke was young, brash and populist – no highfalutin missions for him. A reshuffling of the presenters led to Nick Owen being promoted from sports reporter to main sofa, and he bagged *Nationwide* presenter Anne Diamond to sit alongside him. As for the remains of the famous five, Robert Kee was quietly dropped, Michael Parkinson went on a six-month extended break, and David Frost shifted to Sundays.

Commander Philpott, meanwhile, was also relocated to weekends, with the weather spot given to effervescent Tyne Tees weathergirl Wincey Willis. Also added to the line-up were Jimmy Greaves to talk about television, Jeremy Beadle with an 'on this day in history' slot, Henry Kelly to fill in at weekends, and Gordon Honeycombe to read the news. The Green Goddess, meanwhile, was countered with professional dancer 'Mad' Lizzie Webb, whose routines to get the nation fit included the actions to Black Lace's 'Agadoo'. All of which helped to halt the slide in ratings and gradually helped them upwards again. But it wasn't until the summer break, when Frank Bough and Selina Scott were far away on holiday, that Greg Dyke pulled off his masterstroke and gave *TV-am* its snap, crackle and puppet.

Resting precariously on the top of *TV-am*'s Egg Cup Towers was a rickety, ramshackle old shed, from which *The Spectacular Shedvision Show* was broadcast during school holidays. The programme's host was, of course, Roland Rat – Roland Rat Superstar, to use his full name – the brainchild (hand rodent?) of puppeteer David Claridge. In his autobiography, Greg Dyke describes Claridge somewhat uncharitably as 'a miserable, rather dull man who only came alive when he put his hand up a puppet's rear end'. He was talent-spotted by *TV-am* producer Anne Wood, who later went on to create the *Teletubbies* so obviously had an eye (or even two) for what children want to watch.

Roland Rat was not your average hand puppet. Dressed in a particularly garish selection of Hawaiian shirts and sunglasses, as though he'd just come back from Florida, he had a mouth as big as Alexis Colby's shoulder pads and confidence to boot. Like Del Boy living high up in Nelson Mandela House, Roland was a rat of humble beginnings (he was 'born' in the sewers under King's Cross Station) but with an unerring belief in his own ability. His positivism was underlined by his catchphrase: a long, loud, head-flung-back 'Yeeeahhhhhh!' As far as Roland Rat was concerned, his celebrity status was a given. The viewers were all his 'Rat Fans' ('Rat Feeeeeenns!') and page-three models like Sam Fox were his for the taking. His confidence extended to sending up *TV-am* itself: there was the ironic, 'Hello, good morning and welcome', in a nod to David Frost's 'relatively historic' opening remark, while Nick Owen was sarcastically referred to as 'Nicol-arse'.

Accompanying Roland was his sidekick, Kevin the Gerbil, a fawning little so-and-so who'd travelled down from Leeds to meet his hero and had a fondness for the colour pink. Then there was Little Reggie, Roland's nephew, who was about as high-pitched and irritating as Brian the Weetabix. Errol the Hamster was the behind-the-scenes technician – 'Run VT, Errol!' – and, like most hamsters, obviously, was Welsh. Finally, there was Glenis the Guinea Pig, Roland's long-standing love interest, held captive in a cage at Harrods. The question of whether a rat is actually capable of mating with a guinea pig was never properly tackled – my guess is that the rat would actually try to eat it, but this wasn't really a discussion for the breakfast table.

The Bromley household, like so many others, was not immune to Roland's charms. Joff, in particular, was a big Rat Fan, and had both a Roland Rat and Kevin the Gerbil soft toy. I continued to feed Joff's Rat passion by buying him the picture-disc edition of Roland Rat's debut single, 'Rat Rapping', for his birthday. The single, which went top five, comprised four long minutes of nonsense based around a pun on the word 'scratch': Roland was scratching, you see, not in the sense of mixing a record but because – hold your sides now – he had fleas.

In the days before people got health conscious, Coco Pops were sold as being 'so chocolatey, they even turn the milk brown'. That's sort of the effect that Roland Rat had on *TV-am*: his segment was so success-ful over the summer holidays it even turned the rest of the ratings around. Viewing figures rocketed to more than a million and held firm, even after everyone had gone back to school. Roland Rat's complete confidence in his celebrity was a self-fulfilling prophecy: having told everyone he was a star, he turned out to be just that.

Breakfast Time had, to use the parlance, been 'out-sofa-ed'. Even poaching Roland Rat – as in stealing him to present his own BBC programme, rather than cooking him – didn't dent things much. *TV-am* just replaced him with *Wacaday*. The 'Wac' in *Wacaday* came from *Wide Awake Club*, an already established Saturday-morning programme. Among the *Wide Awake Club* presenters were Timmy Boyd, Michaela Strachan and a pre-*Wayne's World* Mike Myers, which sounds like I'm making it up but is actually true (he had a slot called 'Sound Asleep Club'). The undoubted star, however, was Timmy Mallett, an energetic and exuberant presenter who shared Roland Rat's penchant for garish shirts and boasted a signature selection of spectacles about which even Elton John might have had second thoughts. Echoing Roland's positive 'Yeeeahhhhhh!' catch-phrase, Timmy offered up the slightly less brilliant 'Utterly brilliant!' Shouting this at any given opportunity, he was like Tom Hanks in *Big*, jumping around the screen like a boy trapped inside a man's body.

Wacaday was the school holidays' spin-off from *Wide Awake Club* and very much Mallett's solo show: he presented with only limited help from a cockatiel called Magic and a large yellow-and-pink sponge mallet called Mallet. Mallet came into its own in 'Mallett's Mallet', a word-association game in which contestants were not allowed to either pause or hesitate. If they did, they'd get a bonk on the head like this (cue small child being hit with sponge mallet), or like this (other small child suitably 'bonked'). The child with the least bonks at the end of the game was the winner. The two contestants would first be invited to look at each other, stick their tongues out and go, 'Bleurggh!' They would then turn to the viewers at home and go, 'Bleurggh!' Finally Timmy would ask the viewers at home to respond by going, 'Bleurggh!'

The game would then commence. Timmy would say something like 'sausages'. A contestant might then respond with 'eggs'. The other contestant might come back with 'chicken'. The first contestant might suggest 'yellow'. The second contestant would offer 'blue' and then there'd be a trading of colours until someone ran out and got a sponge smack in the face for their troubles. I'd like to say that I was above such nonsense, but in the period before Timmy Mallett annoyed the living crap out of the nation with his Bombalurina cover of 'Itsy Bitsy Teeny Weeny Yellow Polka Dot Bikini' (a crime against popular culture for which he has yet to be fully forgiven) 'Mallett's Mallet' was compulsory viewing for children of my generation. I don't suppose the Bromleys were the only family to attempt to re-create the game and play it ourselves. Of course it never quite worked at home: firstly, it inevitably pitched children of different ages against each other; and secondly, there was never a big sponge mallet around when you needed one. The search around the house for a suitable weapon usually led to the game being played as 'Bromley's Cushion', which might have lacked the punch of the original title but made up for this with the extra weight (and added zip) administered in the bonks.

By contrast, the BBC got all serious. In the mid-1980s the corporation had a new controller: the same John Birt who had once written a series of articles with Peter 'mission to explain' Jay, arguing that there was a 'bias against understanding' in the media. You can imagine, then, what he might make of Russell Grant telling Sagittarians to keep an eye out for tall dark strangers. Out went the sofas and Frank Bough's naff knitwear, and in came the traditional newsreaders' desks and suits and ties. Out, within the year, went Frank Bough. In his place, among others, came a young Jeremy Paxman and a young Kirsty Wark: the result was a sort of bleary-eyed version of *Newsnight*. By the end of the decade, *Breakfast Time* was *Breakfast News* – all far more laudable, no doubt, but nothing like as fun or popular. The only bias against understanding was that from the top brass about what viewers wanted to watch in the morning.

At least Frank Bough had left the programme before revelations about his sex life hit the tabloid headlines. Bough, it turned out, had brought a generous helping of sausage to his time at the breakfast table. Fern Britton, then a fledgling presenter on *Breakfast Time*, found herself propositioned by the show's main host: 'I wonder how long it'll be before I'm having an affair with you,' Bough notoriously mused to her, 'because I have got a very big cock.' In 1987, the *News of the World* reported that Bough snorted cocaine at 'wild sex parties' (are there any other kind?), and wore a red camisole, stockings and suspenders to have sex with a prostitute. The revelations were big news, not because they were particularly shocking or because they had anything to do with Frank Bough being able to do his job, but because he came across as, well, so straight-laced and boring.

Interestingly, in 1983 *TV-am* had also faced a similar situation with their biggest star. Just as Roland Rat was turning the station round, the *Daily Star* rang to say they were going to run a front-page story alleging that puppeteer David Claridge 'hosted a Soho club called "Skin Two" for rubber and latex fetishists'. As it happened, *TV-am*'s luck held: the story was bumped for Billy Connolly's divorce, and the piece sank without trace in the inside pages. If it had been front-page news, the history of breakfast TV might well have been very different.

*   *   *

Like a couple of Weetabix you'd left in the bowl for just too long, breakfast TV had gone from being crisp and tasty to cold and soggy. The BBC offering had become as boring as All-Bran. *TV-am*, meanwhile, had survived crippling strike action (of which I won't go into detail here, except to mention the sales executive having to man the video machine and broadcasting a backwards version of *Flipper* as a result), only to lose its licence to GMTV in 1991. At the same time, Channel 4 had half-heartedly attempted the *Channel 4 Daily* – a concept consisting of segments, as though it was a grapefruit (and I don't particularly like grapefruit). Hosted by Carol Barnes, it featured a five-minute version of *Countdown* and catch-ups from around the world, including the permanently exhausted-looking 'James Mates in Tokyo'. It didn't survive long.

Some of my sense of breakfast telly becoming boring was undoubtedly due to the novelty of it wearing off. Equally, there was the fact that as a fully-fledged teenager I was far more interested in staying in bed as long as possible than I was in rushing downstairs to watch Timmy Mallett. I'd love to present that as a delayed development in some sense of taste, but suspect that evolution might have a little more to do with it. Anyway, by the end of the 1980s I had a hi-fi system in my room that had the then revolutionary capacity to wake you up with a cassette tape of your choice. I thus was greeted each and every day with 'Beautiful Morning', an upbeat get-up-and-go album track by Roachford, most famous for the hit 'Cuddly Toy'. In my head, I was some cool-living guy like the man from the Kellogg's Start ad. In reality, like the man from the Kellogg's Start ad, I was of course carrying on like a twat.

After the break, a racing driver shows us another use for engine oil, a group of men show us what they can do with a load of balls and a snooker cue, and we almost win a speedboat . . .

Ad Break

Milk

Enter two football-shirted young boys, hot and thirsty after a bit of a kick-about. One of them asks for a lemonade; the other pours himself a glass of milk. The lemonade drinker's response to this echoes strongly the views of Dr Robert, lead singer of the Blow Monkeys, who has in an interview with *Smash Hits* described the white stuff as 'rancid phlegm' . . .

'Eeeurgh!' the boy exclaims in disbelief.

At which point the milk boy responds by saying, 'Swarren Rishdrenks.' Although a definitive agreement on what he is saying will perhaps never be reached, a paper by a group of linguistic scientists at Birmingham University suggests that the message the boy is attempting to get across is that eighties Liverpool striker Ian Rush is also fond of a glass of milk. It should be stated, however, that many other experts still consider this theory to be only conjecture. For example, an ongoing study into Ian Rush's appearances on *Match of the Day* is yet to uncover any evidence of white marks on his moustache.

What is more, while the 'Ian Rush' theory posits that young footballers who don't drink milk will end up playing for Accrington Stanley, there is in fact little statistical evidence to show that the players of this particular football team are known for suffering from malnourishment. As a northern industrial town, Accrington might not be the most prosperous place in the country, but in terms of health it is considered no worse than any other number of similarly sized urban conurbations, some of which, it has to be said, boast far more successful football teams.

It should also be noted that there remains a continued debate as to the correct answer to the lemonade boy's subsequent question: 'Acccchrington Stanley? Oooar they?' The modern favourite is the formulation put forward by Professor Motson from the University of Commentary, who suggests that the correct answer is, 'Well, Trevor, unless I'm very much mistaken Accrington were one of the twelve founding members of the Football League in 1888. When they folded, another local club called Stanley Villa took over the Accrington name and this team joined the football league in 1921, where they stayed in the Third Division North for pretty much their entire career, until resigning with financial difficulties in 1962. They folded four years later, a new Accrington Stanley was formed in 1968 and, after forty-four years of non-League struggle, were promoted back into the Football League in 2006. Ironically, one of the teams relegated from the League to make way for them was Oxford United, the team who had originally gained promotion to the League when Accrington Stanley resigned back in the early 1960s.'

Or, as the milk drinker puts it, exactly.

Episode Eleven

'Let's have a look at what you could have won'

I could not quite believe what I was seeing. It was *World Superstars*, the international version of *Superstars*, where sportsmen from every major sport (plus motor racing) came together to do battle over a range of sporting disciplines, to find out who was the best of the best. The challenges could include anything from archery to kayaking, penalty shootouts to falling off your bicycle on an asphalt running track (if you were Kevin Keegan). The events that really sorted the men out from the boys, however, were the gym tests: the bar dips and the squat thrusts. Both at first glance seemed fairly uncontroversial: for the former, the contestant had to straighten up and down on a pair of parallel bars; for the latter, the athlete crouched down in a squat before thrusting his feet backwards and forwards over a white line, each thrust needing the knees to reach the elbows to be legal. They were events that favoured the fit and muscle-heavy, such as the bubble-permed, long-standing British champion and judo fighter Brian Jacks.

Then along came South African racing driver Jody Scheckter. Motor-racing drivers, as good as they were behind the wheel, were not always the fittest of *Superstars* competitors: Rene Arnoux, a pint-sized French Formula One driver, was very much at the back of the grid when it was his turn to take part. Scheckter, who won the world Formula One title in the seventies, also claimed the *World Superstars* title in the eighties, thanks in no small part to his enormous score on the squat thrusts. Using all of his motoring experience, Scheckter had brought with him a can of engine oil and greased his shoes with it. Rather than going to the exhausting lengths of lifting his feet up over the line each time, Scheckter simply slid backwards and forwards to a record-breaking total.

'That can't be allowed, can it?' I asked my father.

'Of course not,' Dad confirmed, as we watched his score rack up. 'He'll be disqualified for that. Which country did you say he was representing?'

'South Africa. Where those grapes you like came from.'

'John!' Mum exclaimed. 'I thought we'd agreed on a boycott of Cape grapes until apartheid's finished.'

'Yes . . .' Dad shifted uneasily. 'But they are incredibly good value.'

'There's probably a reason for that.' Mum gave him one of those hard stares. 'I mean, look at this man,' she pointed to the blur of greasy feet on the screen. 'Do you really want to subsidize this sort of society?'

As Jody Scheckter's minute of squat thrusts came to an end, so the discussions about his slippery morals began. I waited anxiously for news of his disqualification, which would have the knock-on effect of helping the British competitor for the world title, Rugby Union player Andy Ripley. That seemed a given when Scheckter's only argument was the ever-so-slightly spurious line of defence that nowhere in the rules did it say he couldn't grease his shoes with engine oil. That might have been true, but then there were lots of other things it also didn't say you couldn't do in the rules. Like tickling an opponent when they were doing the bar dips. Or drilling a hole in their kayak. Or kneecapping them.

'I don't believe it.' My father threw his *Guardian* down on the coffee table in disgust. 'They're going to allow his score.'

'But he cheated!' I was confused. I looked accusingly at my father, as though he might be able to sort it out. 'You told me cheats never prosper.'

'Yes,' said my father, thinking hard at how to square the basics of morality he was attempting to teach his children with what was being broadcast on the television screen. 'Um . . .' he concluded.

'It won't help him in the long run,' Mum continued.

'He's just won *World Superstars*,' Joff pointed out, not unreasonably.

'But he'll be feeling bad inside.'

'He looks pretty pleased to me.' I pointed at a smiling and celebrating Scheckter on the television screen.

'Not really,' Mum said, even less convincingly. 'He might look happy, but deep down, he'll be devastated.'

The fact that Jody Scheckter was giving himself a little bit of Castrol GTXtra might seem no big deal. But that someone was prepared to grease the rules of a mere television show − a show that was all about professional pride rather than cash prizes − served as an oily harbinger for the way sport was going to go in the 1980s. Contrary to what Bananarama and Fun Boy Three would have us believe, it was all about what you did rather than the way that you did it. Diego Maradona showed that with his 'hand of God' goal against England in the 1986 World Cup, and bug-eyed pharmaceutical sprinter Ben Johnson did his druggy best to confirm it at the 1988 Olympic Games. When sports stars start to take the P like this, the winner's podium fast turns to odium.

Not that there weren't great sporting moments to enjoy: in fact, compared to the 1970s, there were lots of them. With no satellite broadcasters yet around to snaffle up the rights, these events remained shared national experiences that everyone could tune in to watch. It was, as the Dickie Davies-hosted ITV programme had it, a *World of Sport* – and (to name-check the BBC alternative) we had a *Grandstand* seat. To a young boy growing up it felt like a golden ticket to a golden era, and founded a love of sport that I'm not sure television coverage could instil now. Take the 1981 Ashes series between Australia and England, for example, in which Ian Botham took the fight to the Aussies, and of which the nation enjoyed ball-by-ball coverage. These days, unless you are a satellite subscriber, you're reduced to forty-five minutes of highlights on Channel 5: consequently an Ashes victory does not quite feel the same.

My interest in sport was awakening just as the British started to be a bit more successful again. Not only had the England cricket team regained the Ashes, but also in 1982 England, Scotland and Northern Ireland all went to the World Cup finals in Spain. It was the first time England had made it since 1970, and in their accompanying single they promised that 'this time, we'll get it right'. As it turned out, the only thing that went right was Kevin Keegan's header in the crucial match against Spain. Right past the bloody post. My disappointment there was tempered by my first-ever sighting of the yellow shirt of Brazil. The 1982 vintage remains the most exciting side I've ever seen, and for all England's presence in the finals it was Socrates, Falcao and Zico who everyone was pretending to be in the playground.

The British had picked up the pace in the Olympics, too. Though that was no doubt helped by the fact that the United States boycotted the 1980 Games in Moscow (because of the invasion of Afghanistan) and the Soviet Union retaliated by not turning up in Los Angeles four years later. Seb Coe and the Steves – Ovett and Cram – traded medals in the 800 and 1500 metres. Daley Thompson, who caused huge controversy by whistling during the national anthem, won the decathlon gold medal at successive games. Britain even had the fastest man in the world (at least, the fastest man who'd turned up) in the shape of Allan Wells.

Away from the athletics, Duncan Goodhew left his competitors behind in the swimming pool (possibly they were all weighed down by having to wear caps). And in the Winter Games there was success, firstly for Robin Cousins and most famously for Jayne Torvill and Christopher Dean. On Valentine's Day 1984, their purple-costumed dance to Ravel's *Bolero* was the first to ever be awarded a full set of 6.0s. Sitting ringside was a surprising part of their team: Michael Crawford, the star of *Some Mothers Do 'Ave 'Em*, who'd helped with the acting part of their routines. Presumably the bit where Torvill slipped on the little whoopsie the cat had done was taken out at the last minute.

British success on the ice rink was not replicated on the tennis court, however. The only match of local interest at Wimbledon was that between Sue Barker and Cliff Richard. Instead, all eyes (and ears) were on one of the greatest rivalries that tennis had ever seen: that between the cool, suave and silent Swede Bjorn Borg and the brilliant, brash, head-banded New Yorker John McEnroe. In the dying days before technology made the sport a boring exchange of power play, McEnroe was a genius — if a temperamental one. 'You cannot be serious!' was his catchphrase, and no match was complete without a discussion about chalk dust and an umpire's warning of racket violation. The 1980 final, which Borg won 8–6 in the final set, was famous for the fourth-set tie-break. Lasting twenty-two minutes, it eventually went McEnroe's way 18–16. Like Torvill and Dean's perfect 6.0s, the numbers tell only half the story. It was a moment that everyone who watched it would never forget.

Another strong memory is the 1981 FA Cup final replay between Spurs and Manchester City. Spurs were one of the first clubs to bring in players from abroad, and had signed the Argentinean duo Osvaldo

'Ossie' Ardiles and Ricardo 'Ricky' Villa. It might have been Ossie who Chas and Dave celebrated in 'Ossie's Dream (Spurs Are on Their Way to Wembley)', but it was bearded Ricky Villa (who bore a passing resemblance to Chas or Dave) who ended up stealing the show. With commentator John Motson disbelievingly shouting, 'Villa. And still Ricky Villa . . .' the Argentinean weaved his way through what seemed like the entire sky-blue half of Manchester before slotting the ball past the goalkeeper. For a brief while, Joff and I made Tottenham our second team (after York City, of course) and religiously wrote off to each and every player in the hope of getting a signed photo or programme back – Steve Perryman and Gary Mabbutt were always friendly to our fawning letters. Joff, meanwhile, got so cross when Glenn Hoddle was dropped from the England squad that he offered to write to Ron Greenwood on Glenn's behalf, to tell him what he thought of his decision. Glenn wrote back pretty sharpish to that one.

Ricky Villa's goal remains deserving of the regular dustings-down the TV footage still gets. But its resonance also has something to do with the limited amount of football shown on television in those days. Live football, in particular, was something of a rarity: it wasn't until the mid-1980s that live League matches were shown on BBC and ITV. As for highlights, even if I had been allowed to stay up to watch it, *Match of the Day* showed only a limited selection of games – unlike now, when every goal from every game is recorded for posterity. For cameras to be there when a great goal was scored was one thing; to watch it happen live made it, to borrow a modern footballing phrase, a special one.

Of course, part of the power of these particular moments was because they happened when I was an impressionable age. There was also the factor of rain repeats: whenever there was a washout at Wimbledon or the Test Match it was Borg and McEnroe or Botham and Australia that the BBC would pull off the shelf. Undoubtedly, re-watching the clips again and again reinforced the memory of them. These days, with Centre Court having built itself a retractable roof, the tennis might continue uninterrupted, but that link with the sport's history has been lost.

The other factor was that football was yet to become the all-powerful, all-encompassing uber-sport it is today. The eighties was not a great decade for football – there was hooliganism, declining crowds and terrible tragedies such as Heysel, Bradford and Hillsborough – and as such the clamour for more coverage was never overwhelming. Football had its slots – like the Saturday-lunchtime fare of *Football Focus* with Bob Wilson and the Smashy-and-Nicey punditry of *Saint and Greavsie* – and had the sense to keep itself to itself. This gave space, and weight, to other sports, which made the coverage feel richer and more colourful than the football-heavy schedule today.

Nowhere was the contrast in the variety on offer clearer than in the Sunday-teatime slot. On BBC2 there was *One Man and His Dog*, which in the early eighties pulled in an audience of eight million viewers to watch Britain's leading shepherds lean on their crooks and call 'Away!' and 'Come-by!' to guide a small flock of sheep around a course and into a pen. The setting was a picture-postcard version of the British countryside, all rolling hills and dry-stone walls. This was accompanied by a soundtrack of long pregnant pauses as the sheep waited for the sheepdog, who waited for his master to give him the all-important whistle.

Channel 4, meanwhile, went for a sport as far away from this gentle British pastime as it was possible to be: American football. The theme tune to the programme was Bonnie Tyler's 'Holding Out for a Hero', in which she belted out her croaky search for good men and gods and 'street-wise Hercules'. The white knight Bonnie was looking for had to be both strong and fast, an ideal combination I was never completely convinced could exist in one man. Strong? Yes. But fast as well? That's not the sort of man who's going to be around 'till the end of the night', as any of my former girlfriends will sadly testify. On Channel 4, while the music thumped out so the introduction showed American footballers thumping hard into each other, helmet cracking against helmet, shoulder pad crunching against shoulder pad. This came with a soundtrack of manly grunts and groans, which was perhaps a little bit too *Debbie Does Dallas Cowboys*, or maybe that should be *Dallas Cowboys Doing Debbie*. (Or maybe Debbie wasn't involved at all and it was just a bit *Top Gun* in the locker rooms. Either way, this wasn't the sort of debate you got into about the opening credits of *One Man and His Dog*.)

Unlike British football clubs, which had everyday names like United or City, American-football teams were called Vikings or Raiders, Giants or, er, Packers. After some careful research I decided which team I would add to my roster of York City, Yorkshire County Cricket Club and England (all competitions).

'The Redskins?' Mum looked pleased when I announced it over potato croquettes at tea. 'Well, we must be doing something right if you're naturally drawn to a team named after America's indigenous people.'

'In digit what?' I looked blank. 'I'm supporting the Washington Redskins because they won the Superbowl last year.'

That might seem a bit of glory-hunting on my part, but I felt it was allowed given my support of York City, who in 1981 had finished 92nd out of the 92 Football League clubs. Anyway, I was the eldest child so I got first pick. Joff went second and plumped for the Superbowl runners-up, the Miami Dolphins.

'Dolphins?' I pulled a face. 'What sort of cissy name is that? They're so rubbish their stadium is called the Fruit Bowl.'

'It's called the Orange Bowl, actually,' Joff responded a little grumpily.

Somehow we persuaded our parents that we absolutely had to have sweatshirts to support our new teams – I can only guess that a combination of the garish colours, the artificial scratchy fabric and the sheer Americanization of the imagery made Mum pass into some sort of trance when we entered the sport shop. Her one note of hesitation was to suggest that Joff and I swap teams, as the turquoise of the Miami Dolphins suited my colouring better. Which was just a so-typical 'Mum' comment to make, and ranked only second to the time she'd taken Joff and me to watch York City because Dad was away: York somehow managed to win by the extraordinary scoreline of 7−1, and all she could say was, 'Is it always this boring?' So her suggested team swap simply furthered the strength of my support of the Washington Redskins, and meant that I wore the clashing crimson sweatshirt against my bright-red hair at every given opportunity.

The Channel 4 coverage was hosted by Nicky Horne, a small and bearded radio DJ who was undoubtedly extremely amiable but did not look the sort of person that Bonnie Tyler was holding out for. He did, though, have a fantastic three-dimensional map of America in the studio, complete with team helmets rising out of each of the relevant cities. The Sunday-teatime show was a magazine format of match highlights, league round-ups and features where Horne and friends gamely attempted to explain to the British public how the game was a bit more than just rugby with a lot of adverts.

By the time I'd sort of worked out what was going on, I'd also worked out that I'd chosen to support a bit of a duff team. Yes, the Redskins had won the Superbowl in 1983, but they failed to do so again for another five years, by which point I'd begun to lose interest in the sport. Despite hardly ever winning, they were always expected to do so − which made even their victories disappointing. And their way of playing was dreary: the Redskins appeared to be managed by a gridiron George Graham, grinding out the results rather than turning on the style.

By contrast, Joff had lucked out with the Miami Dolphins. They didn't win the Superbowl in this era either, but in the young and dashing Dan Marino they had the equivalent of Zico playing at quarterback and they were always great to watch. Not only that but, thanks to the exploits of Crockett and Tubbs, even the city of Miami was cool. And the turquoise sweatshirt went with my eyes. Much as I hated to admit it, Mum had been right again.

Football was not the only sport that tickled Chas and Dave's musical tastebuds during the eighties. In 1986 they teamed up with the so-called 'Matchroom Mob' for their Top Ten hit 'Snooker Loopy'. With badly sung cameos from all the nation's favourite snooker players, the group threatened to show what they could do with a load of balls and a snooker cue. This involved potting the red, and then screwing back for the yellow, green, brown, blue, pink and black.

Snooker loopy nuts were we in the 1980s – we were all snooker . . . loopy. I think this can be put down to the fact that colour TV sets were by now the norm: it wasn't until the late 1970s that they made up the majority of the nation's televisions. Snooker on a black-and-white set had never been the most enjoyable of televisual experiences. In colour, though, the game had and still has a strange sort of hypnotic quality on the male of species. You think you're going to watch for only five minutes, but three and half hours later you wake up to discover that what's on the screen isn't the white ball but the white dot that tells you the day's television's over.

Snooker was one of those *Going for Gold* sports in which the contestants were predominantly from the British Isles, with a couple of token foreigners thrown in to give the 'World' Championship a sense of international legitimacy. The main man was undoubtedly Steve Davis – or Steve 'Interesting' Davis, to give him his full *Spitting Image* moniker. Steve won the title six times in the eighties, and was runner-up twice. With his unshakeable persona and carrot-red hair, he looked more like an insurance clerk than a world champion of anything, but the funny thing was that underneath he *was* actually quite interesting and a bit of an expert on soul music.

Far more immediately intriguing were the exploits of some of the other players. There was Tony Knowles, the resident sex symbol, who had female fans queuing up to have him sign their breasts and was exposed in the tabloid press for his penchant of threesomes. Then there was Kirk 'White Magic' Stevens, whose choice of nickname was unfortunate given his cocaine addiction. Alex 'Hurricane' Higgins, meanwhile, was the sport's McEnroe figure, his wayward genius marred by an occasional tendency to punch or head-butt officials with whom he disagreed. The cult figure in the Bromley household, however, was undoubtedly the Canadian Bill Werbeniuk. Werbeniuk was the sort of man who made John Candy look svelte. The size of his frame was matched by the amount of alcohol he could get through – up to thirty pints a day – which he claimed was for medicinal purposes. Werbeniuk once famously split his trousers live on air, while trying to reach a difficult shot (his response to the rip was to ask, 'Who did that?'). He also performed one of the pots of the century in bouncing the white over one ball in order to pot another.

In 1985 the World Championship final was between Steve Davis and Dennis Taylor, an unfancied Irish player who looked as though he wore his glasses upside down. It was one of those finals that was nip and tuck all the way, and everyone in the country (who didn't have to go to bed) stayed up to watch the conclusion (Dad helpfully stayed up until the bitter end to let us know who won). The match came down to the last frame, and then down to the last black: whoever could pot the last ball would be champion. It was well past midnight by this point, but 18.5 million viewers sat on the edge of their seats as Steve Davis missed a difficult pot then Dennis Taylor buried the ball to huge cheers. For all the relevance of colour television in the popularization of snooker, it was a battle with a black ball and a white ball that became the sport's defining moment.

*　　*　　*

If all of this variety of coverage wasn't enough, there were also plenty of eighties entertainment shows that attempted to add a bit of sporting stardust to proceedings. The granddaddy was *A Question of Sport*, which felt like it had been around forever – and given that it had started in 1970, two years before I was born, it sort of had. The eighties was the programme's high point (everything is relative) with David Coleman hosting captains Bill Beaumont (who always looked bemused) and Emlyn Hughes (who always looked out of control). Hughes famously managed to mistake Princess Anne for a male jockey the week before she came on the programme. God only knows why they didn't put her next to Bill, because Emlyn was unable to curb his natural instinct to hug his team-mate, however royal they were, when they got a question right.

Children's telly also had its own slew of sports programmes. There was *We Are the Champions*, at the end of which host Eddie Waring would shout, 'Away you go!' and all the contestants would pile into whichever municipal swimming pool that week's heat was being filmed at. At least the children seemed to be having fun there, unlike in *Junior Kick Start*, where the only one enjoying himself was host Peter Purves. He would spend the programme trying not to laugh as ten-year-old boys fell head first into bales of hay as they failed to navigate their motorbikes over logs.

The success of snooker, meanwhile, led to the BBC's *Pot the Question*, a 1984 quiz show that combined snooker and general knowledge and featured host Stuart Hall and team captains Patrick Mower and Denis Law. It disappeared as quickly as one of Bill Werbeniuk's lagers, and the idea was shelved for the rest of the decade – until Jim Davison and John Virgo turned up with the not un-similar *Big Break* in 1991. The only place where snooker and general knowledge worked in the eighties was on the wireless, in the form of Dave Lee 'Hairy Cornflake' Travis' Radio One quiz, *Give Us a Break*. Contestants would attempt to rack up as high a score as possible – different-coloured balls reflecting the relative difficulty of the questions – and avoid the 'Quack-quack-oops' sound that denoted a wrong answer. If a snooker quiz show worked on the radio, but not the television, the opposite was true of that other pub staple: darts. DLT attempted that too, in his game 'Treble Top', but it never caught on in the same way. The home of darts and questions, it turned out, was very much on the small screen, not the radio.

Bullseye wasn't the first time that television had tried darts as entertainment. An honourable mention has to be made to Fred Trueman's *Indoor League*, a mainstay of 1970s television in which the fiery Yorkshire bowler, pint in hand, presided over bar billiards, shove-ha'penny, skittles and, above all, 'real darts on a Yorkshire board'. God's own dart board, it might not surprise you to hear, is harder to play on than a normal one: less generous in the points it hands out, and far more unforgiving. It eschews such fancy rubbish as trebles and the outer ring of the bullseye for a simpler, no-nonsense design: a single ring of red and green doubles on the outer rim; coal-black and Wensleydale-white cheese slices within it. Even the bullseye on this sparse-as-the-moors board is parsimony itself, smaller in size than the 'luxury' centre circle usually offered.

Fortunately for viewers, Yorkshire TV decided not to follow the format of the local dartboard and thus reduce the size of *Bullseye* the programme. Because from the moment it started in 1981 the programme was very much double top. It was hosted by Jim Bowen, a Cheshire-born stand-up comedian, who may have lacked Fred Trueman's pint and pipe but made up for this with his dead-pan delivery and string of superlatives. Bowen's three killer-catchphrase arrows were 'super', 'smashing' and 'great', the combination of which would have sounded over the treble top, if Bowen didn't deliver them as though he'd just been given a parking ticket. My personal favourite word of his was 'marvellous', with the emphasis on 'mar'. Like an out-of-date Dairylea triangle, he couldn't say this without sounding thoroughly cheesed-off.

It might be fairer to describe Jim Bowen as co-host of the programme, because centre stage was shared with a jovial cartoon bull called Bully. The animated opening credits featured Bully driving a coach whose passengers included Jim Bowen and a selection of leading darts players – Eric 'Crafty Cockney' Bristow and the like. One feared for their safety as Bully hit an ejector seat and caught a ride on a passing dart, which he held on to as it flew to the centre of an enormous dartboard. 'It's a bullseye!' shouted the voiceover man to huge cheers from the studio audience.

Bully appeared throughout the programme, offering a loud 'Moo' if contestants ran out of time answering a question. The format was that three pairs of contestants would fight it out for the star prize; one half of each partnership was a darts player and the others were the general-knowledge buffs, and play revolved around three different dart boards, none of them the Yorkshire variety (Fred Trueman would no doubt have been spluttering into his Old Peculiar). The first round employed a 'category' board, which was split into various question themes rather than numbers. So (for example) the general-knowledge guy would ask his darts player to hit 'Places', but he'd miss and land on 'Spelling' instead. At the end of the round the lowest-scoring pair of the three would be knocked out and the remaining contestants would then move on to play a traditional board in round two. Here it was 'pounds for points': the higher score the darts player got, the more each correctly answered question was worth.

By the end of this round there'd be one pair of contestants left. Not that the other contestants went home empty-handed – there were consolation prizes of *Bullseye* darts, *Bullseye* tankards and the 'Bendy Bully': a pint-sized rubbery replica of the great bull himself. There was also any cash that had been won – this Jim Bowen would take from a wad of notes he kept in his jacket pocket.

'This'll take me a couple of minutes to count out,' Jim would say, cueing up the ad break. 'Why don't you come back in two minutes?'

Surely it couldn't really take two minutes to count out £100 in £20 notes? And it meant that we never got to see the less-evenly rounded-up second-round totals, and Jim Bowen jiggling around in his trouser pockets for a bit of loose change. All this was soon forgotten, however, when it was time for the winning duo to win, or at least attempt to win, a selection of prizes. First up was Bully's non-Yorkshire prize board, which was made up of eighteen alternate red and black segments: the red ones each denoted a different prize, while the black ones meant a miss. Or, as Jim's somewhat convoluted catchphrase put it: 'Stay out of the black and in the red, there's nothing in this game for two in the bed.'

The prizes were a notch up from those that, say, Terry Wogan was offering on *Blankety Blank*, but because they were presented so excitedly they didn't always come across as much better.

'Innnnn One . . .' Bully would bellow, as though he couldn't quite believe what was being given away.

'. . . a selection of house plants,' Jim Bowen would deadpan in return. 'Plus a bamboo stand to store them on. Marvellous.'

Although it was theoretically possible to win all nine prizes, in reality the six darts of the darts player and the three darts of the non-darts player would usually snare two or three at best. This would then leave the duo with a difficult decision to make: as the prize board disappeared and the regulation dart board returned, the contestants had to decide whether to keep what they'd already won or gamble it all for 'tonight's star prize'. To achieve that, they needed to score 101 or more in nine darts: again, six for the darts player and three for the non-darts player. Considering your nine darts could net you a maximum 540 points, and that the prizes won were hardly worth Bully shouting home about, it might seem surprising how many contestants would tell Jim that they'd had a 'lovely day out', and were going to stick with what they'd already won.

But perhaps during the ad break, while Jim counted out the losing contestants' cash, the winning duo peeked behind the curtain to see whether Bully's star prize was yet another speedboat. The star prize wasn't always a speedboat – sometimes it was a car, or a set of dining-room table and chairs – but it did feel as though it was more often than not. Part of this, to be fair to *Bullseye*, was because of the limitations on the size of prizes you were then able to give away on TV: if Chris Tarrant had done his quiz show in the eighties, it would have been called *Who Wants to Be a Few Thousand Quid Richer?* A speedboat was simply about as expensive a prize as was allowed.

Bullseye did seem to have a lakeful of the things up Bully's shirt sleeves: it was almost as if Jim Bowen had met some dodgy bloke at a service station up the M6 and bought a job lot with the wad in his jacket pocket. As flash as it might appear, a speedboat was a bit of a rubbish prize. Unless you happened to live by Lake Windermere, what were you going to do with it? How were you going to get it home from the studio, for starters? Were you going to have to take lessons before you'd be allowed to ride it? Would you need to pay out to join some boating yard to store it? Or would it just end up dumped in the driveway, blocking the view for twenty years until your wife could take it no more and you found yourself giving Jim Bowen a ring to see if *Bullseye* was coming back and was in need of a spare star prize?

The programme was not known for letting its losing contestants down gently: as the non-darts player's arrows bounced off the board and were handed back by commentator Tony Green, Jim Bowen would note the combined total score of 17 and say, 'Let's have a look at what you could have won.' Why? That's what you always wondered as the stage-hands wheeled out Bully's boat booty. They hadn't won it, and now they were never *going* to win it, so the only possible reason for showing it to them was to rub their noses well and truly in the bull.

It was always a cruel moment, but in a funny kind of way it also summed up the period: for all the growing commercialization, and the win-at-all-costs philosophies of the professionals, the spirit of what sport was originally about lived on. For as Jim Bowen said, 'Let's have a look at what you could have won,' the camera would zoom in on the contestants' faces for a reaction. And rather than despair or disappointment, you could usually detect a 'thank fuck for that' look in their eyes as the speedboat was wheeled out. No one really wanted to win such a pain-in-the-arse prize: all anyone who went on the programme really wanted was to meet Jim Bowen, have a 'lovely day out' and go home with a Bendy Bully to show their friends back at the pub. While the same might not have been true for a Jody Scheckter or a Diego Maradona, it was warming to see that in the *Bullseye* studio at least it remained the taking part, and not the winning, that really counted.

After the break, we play catch-up, say what we see and get our fingers in a twist . . .

Ad Break

Stork

There is a danger that lurks in British supermarkets of the 1980s – a stalker (or should that be storker?) who lies in wait by the dairy counter for his unsuspecting victims. One minute they're there, quite happily putting a pat of butter or tub of margarine in their shopping basket, and the next they have smooth-talking TV presenter Leslie Crowther leaping out at them with a camera crew and host of accusatory questions.

'You haven't chosen Stork SB margarine,' Crowther both observes and chides. 'Now, why haven't you?'

To be honest, it won't matter what their reply is, because before they know it Crowther has whipped them off for a 'taste test' – a challenge which he gives to the husband rather than to the non-Stork-buying wife. The husband does, unsurprisingly, prefer the taste of Stork SB, so Crowther turns back to the non-Stork-buying wife and asks what she's going to do about it. The implication, presumably, being: 'Listen up, women of Britain! Don't deprive your hard-working husband of what he really likes, or you'll only have yourself to blame!'

On one particular occasion, Crowther is talking to some more non-Stork women when a slightly pushy older woman sees him from across the aisle and barges into the conversation. This woman loves Stork, and can't wait to tell Crowther and his interviewees how great the margarine is.

'You're not married yet then, are you?' she asks a non-Stork woman. No. 'That's it, then,' she says conspiratorially. 'When you get married, you'll know.'

Know what? I've been married for five years and I'm still not really sure what she's on about. All I can think is that she's suggesting that margarine is what lubricates a successful long-term relationship, while butter is only good for a quick *Last Tango in Paris*.

If you're eating toast while you're reading this, I'm really sorry.

Episode Twelve

'See what you say and say what you see'

Every summer holiday, we the Bromleys would pack our worldly belongings into our white Peugeot 504 and set off on the six-and-a-half-hour drive from York to the south coast. The journey would be punctuated by the pulling over to the side of the road for someone to be sick, and the sound of *The Swinging Sixties* rattling out from the car stereo. I say car stereo: what this actually was was a cassette player plugged into the cigarette lighter and stuck down on the dashboard with thick black tape. Once we had finally arrived at our given destination, holidays followed a regular pattern: one of my brothers or sisters would retire to bed with one of the major childhood illnesses (one year it was chickenpox, another it was mumps); and as the inevitable rain starting pouring down the family would christen that year's addition to our collection of board games.

Travel games seemed to be a theme for a while: there was The Game of Great Britain (or was it The Great Game of Britain?), which involved catching trains round the British Isles to visit all the exciting tourist locations from Stonehenge to Stornoway (if you got the card for the latter in your hand, you may as well give up before you started). Then there was The London Game, which was the same sort of thing except it involved travelling around by tube. It says much about my childhood that this seemed fantastically exotic at the time – a feeling that did not return when I became a commuter. There were some wonderfully middle-class games thrown in for good measure: The Peter Rabbit Race Game involved guiding one of Beatrix Potter's characters around a board, though some of the creatures seemed more equal than others (put it this way, it wasn't called The Jemima Puddleduck Race Game); we also had a particularly mind-numbing game from the RSPB, which was less about fun and more about learning about rare birds.

These were bored games rather than board games. In our house there was no Operation, or Buck-a-roo, or Ker-plunk!, or Hungry Hippos or Mouse Trap, or any of those cheap-and-cheerful games that were advertised by shouting children on TV. We played Cluedo, though I could never see the point (where's the skill?), and only if the rain really set in did Monopoly get dusted down. This inevitably ended in tears, which, with a knowing nod, would confirm my parents' political beliefs. We played Trivial Pursuit, too (who didn't in the eighties?), though we never did so obsessively like those who referred to it by such smug shorthands as 'Triv', or 'TP'. For me, the game was always hampered by the fact that Joff and I were just too old for the 'Young Players' edition and just too young for the proper adult questions. Which meant we either won easily or lost heavily, depending how competitive our parents were feeling.

One game that always puzzled me was Mastermind. Now, I'd seen *Mastermind* on the telly. It had a big black chair in which sat a contestant whom Magnus Magnusson asked questions about Napoleon or the life and works of Elizabeth Gaskell, and if Magnusson got interrupted by the beeper he'd stubbornly say that he'd started so he was also going to finish, thank you very much. Not much of this was in evidence in our board game. Gone was Magnus Magnusson and in his place was a slightly menacing-looking man with his fingertips pressed together and a stare that said, 'I have started, Mr Bond, so allow me to finish.' Standing behind him, with her hand on his shoulder, was an attractive Asian lady in a slinky white dress – the bad variety of Bond girl who'd sleep with James then steal his gun while he slept. In order to impress this incredibly sophisticated couple, one didn't need to know about British prime ministers from 1841 to 1911 but to correctly guess a sequence of four coloured pegs – your guesses were rewarded by black and white pegs, depending on accuracy. Which might not have been the greatest concept ever but probably made for a better evening than if the real *Mastermind* had been turned into a board game, and was certainly no less random than many of its many rivals on TV.

The makers of our board game weren't the only ones to attempt *Mastermind* with a twist. The biggest game show of the 1980s – in terms of money won, at least – was *Ultra Quiz*, which ran for three series from 1983 to 1985. *Ultra Quiz* was the British version of the hugely successful Japanese show *Trans America Ultra Quiz*, one of those funny foreign programmes about which Clive James would raise his eyebrows on his television show. The Japanese version involved the contestants answering questions as they crossed the United States, where the prizes were big (for example, a helicopter) but so were the forfeits for losing (for example, being chucked off a ship).

With no racial undertones whatsoever, the British version was originally sold to viewers as 'kamikaze *Mastermind*'. It wasn't that – unfortunately, as it would have made for gripping TV, pilots trying to answer as many questions on Charles Dickens as possible before crashing their plane into the side of an American ship. David Frost, who hosted the second series, described it slightly more accurately as 'a cross between *Mastermind* and *Around the World in 80 Days*'. Beginning in Britain, a ridiculously huge number of contestants (2500) would be whittled down as the show globe-trotted to increasingly exotic destinations: if you got through to show two, you got to go on a cross-channel ferry; if you got through to show seven, you found yourself in Hong Kong. Unless, that is, you found yourself a contestant in series three: in which case, due to cutbacks, you weren't going to leave the British Isles (what's more, you got Stu Francis as a presenter, rather than Frost or Michael Aspel).

So, if the programme wasn't always quite Jules Verne, it wasn't quite *Mastermind* either. Part of the show involved contestants running to giant ticks and crosses painted on the ground, to indicate whether they thought a given 'fact' was true or false; get it wrong, and you were out. The questions were quite often linked with stunts. So in the opening programme, for example, possibly to add a Japanese flavour to proceedings, the Nottingham karate team were given five minutes to destroy a piano with their bare hands and post it through a hole the size of a letterbox – all the contestants had to do was guess whether or not they would succeed. Perhaps unsurprisingly the karate team failed, which created a problem for the opening programme: most of the contestants had given them a sporting chance, thus eliminating far more people than had been the intention.

Ultra Quiz might have lacked that kamikaze killer touch, but it maintained the cruel streak of the original Japanese programme. So, rather than finding themselves thrown off a ship, losing contestants on the cross-channel ferry were given mops and told to clean the deck. There were also lots of switchback tricks, where the people you thought had lost actually turned out to have won. This continued right up to the winner being given his prize money – £10,000 – in pound coins. Oh, how their bank manager must have laughed the following Monday morning.

Ten grand might not sound like much of a prize but for quiz shows in the eighties it was by far the largest on offer. This was because of the aforementioned strict rules laid down by the powers that be regarding how much could be won. Prizes on a programme could total no more than £1750 a week; once a month 'a small car costing between £4500 and £5000' could be won, as long as this didn't mess up the £1750-a-week average. *Ultra Quiz*, which ran for a couple of months, was therefore just about allowed to give away its solitary prize of £10,000. Maybe they got their special dispensation because it was all in loose change.

The relaxation of these rules about prize money hasn't been the only change in this area since the eighties. Another stipulation back then was that no quiz show could be based on pure chance: there always had to be an element of skill involved somewhere along the line – unlike in say, *Deal or No Deal* (unless having a 'system' is an example of skill). In the same way that any giveaway on the television always comes with a question, however ridiculously easy, so you had to answer something correctly before Brucey would let you shout 'higher' or 'lower' in *Play Your Cards Right*.

The one quiz that pushed this ruling to the limit was *3-2-1*. Not because the questions were so easy, but because they were so impossibly hard. While *Ultra Quiz* had taken its influence from Japan, *3-2-1* took its inspiration from the wrong-way-round-sounding Spanish quiz show *Uno-Dos-Tres*. 'It's a quiz!' the opening credits helpfully explained. 'It's a game!' they continued, muddying the waters a little. 'It's fortune and fame!' it finished up, which not only confused things further but was also a bit of a fib, given the £1700 prize fund and the fact that the only person to get fame from the programme was a rubbish bin.

The host was Ted Rogers, who brought to the show his own visual catchphrase of flicking his wrist round to show three fingers to two to one in a way that was difficult for anyone watching to resist instinctively trying to imitate. Having failed – no one could do the proper finger swivel quite like Ted could – you'd resort to doing the fingers the wrong way round, so the middle V for victory became 'up yours' instead. Although his jokes were occasionally a bit Ted Rogers in the nineteenth century, Ted was an amiable enough host – especially when you consider that rather than being given the help of a lady lovely he'd found himself sharing the screen with a remote-controlled rubbish bin. Dusty Bin was to Ted Rogers what Bully was to Jim Bowen, a comic sidekick who was wheelie-binned on to huge applause. As well as being Rogers' assistant, he was representative of the show's booby prize – a dustbin – which final-round contestants had to do their best to avoid.

This final round, like some sort of light-entertainment wet dream, combined variety performances with a game-show challenge. A string of singers and comedians, impressionists and magicians would come on and do their acts before wandering over and leaving the contestants with a clue to the identity of a prize. These clues came in two parts: first, a physical object, which seldom related to the act they'd just performed, and then a riddle, which seldom related to anything whatsoever. In fact, so open-ended and indecipherable were the clues, the skill stipulation pretty much went out of the window. It was pot luck, frankly, whether you got the dream holiday or the Dusty Bin.

Here are three clues from one typical episode of the programme, one of which won a holiday to New York, one of which won Dusty Bin, and one of which won the star prize of a small car: see if you can work out which was which. Clue one, delivered by an impressionist pretending to be Angie from *EastEnders*, was: 'This one's from the other end/ My name's a clue for a little friend.' The object was a miner's helmet. Object two, presented by a group called Wall Street Crash, was a mass of shredded paper, and its associated couplet was: 'Peace and agreement at speed/A crash is not what you need'. Finally, object number three was a tinder box, and its riddle was: 'Anyone can get the German out/You're well on the way without a doubt'.

What do you mean, you can't work it out? Isn't it obvious that the New York holiday was clue number two: peace and agreement at speed – that obviously referred to Concorde; the clue was presented by Wall Street Crash, and as 'crash' is not what you need, that leaves you with Wall Street; Wall Street is in New York, where they have ticker-tape parades, hence the paper. Dur! And I'm sure I don't need to tell you that clue number one was the car: 'my name's a clue for a little friend', that's obviously a mini; 'Angie' from *EastEnders* is from the East End, the other 'end' is the West End, therefore the car is quite clearly a Mini Mayfair. And as for number three being Dusty Bin? Well, anyone can get the German out – German for 'the' is '*der*'; take '*der*' out of tinder box, and you're left with tin box: Dusty Bin. Honestly. It's really quite simple when you put your mind to it.

It was at this part of the programme that Ted Rogers really earned his money – reading out the clues and answers with a completely straight face. It was at this point, too, as Ted read out the ridiculous reasoning that led to them winning a bin, that the losing contestants must have been sorely tempted to give Dusty the Ted Rogers salute, and not the right way round.

There was only one quiz that could match *3-2-1* for the sheer diffi-culty of its clues, and that was Channel 4's *Treasure Hunt* ('155 degrees magnetic, 3.5 miles from breakwater light . . . a visit to the home of the Gods is your reward'). Unlike *3-2-1*, however, at least here the contest-ants had access to all sorts of reference facilities to help them work out what was going on. Gently prodded by host Kenneth Kendall, and watched over by weatherperson Wincey Willis, the contestants would attempt to decode various cryptic messages in order to guide their 'skyrunner' to where the treasure was.

The skyrunner, of course, was Anneka Rice, who wore a large set of headphones and bright-pink jumpsuit. According to what the contestants told her to do, she'd either dash around the countryside in a helicopter or run around shouting for help at startled-looking locals, all while a slightly less fit cameraman followed behind. Quite literally, in fact: for all the clever crossword-type clues, Anneka's bottom was one of the stars of the show and the inevitable winner of Rear of the Year. In later years, Anneka's jumpsuit would be passed over to tennis failure Annabel Croft, who got so good at jumping in and out of helicopters that she also took part in the not-similar-whatsoever programme *The Interceptor*. The twist to the *Treasure Hunt* format in this version was that the contestants were let loose in the countryside, attempting to unlock the winning cash before being caught by and zapped by the eponymous 'Interceptor', a laser-wielding Sean O'Kane, complete with long black coat and pantomime laugh.

Helicopters weren't the only gimmicks that game shows added to the mix in eighties. Another popular programme was *Child's Play*, hosted by Michael Aspel, in which young children were asked to describe things (Australia, or Father Christmas, or Boy George) so the contestants could then try to guess what the heck they were talking about. Whenever the kids said the word in their description, a cartoon 'Oops' appeared over their mouths – which pretty much summed up the cutesy feel of the programme. To be fair, it was actually quite funny – often the children had only the vaguest idea of what it was they were trying to describe, which led to lots of unintentional humour and the sort of bizarre answers that Ted Rogers would have been proud of.

Equally bizarre was *The Adventure Game*, in which various minor celebrities, such as a Bonnie Langford or a Richard Stilgoe, found themselves transported through space to the planet Arg. Arg was home to a group of dragons called Argonds who could change themselves into different things, including Moira Stuart (under the name of Darong) or an aspidistra plant (the Rangdo). The celebrities played various games in the hope of winning crystals to power their spaceship back home, and had to attempt to get over a criss-cross grid without being evaporated by the 'Vortex'.

Catchphrase, meanwhile, swapped dragons for swanky computer graphics. The programme was hosted by Roy Walker, who urged contestants to 'see what you say and say what you see'. A well-known phrase or saying would be displayed on a giant computer screen in the studio, and the contestants had to guess (which they often did badly) what the catchphrase was. So for example you might have a picture of a hand with a bird perched on it, an 'equals' sign, and a bush containing two further birds. At which point Julie from Chichester would buzz in to say, 'Is it a stitch in time saves nine, Roy?' Then Roy would smile warmly and say with silky-smooth sincerity, 'It's good, but it's not right.'

Not everything was as high-tech as this. *That's My Dog!* was the hound of a quiz where the contestant couples were owner and pooch. The dog got the inevitable obstacle course to navigate, while the owner was asked suitably canine questions. There was also a round where the dog was shown a variety of objects and had to sniff out which one had the scent of its owner. I can't recall what the star prize was – a Rover was presumably too big to be considered a 'small car' so maybe it was just a nice bone from the butcher's instead. And when all else failed, there was always the television quiz about television itself. Noel Edmonds' *Telly Addicts* was the show where television-watching families tuned in to watch television-watching families compete with other television-watching families. Which was all either incredibly post-modern or an excuse to squeeze yet another programme out of some old clips.

If helicopters or children, dragons, computers or animals weren't quite your thing, there was always one more thing you could throw into the game-show mix: foreigners. In 1987 Henry Kelly launched the supposedly pan-European quiz show *Going for Gold* (the show was so called because the prize for the first series was a trip to Seoul for the 1988 Olympic Games). The programme was basically quiz show meets Eurovision, except with all the questions in English. And about English subjects. To be honest, the nationalities thing was always a little bit stretched, given that the programme not only divided the UK up into England, Scotland, Wales and Northern Ireland but also created further countries such as Gibraltar – which would have pissed the Spanish off something rotten had they not been having their siesta at the time it was on air.

Anyway, in this thoroughly unbalanced quiz, Henrik from Sweden found himself answering questions on the royal family (ours, not his) and being thoroughly trounced by Chris from Jersey. The bit I always remember was the complicated final round, in which contestants had to guess 'Who Am I?' They could buzz in only when the ticking clock was in their 'time zone', with play switching back and forth between each person's zone and the answer being worth less as more clues to the person's identity were revealed. If a contestant guessed incorrectly, 'control of the game' passed over to the other player. When a contestant was losing they found themselves 'playing catch-up', as Henry Kelly described it: meaning that they could choose whether to 'pass or play'. (I appreciate this is quite anal, but I watched the programme a lot as a teenager and as a student. Which probably explains why I'm writing this book rather than doing a proper job.)

The other thing that was particularly memorable about *Going for Gold* was its theme tune. The intro started with a ring of circles flying over a desert before turning golden as they flashed through a rainbow. Then a sun would rise over the horizon, except that it wasn't a sun after all but a gold medal, with the little circles from earlier being the decoration around its rim. After a heavenly choir had sung the show's title, the gold medal flipped over to reveal a map of Europe – followed by a cheery wave from that day's contestants. All of this to a soundtrack of lyrical clichés about how the heat was on (well, it was in terms of your essay) and the time was right (for another cup of coffee), and how everyone was gathering together and going for, going for Gold.

The sad thing was (bearing in mind my joking about the thoroughly loaded deck) that the British only won four out of the programme's ten series. And one of those, the last one, was open only to UK contestants. So that's basically a one-in-three success rate despite the huge advantage. Which is not exactly what I would call a gold standard.

Giving your game show a gimmick came second to what every producer really wanted: the big-name host. The biggest name in the pack at the start of the eighties was, of course, Bruce Forsyth. Bruce, who'd left the BBC and *The Generation Game* behind at the end of the seventies, was now on ITV, where he was the host of *Bruce Forsyth's Play Your Cards Right*, among other things.

I don't know if it was deliberate, but I always liked the fact that in the opening credits of the show, where a pack of cards orbited as though you were looking at them through a kaleidoscope, Bruce's name came up just as the king appeared. Certainly Bruce was king when it came to the catchphrases. The audience would be started off with a classic, 'Nice to see you, to see you . . . nice!' Then there'd be a joke about how this audience was so much better than last week's – funny because the shows were recorded back to back, meaning last week's and this week's audiences were one and the same. And as the game got going Bruce would be reminding contestants that there was 'nothing for a pair in this game' and asking, 'What do points make? Prizes!'

The pair reference relates to the main hook of the show, which was for the contestants to shout 'Higher!' or 'Lower!' as Bruce turned over a succession of oversized playing cards. If you got to the end of the line you won a prize or a Brucey Bonus; if you guessed wrongly or bagged a pair, you didn't. The points/prizes catchphrase, meanwhile, referred to the fact that contestants didn't play for pounds but rather for points, which could be converted into prizes. What you did with any points left over, I'm not completely sure.

If you couldn't get Bruce, then second-choice game-show host was probably Bob Monkhouse. Bob was both the original host of *Family Fortunes* and, subsequently, the presenter of his very own *Bob's Full House* (if Bruce wanted to do playing cards, then Bob was going to bag himself bingo). *Bob's Full House* always felt a bit complicated to me, but essentially you had to answer questions right to fill your bingo card; if you got questions wrong, you got 'wallied' and couldn't answer the next question. The final round was Bob's 'Gold Card', during which every correctly answered question revealed a letter of the star-prize holiday destination. Bob would end the programme telling the viewers that in *Bob's Full House* 'the doors are always open to you'. In the 1990s a thief took advantage of this and nicked his joke books.

And if you couldn't get Bob, then you'd probably give Tarby a ring. (Actually, you might find him playing golf with Brucey.) Tarby's main game-show vehicle (if one can have a game-show vehicle, Dale Winton's *Touch the Truck* aside) was *Winner Takes All*, whose main selling point was the bit of gambling it brought to the table. Questions were multiple-choice, with possible answers given different odds from 2−1 to 10−1. The contestants would then decide how many of their points they would like to bet against which answer. By the end of the programme, as the title suggested, one player went away with all the cash. By the mid-eighties, possibly jealous about both Brucey and Bob having their names in their game-show titles, Tarby had a new show, *Tarby's Frame Game*. This had nothing to do with snooker and everything to do with finding the word that linked 'pot' and 'adder', or 'Wendy' and 'Bond', or 'Hanna' and 'Woodhouse'. (Award yourself a bonus point if you spotted the deliberate mistake among those. 'Ho ho,' as Tarby would say.)

For all the importance of Brucey and Bob and Tarby, perhaps the key figure in British game shows in the eighties was William G. Stewart. Stewart was host of *Fifteen to One*, the Channel 4 teatime show when

Countdown was off the air. Each show started with fifteen contestants, and via a series of general-knowledge questions the number would be knocked down until only three were left for a head-to-head (-to-head) decider in the second half of the show. What gave the programme its edge was that contestants could 'nominate' who'd get the next question. Consequently it all got a bit nasty between the eggheads as they tried to take out their biggest rivals before the final showdown.

Fifteen to One was only part of William G. Stewart's contribution to the quiz shows of the eighties, though. For it was in his role as producer that he really delivered – in particular with his two huge successes, *Family Fortunes* and *The Price is Right*. The former started on ITV in 1980 in the capable hands of Bob Monkhouse, before 'Our survey says' was said by first Max Bygraves and then Les Dennis. The programme was based on the American show *Family Feuds*; the title was changed at Bob Monkhouse's suggestion. Two families would compete to guess what answers a survey of 100 people had come up with when asked to list 'Things you'd take on holiday' or 'What you'd find in the kitchen'.

In a similar way to *Child's Play*, the set-up created much of the humour, and under the pressure of the studio lights family members would find themselves coming up with all sorts of bizarre answers. When asked to 'name something that flies without an engine', one contestant answered 'a bicycle with wings'. Another, asked to 'name something people might be allergic to', answered 'skiing'. And, when prompted to 'name something in the garden that's green', another contestant confidently replied 'the shed'. At this point the host would make a joke about how he'd give them the money himself if their answer was right – then a large 'X' would flash up on the screen, complete with 'eugh-eugh' sound.

As successful as *Family Fortunes* was, not even that could top *The Price is Right*, which within weeks of starting in 1983 had overtaken *Coronation Street* as the biggest show on ITV. The programme, perhaps unsurprisingly, was American, and had been racking in the ratings Stateside since its launch in the early 1970s. British producers, while long aware of the show, had always felt it would never work in Britain. This wasn't so much because of the quiz itself, which was a fairly straightforward idea based on guessing the price of a soda stream or exercise bike in a variety of games, but was really because of the whole *feel* of the show. With every member of the audience a potential contestant, the atmosphere was whipped up into a crazed frenzy – somewhere between a political rally and a Kajagoogoo concert.

British audiences were seen as somewhat more sedate: whooping and hollering was not the British way of doing things; we were more for a polite round of applause and on your way, sonny Jim. This was not the only difference between the British and American audiences: a survey carried out in the eighties showed that British audiences broadly wanted the contestants to win, whereas American audiences tuned in to watch them lose. This was probably in part to do with the regulations on British TV: contestants over here had to work hard to get their rubbish prizes, while contestants over there got given riches far more at random. My guess is that British audiences felt that our contestants deserved their prizes, so rooted for them as a result.

The Price is Right stood all this conventional thinking on its head. William G. Stewart managed to successfully gee the audience up, though in a peculiarly British manner: part of his pre-show warm-up was to play 'Land of Hope and Glory' and get the audience to sing along, in a *Last Night of the Proms* sort of a way. The reins were then passed over to main man Leslie Crowther, who, as a former host of children's programme *Crackerjack*, was well versed in dealing with hyper crowds. Without so much as a good evening, he'd yell out for four members of the audience to 'Come on down!'

These four contestants would find themselves on Contestants' Row; if they escaped from there, they'd get to guess some prices and win some prizes. The show had a wider variety of games they could play than the Los Angeles Olympics: the 'Race Game', for example, involved putting prices to prizes against the clock, with Crowther telling contestants how many they'd got right; then there was 'Cliffhanger', in which a tiny figure climbed up a mountainside for every pound out the price guess was – go too far out and he'd fall off the top; at the end of the show was the 'Showcase' finale, in which the remaining contestants had to guess the total cost of a whole load of booty – the one who was the nearest won the lot.

The Price is Right was either an appalling dumbing-down of British television (nearly all the critics of the time) or the British public being given what they wanted (the 16 million plus viewers). It should hardly come as a surprise that the programme was not exactly compulsory viewing in our house. One could have probably worked that out from the title alone – the price (in other words, monetary value) is right (i.e., is what is important). Or, as Gordon Gekko put it in the film *Wall Street*, greed is good. Certainly, the programme couldn't have been less middle class if it tried – not only was there all the shouting and screaming and the grasping nature of the contestants, but there was also all that gold: in the credits, in the logo, in the backdrop. I guess my middle-class upbringing had rubbed off on me: the more I watched the gold sparkle, the grubbier I felt from watching it.

The Bromleys weren't the only people to feel rather British about the whole thing. When Leslie Crowther shouted his famous 'Come on down!' for the first time, the chosen contestant stayed in her seat and refused to do any such thing. When that first programme got to the end of its nail-biting climax, the man who'd beaten his female rival for the star prize of the holiday didn't just grab his winnings for himself, but instead asked the person he'd just beaten if she'd like to share the holiday with him. In quiz-show terms this was the equivalent of the first-ever London Marathon, where the leading two runners went over the finishing line in joint first place. Or maybe he just fancied her.

It'd be nice to say that such a selfless streak became a hallmark of the programme over the years. Sadly, though, that was not the case. *The Price is Right* ran right through the boom years of Thatcher's Britain, its ethos nicely echoing a sizzling stock market, the arrival of the yuppies and that general Thatcherite principle of putting yourself first. Although the ratings remained huge, the audience reaction was noticeably different from that of the other quiz shows on TV – for once, the British viewers were behaving more like their American cousins, and weren't rooting for the contestants to win.

Was *The Price is Right* the start of the slide towards a new era of quiz programme, where the rules and regulations became relaxed, prizes became bigger, the skill element became smaller and the pitfalls of losing were laced with nastiness? Did it lead to standards coming on down? I'm not sure Oscar Wilde ever got to see the show himself, but his definition of a cynic feels similarly applicable to any one of the programme's overexcited contestants: someone 'who knows the price of everything and the value of nothing'.

After the break, we say farewell to a couple of comic legends, keep a careful eye out for small men with beards, and say, 'Yes, Paul' . . .

Ad Break

Atari

To a party round at comedian Ernie Wise's house. Wise's guests are looking bored and distracted as he talks them through a photo album of his theatre memories. Then, with a slam of the door and a shout of 'Sit!' to the ornamental dog in the hallway, help is at hand with the arrival of Eric Morecambe. What has he brought with him to get the party started? Why, the very latest from computer manufacturer Atari: the 2600 video-computer system.

As the guests gather round excitedly, Morecambe reveals a selection of games from the inside of his raincoat: *PacMan*, *Missile Command*, *Super Breakout* and *Haunted House*. Morecambe shoves the latter into the console and begins his search round said spooky abode for the magic pieces of a different sort of urn. When one of the other guests tells Eric he'll have to be nimble on his feet, Ernie takes this as his cue to show off his tap dancing.

*   *   *

Despite some strong lobbying on my behalf, and the official endorsement of Eric and Ernie, the Bromleys didn't end up with an Atari 2600. When we finally got kitted up, it was with the somewhat less game-friendly BBC Micro 32K computer. Micro, in retrospect, was the important word – the BBC's memory was smaller than that of either the ZX Spectrum (48K) or the Commodore 64 (64K, obviously), which meant that it was too feeble to play even some of the most basic games. (In fact, there was only one worse computer on the market, and that was the Acorn Electron – which used up all of its 16K just switching itself on.)

The BBC was very much the 'educational' choice among home computers: even its colour (beige) was boring. Still, one of its plus points was that it allowed me to learn how to program. After years of studying the secrets of coding and various IT languages, I managed to distil my knowledge into the following early-eighties masterpiece:

```
10 Print 'If only my parents had listened to Morecambe and Wise'
20 Goto 10
End
```

Episode Thirteen

'You'll like this – not a lot, but you'll like it'

On a Sunday evening in mid-April 1984, ITV were showing
the latest edition of their variety show *Live from Her Majesty's*.
Broadcast live from Her Majesty's Theatre in the heart of London's
West End, the programme was hosted by Jimmy 'Tarby' Tarbuck,
who introduced a variety pack of comedians and musicians. On
this particular occasion the music was provided by American actor
Howard Keel, *a capella* group the Flying Pickets and the evergreen
Donny Osmond; the comedy star turn, meanwhile, was Tommy
Cooper.

Cooper, it goes without saying, was a once-in-several-generations
comedian who combined Caerphilly-cheesy one-liners with apparently disastrous magic tricks – the real conjuring trick being in giving
the impression that things were going horribly wrong; something
only an extremely good magician can pull off. As ever, Cooper was

performing in dishevelled black tie and Moroccan red fez, complete with hassled black tassel hanging down the front.

Towards the end of Cooper's routine, he looked across stage left with his arms held out. This was the cue for his assistant, the regulation young peroxide blonde, to bring out his golden gown – the sort of garment that a heavyweight boxing champion would wear before and after a fight. The gown was worn for the part of Cooper's routine where he would magic items out of his sleeves: the 'magic' being that he'd stand with his back to the stage curtains, behind which was a helper who would pass him the various objects.

To giggles from the audience, the assistant helped Cooper put on the gown and did up the catches at the front. She had barely finished before Cooper, to huge laughs from the audience, crumpled to his left and collapsed on to the floor, slumped forwards like a dishevelled comic Buddha. The assistant looked across at him and smiled at this new addition to the routine, then walked back off stage with the microphone stand. As Cooper sat slumped, waves of laughter continued to wash backwards and forwards across the auditorium. The longer he stayed there, the funnier the joke seemed to become. Then, to one final appreciative roar, he fell backwards, flat on the floor against his final curtain.

With a shard of irony as black as the tassel on his fez, Tommy Cooper, a comedian so good he had never died on stage, had finished his career by doing just that. This same irony was to be repeated in an unwanted encore just six short weeks later. Treading the boards of another theatre (this time the Roses in the Gloucestershire town of Tewkesbury), Eric Morecambe was taking part in a show hosted by his friend Stan Stennett. Remarking on the death of Tommy Cooper, Morecambe commented how he would hate to die in that way. Moments later, after six curtain calls and a farewell shout to the audience – 'That's your lot!' – Morecambe returned backstage, commented, 'Thank goodness for that,' and also collapsed from a heart attack. It was his third attack, and this time it was fatal – he died in hospital in the small hours of the following morning.

In the space of little over a month, by far the brightest lights of British light entertainment had both passed away. The tributes to both were fulsome and heartfelt. Morecambe led the tributes to Cooper – 'He was one of the great funny men . . . His greatest talent was not that he could get tricks wrong but that he could tell you something very real and sad and still make you laugh.' Ernie Wise described his comedy partner as 'a genuinely funny man, like Buster Keaton or Charlie Chaplin', while the *Sun* simply called him 'one of the good things in life'. More than 1000 people were unable to get into the church for Morecambe's funeral and listened outside via loudspeakers as Wise read out the words to 'Bring Me Sunshine'.

Back on *Live from Her Majesty's*, as the realization finally hit home that Tommy Cooper wasn't messing around, the conductor signalled to the orchestra to play some music and ITV cut to an unscheduled break. During the course of which it was decided that, in true show-business style, the show must go on. Like the final act of a Shakespearean tragedy, where the presence of a young prince is meant to restore order following the death of the king, so the baton (or, in stand-up parlance, the microphone) was passed over to the then rising comedy duo of Les Dennis and Dustin Gee. The double act were given the all but impossible task of somehow trying to keep the audience laughing while a few feet away, behind the stage curtain, desperate attempts were being made to resuscitate Tommy Cooper. It was a situation as black as comedy can get, and one that, with hindsight, remains hugely resonant: a macabre moment that captures both the sudden coming of age of the next generation of light entertainers and the presence of their forebears in which they would always be performing.

Les Dennis and Dustin Gee were nothing if not prolific in the mid-1980s. They were stalwarts of *Russ Abbott's Saturday Madhouse*, a

Saturday-teatime selection box of sketches and Russ-foolery (Abbott himself had a touch of the Coopers in his ongoing ability to 'spoil' sketches by 'forgetting' lines or bursting into 'spontaneous' laughter). From this they went on to be regulars on the impersonations programme *Go For It* before getting their own prime-time vehicle, *The Laughter Show*, on BBC1. The duo's set piece was undoubtedly their impression of *Coronation Street*'s Vera Duckworth and Mavis Riley ('Well, I don't really know . . .'); their sign-off was saying goodnight to 'each and every one of you'.

They were unfortunate in that they were the ones on next when the merry-go-round stopped, but their sad moment in the spotlight could have belonged to any number of acts. More fitting under the circumstances might have been (Tommy) Cannon and (Bobby) Ball, whom Eric Morecambe once described as his natural successors. A pair of former welders from Oldham, Cannon and Ball enjoyed a Saturday-night run that ran from 1978 until 1990. Cannon played the straight (i.e. boring) one, while with his bubble perm and moustache Bobby was given the cheeky (i.e. irritating) role. His catchphrase was to pull on his braces and say, 'Rock on, Tommy'; this was something that several classmates thought it hilarious to repeat back at me.

It could equally have been Little and Large, whose cleverly titled *The Little and Large Show* was another piece of companion viewing for Saturday teatime's beans on toast (with little sausages, if you were lucky). Matching Cannon and Ball bad joke for bad joke, Little and Large enjoyed a similar run from the late seventies until the early nineties. Syd Little (real name Cyril Mead) and Eddie Large (Eddie McGinnis) were a bit like a Lidl Laurel and Hardy. Sid, a sort of a Jim Bowen meets Mr Muscle, was the main butt of the jokes from the larger Eddie Large, who was more like an inflatable version of Kevin Keegan.

Then there was Keith Harris, who also must have thought long and hard before calling his own programme *The Keith Harris Show*. Harris was a ventriloquist, a practitioner of one of those gently dying crafts – like being a coal miner or the one in the band who plays the saxophone – and his sidekicks were the nappy-wearing green duck Orville ('I wish I could fly') and the sniffing orange monkey Cuddles ('I hate that duck'). I always thought Cuddles had it about right there.

It could have been the Krankies, whose various programmes and appearances included *The Krankies Elektronik Komik* – another reason not to rush back from town on Saturdays in 1986 and 1987. The Krankies were real-life married couple Ian and Janette Tough: in their act, Ian played Ian and Janette was 'wee Jimmy', joining AC/DC's Angus Young in that select group of adults who make a living out of dressing up as schoolboys. The Krankies gave a lot of thumbs-up and said 'Fandabbydozi'. I gave them the thumbs-down and fandabbydozed off.

'And there's more,' as Jimmy Cricket would say: Bob Carolgees (with his hilarious comedy spitting dog, Spit the dog); Frank Carson ('It's a cracker'); Roy Jay ('Spook!'); Jim Davidson (with his modestly named *Jim Davidson's Special*); and Freddie Starr (who, it turns out, never did eat a hamster in 1986 – though he did put a live one, called Supersonic, in between two pieces of bread at a model's house and pretend to munch away). Between them, these were the acts who formed the eighties comic establishment: traditional performers who'd learned their trade and paid their dues and were now ready to reap what they felt were their just rewards.

The deaths of Tommy Cooper and Eric Morecambe, however, had left that establishment without its figureheads – and this just as alternative comedy was beginning to make its mark. With the standard-bearers gone, it looked very much like the standard of what was left had slipped. It was the beginning of a process that would see alternative comedy take over – to the point that, ultimately, alternative comedy became the mainstream and old-school comedians became the alternative, a cast-aside tradition playing to an ever-decreasing (and ever-older) audience. Whatever you think of the different kinds of comedy, there's a wistful sort of sadness here: the sort given off by former football grounds, overgrown and overtaken by the replacement development out on the ring road.

This sadness continued to resound in the career of Les Dennis. Two years after the death of Tommy Cooper, Dustin Gee was performing in pantomime when he too suffered a fatal heart attack. Having been unfairly required to follow in the footsteps of one of the comic greats, Les Dennis now found himself left with only half an act – and, if one is being brutally honest, the slightly less funny half at that. *The Laughter Show* continued without Dustin Gee, and also without as much laughter: the couple's trademark *Coronation Street* skit was now a somewhat poignant solo sketch. It wasn't long before Les Dennis made the switch from stand-up to game-show host, taking over the reins of *Family Fortunes*. Our survey says that this was the right answer.

It was a tradition in the Bromley household that each child on their sixth birthday had a magician at their party. He was a local turn, called Uncle Paul – though as far as I'm aware he was not actually a relative, not even one of those 'uncles' you sometimes get who are really just family friends. As the eldest child I inevitably got hauled up to be his assistant, a job which consisted mainly of being the butt of his jokes and looking after his magic wand. The magic wand itself was a set-up: every time I was called upon to produce it, it predictably went all floppy in my hands.

Uncle Paul might not have been a real uncle but I knew he must have been a real magician because his name was Paul, just like that magician off the television. Paul Daniels was one of many eighties stars to have appeared on a talent show – in his case *Opportunity Knocks*. In 1979 the BBC decided to give him his own show, which was to run for fifteen years, until 1994. This was no mean feat – apart from David Nixon (host of *It's Magic* back in the day), Daniels was the only magician to have been given a prime-time series on British TV.

Unlike the Derren Browns and David Blaines of today, tall and dark with goatee beards and staring eyes, Paul Daniels was a more concise kind of conjuror with a twinkle in his eye and the eight of spades hidden under his toupee. Daniels was a natural sort of showman, as fast with his words as he was with his hands: playing daft to conceal his deft handiwork. Unlike that of the most successful American magician of the era, the ever-so-slightly copper-coloured David Copperfield, Daniels' skill lay less in the big showy illusion (for example, making the Statue of Liberty 'disappear') and more in the close-up, fast-hand-movement sort of trick. A trademark trick would be the one where a ball repeatedly disappeared and reappeared underneath a cup, before finally being replaced by a lemon. It was fast without being flashy, with the rapid-fire repartee with the audience masking the technicalities.

Regular features on *The Paul Daniels Magic Show* included the 'Bunco Booth', in which Daniels looked at the tricks of street magicians (in the days when people went to the trouble of doing a bit of dodgy magic before making off with your wallet); special guests, such as Hans Moretti, who did complicated and dangerous things with crossbows; and Paul's assistant, Debbie McGee, or 'the lovely Debbie McGee', to use her full title. McGee was originally a dancer and a member of the Iranian National Ballet, before fleeing the country because of the Islamic Revolution. On her return to Britain she ended up as Paul's assistant, smiling pleasantly even when she was being sawn in half. Whatever it was that attracted Debbie McGee to the millionaire Paul Daniels (as Mrs Merton would later ask), she said, 'Yes, Paul,' in 1988 and the couple married.

'Yes, Paul' was just one of the many catchphrases that were sprinkled throughout the programme. Another was, 'You'll like this – not a lot, but you'll like it,' which managed to sound both self-deprecating and vaguely threatening at the same time. By contrast, there was the almost musical manner in which Paul Daniels would say, 'So . . .' or, 'Ho . . .' – high-pitched and mellifluous, in a faux-thoughtful attempt to suggest that he didn't know what he was going to do next. And, of course, once the trick was complete there was a final flourish of, 'That's magic!'

'How did he do that, Dad?' Joff and I were never quite satisfied with 'That's magic!' as an explanation for what we'd just seen, and so usually turned to our father for a fuller answer. Obviously, being a dad by definition meant he knew everything there was to know. But our general faith was doubled in his magical knowledge because not only did he know a real magician (or how to find one in the *Yellow Pages*) but he could also pull off a card trick of his own. This involved a long and slightly complicated story about four jacks wanting to hide from their father. Dad would show us the four jacks, held suspiciously tightly in his hand, before hiding them in a castle (the rest of the pack of cards). Then three of the jacks would hide at different points in the castle/pack, with the fourth one staying on top as lookout. Once the coast was clear, the lookout jack would call to the other jacks to rejoin him. There followed a lot of banging on the pack to denote the jacks running back up the stairs to the top, where they would all be produced with a flourish.

It's a nice trick, as long as you remember to make sure you have three cards hidden behind the jacks at the beginning, which then become the 'jacks' hiding in the castle. If you forget to do this then – let me tell you – it's a bit less impressive. Which probably explained why Dad was sat at home watching the magic with the rest of us. So I wasn't about to be fobbed off with his, 'But it really is magic.' Or that he could tell us, but then he'd have to kill us afterwards. Or that if we knew how it worked, it would spoil the illusion. Dad would eventually sigh, and say, 'I don't know, some sort of distraction. And a false bottom.'

I got a better bit of insight one Christmas, when I was given an official pack of Paul Daniels magic cards (complete with picture of Paul and his signature on the front). The pack was a 'svengali' pack, which is a specially designed deck where half the cards are (a bit like Paul Daniels) slightly smaller than the rest. At first I thought I'd been given a dud pack, as this half all seemed to be the nine of diamonds, but as I read the instructions it became obvious that this was part of Paul's cunning master plan. This was the card I was going to 'force' on to my unsuspecting volunteer. So *that*'s how he does it, I thought, as I taught myself a trick and searched for my first victim.

'You'll like this − not a lot, but you'll like it,' I said to Joff, as I followed Paul's instructions and stuck him with the relevant card. 'Is it . . . the nine of diamonds?'

'Wow,' Joff said, as he did indeed have the nine of diamonds. 'How did you do that?'

'That's magic!' I said triumphantly, running back upstairs to learn another trick.

It was at this point that I realized that Paul Daniels − if he really did use these cards in his act − must have quite a few different sets at his disposal. Joff was slightly less impressed when, twenty minutes later, he managed to pull out the nine of diamonds again. Another twenty minutes later, when I came downstairs for my next trick, he pre-empted me by asking, 'It's not going to be the nine of diamonds again, is it?' My fledgling magic career, alas, was over before it had begun.

Paul Daniels was also slated as the presenter of another, non-magic show called *Gotcha!* The BBC decided that the pilot episode looked a bit tacky, and dropped the idea. This might have been the right call in terms of taste, but in terms of ratings it was the wrong decision. Re-tweaked and reformatted − and under a different name – *Gotcha!* ended up being the show that would help ITV beat the BBC in the Saturday-night ratings for the first time.

Game for a Laugh started with the show's four hosts running down the stairs through the audience to huge cheers. The four original hosts were Henry Kelly, Matthew Kelly, Sarah Kennedy and Jeremy Beadle. The show was Beadle's brainchild (he'd written the original *Gotcha!* pilot) and he was the only presenter to last the course (the other three left to be replaced by Rusty Lee, Lee Peck and, in a neat bit of television symmetry, Paul Daniels' son, Martin). Beadle had that sort of poncey pirate's beard where a thin line linked the sideburns and goatee beard, nestled in which was a row of brilliant white teeth that were trying only moderately hard not to giggle at what was about to happen next. He was a television enigma, and a classic love-to-hate figure: he may have been voted the second-most hated man in Britain (after Saddam Hussein, who wasn't even *in* Britain), but in the early 1990s his *You've Been Framed!* nudged out *Coronation Street* to briefly become the biggest programme on TV.

Jeremy Beadle was also a television original. His move into TV and radio originally came about because of his phenomenal knowledge of bizarre facts, and he found work writing for, among others, Bob Monkhouse and Terry Wogan. He used his knowledge for a regular 'on this day in history' slot on Greg Dyke's revamped *TV-am*, and in later years wrote a fiendishly difficult quiz for the *Independent*. As well as this long-standing interest in trivia, Beadle had also long developed a love for hoaxes and practical jokes. This latter interest had surfaced in the various menial jobs he had undertaken before getting his big break: cleaning lavatories in Germany, he would fill the urinals with tea to make them look like they were overflowing; working on a bakery production line, he made the dough into penis-shaped 'rude rolls'.

In *Game for a Laugh* Beadle had the platform – and the budget – to bring his practical jokes into the public eye. The basic tenet of the show was non-stop japes and set-ups, in which members of the British public were made to do extremely silly things and then made to demonstrate that they were jolly good sports by laughing about it all afterwards. It was a new kind of show in that ordinary people were the stars – a people show, if you will – but only at the cost of being made to look complete Charlies in the process. On one programme, selected members of the audience were asked to sign a contract just before filming was about to start – except that filming had already started; and the key line in the contract was the one at the top of the second page, which said that whoever read it first was to plant a custard pie in the other person's face. On another occasion a member of the audience volunteered his wife for a pop quiz, only to find himself sitting above a 'dunk tank' in case she got the questions wrong – and his wife being given popular opera tunes to name instead of chart hits. In another elaborate stunt the show secretly taught a man how to fly, and then watched his wife's reaction as he got into a plane and started the engine.

Each show ended with a complicated catchphrase that had one presenter saying, 'Watching us . . .' then another saying, 'Watching you . . .' and a third saying, 'Watching us . . .' before Beadle finished: 'Watching you', then wishing the viewers goodnight. While the other founding hosts ended up on other more respectable shows – *Going for Gold* (Henry Kelly), *Stars in their Eyes* (Matthew Kelly) and early-morning Radio Two (Sarah Kennedy) – Jeremy Beadle continued the japes in his solo show, *Beadle's About*. (Or 'Beadle's a Complete ****', as the public were inevitably bleeped-out saying when the host revealed it was all just one big funny joke.) The hoaxes here became bigger and ever more elaborate. On one occasion Beadle faked a UFO landing in some poor woman's back garden. When the spaceship opened and an alien poked its head out, the woman did her country proud by asking if it would like a cup of tea.

The woman's response to such a convoluted set-up was a rare piece of dignity in the face of what some saw as a symptomatic decline in television standards. Beadle's success went hand in hand with opinion pieces in the newspapers (not for the last time) about whether TV was dumbing down. The specific concern in the mid-eighties was that the launch of Channel 4 had freed ITV from some of its public-service obligations, leaving ITV able to go downmarket for big audiences and a hefty profit: the BBC would then be forced to follow suit in order to keep up. Whether that was true or not, the success of *Game for a Laugh* saw the end of the BBC's dominance of Saturday nights, and the cancellation of its long-running *Generation Game* (then in the hands of Larry 'Shut That Door' Grayson).

I don't know if the BBC specifically put the call out to find themselves a rival small giggly bloke with a beard, but they found one in the shape of Noel Edmonds. Noel had already made the leap from hosting the Radio One breakfast show to his Saturday-morning television show, *Multi-Coloured Swap Shop* (along with Keith Chegwin, Maggie Philbin, John Craven and Posh Paws). In 1982, elements of both of these, along with bits of Beadle, were stitched together to become *The Late, Late Breakfast Show*. The show was a mish-mash of features, including set-ups by the Beadle-esque 'Hit Squad', bloopers and outtakes in 'The Golden Egg Awards', proper pop stars (the programme boasted Abba's last-ever TV appearance) and, somewhat randomly, a cheesed-off-looking John Peel.

If Beadle's skill was to get members of the public to do increasingly ridiculous things, Noel Edmonds' trump card was to get them to participate in increasingly hair-raising stunts. The feature was called 'Give It a Whirl' and the gist of it was that the 'Whirly Wheel' was spun to pick a punter completely at random and a stunt slightly less at random (the theoretically free-wheeling wheel would stick at whichever stunt had been chosen for the following week's programme). The selected member of the public would then be trained for a week, before performing the stunt live during the following Saturday's show. Mike 'Smitty' Smith was the outside-broadcast presenter, given the job of moaning about how cold and dark it was.

The stunts, which ranged from firing people out of cannons to Evel Knievel-type leaps in a car, both *looked* dangerous and indeed *were* dangerous – on more than one occasion the participant went away with broken bones. The stunts, though, were the biggest draw on the show and, like Beadle's jokes, got more daring as the series went on. In November 1986 an unemployed builder called Michael Lush was chosen to attempt something called 'Hang 'Em High'. The trick involved being tied up Houdini-style in a metal box that was to be suspended 120 feet in the air by a giant crane. Lush would have a limited amount of time in which to work himself free and then bungee-jump to safety before the box exploded.

In rehearsals, however, everything went horribly, tragically wrong. On the Thursday before the show, Lush was winched up in the box in order to practise the bungee-jump element of the stunt. But when he leaped out the clip on which his rope was attached came undone and he fell, Icarus-like, to his death. The title of *The Late, Late Breakfast Show* felt eerily prescient, and the BBC response was swift: 'Because of the tragic accident involving Michael Lush,' the continuity announcer said the following Saturday, 'the BBC has decided to cancel . . . all further editions of the programme.' Its immediate replacement was a re-showing of the dreary old film *One of Our Dinosaurs is Missing*.

In the aftermath of Michael Lush's death the BBC faced criticism for its preparations, both at the inquest which gave a verdict of death by misadventure – and in a court case brought by the Health and Safety Executive (which fined the corporation the pathetic maximum of £2000). Noel, meanwhile, did not return to Saturday nights until almost two years later. The successor programme, *Noel's Saturday Roadshow*, was in theory broadcast 'on the road' from exotic locations – in reality, from cheaply knocked-together studio sets – and it was pre-recorded rather than live. It was safer than its predecessor in many respects but, like Jonathan Ross after Sachsgate, had lost a little of its edge in the process.

After Eric Morecambe died, Ernie Wise said, 'Through the years people will realize how great he was.' While that is certainly true, so is it that through the years one also realized how far from great many of the other acts from the period were. While Morecambe and Tommy Cooper still loom large in the public imagination, it says much that the eighties generation of light entertainers are no longer anything like as prominent: instead, it is the alternative stars, such as Stephen Fry or Dawn French, Harry Enfield or Alexei Sayle, who have enjoyed far greater longevity and 'national treasure' status.

What made up for the shortfall in star quality in the eighties was inclusion of people like you and me: the Great British public. *Beadle's About* and *Blind Date*, *Surprise Surprise* and the *Late, Late Breakfast Show* were all based more around the ordinary punter than they were the celebrity act. What this shift in programming demonstrated was that members of the public could be as entertaining as the entertainers themselves and a damn sight cheaper too. I guess you could argue that this was democracy in action, except that what the public were asked to do – and indeed what they fell over themselves to take part in – involved everything from ritual humiliation to risking life and limb. Which frankly is not a great indictment for anyone involved. The eighties was the decade when the lights in light entertainment were undoubtedly a little dimmer.

After the break, we can't decide whether that singer is a boy or a girl, meet some very, very young pop stars and get sworn at by a tired-looking Irishman . . .

Ad Break

Kit Kat

A record company's office, the mid-eighties. Squeezed on to a single black sofa are the four members of what could be the next big thing in music. Quite what that thing is is not immediately clear: the foursome are dressed respectively as though they are members of Brother Beyond, Bananarama, Amazulu and Spandau Ballet. On the table in front of them is a ghetto blaster on which their demo tape is playing, and the one who looks like he wants to be in Spandau Ballet (bright billowy orange shirt and sunglasses), is banging out the rhythm on a white vase with a pair of drumsticks. The music, if one can call it that, is sort of Haysi Fantayzee meets China Crisis, with the high point, quite literally, being a shriek that causes the record-company executive to wince.

Ah yes, the record-company executive. With his thick black hair and look of utter disdain at what is making its way through his eardrums, this might just be the man on whom Simon Cowell has modelled his whole career. The executive (who actually turns out to be Terry from *EastEnders* in a previous life) switches the stereo off and calls for a break. Enter a tea lady with a tray of Kit Kats – the four- rather than two-fingered variety, by the way, showing just how extravagant the music industry really is.

At which point our record-company executive goes off on one about how terrible the band are. The singing? Shit. The music? Crap. The look? Completely ridiculous. It's the sort of diatribe you now get week in, week out, on *The X-Factor*: all that's missing are the boos from the audience and the 0898 number scrolling across the bottom of the screen. But then, just as Simon Cowell has the chutzpah to royally slag off Jedward before voting to keep them in the competition, so the record exec puts on his very best sneer and says, 'You'll go a long way.'

To be honest, the group are lucky that the tea lady was serving Kit Kats, because this allowed the record executive to give them a break. The previous week, another band had found their meeting interrupted by the cleaner popping in to do the Shake 'n' Vac. Rather than receiving a record contract the group were sent packing: according to the executive, they needed to find a way to bring the freshness back into their music.

Episode Fourteen

'Be there or be a completely ungroovy fucker'

'It is a boy?' Joff asked.

'Don't be silly,' I replied. 'Of course it's a girl.'

'It's got a dress on,' Helen offered helpfully.

'Well, I think it's a boy,' Joff said, determinedly.

'It's a girl,' my mum answered. 'In fact, doesn't she look like someone you used to go with, John?'

'It's a man,' said my father, after a long, studied stare. 'Look at his hands. He should be on a building site with those.'

It was an early Thursday evening in 1983, which – this being before the BBC started messing around and showing it on a Friday night, screwing up the ratings and eventually cancelling the thing – was the long-standing home for *Top of the Pops*. As for many families, for us the weekly run-down of the charts, introduced by a Gary Davies or a

Peter Powell, was staple viewing – a ritual of children nodding along approvingly while the parents tutted and moaned and looked down the back of the sofa to find out where the tunes had all gone.

I don't think that the Bromleys were the only viewers that particular evening to find themselves confused at the appearance of Culture Club singing their debut hit, 'Do You Really Want to Hurt Me?' The topic of discussion wasn't the band's cod-reggae sound (whatever cod reggae is – presumably a distant cousin of sole music), but was the look of the lead singer. Growing up in York, the likes of Boy George were not something one bumped into on a regular basis: men wore the trousers, and that was that. And Boy George was not only not wearing trousers – he was actually wearing a dress. And make-up too. For a young boy with my limited life experience, it was all rather confusing.

'He's called Boy George!' Joff shouted triumphantly as the song ended and the presenter DJ gabbled away. 'I *told* you he was a boy.'

'What about that girl in the Famous Five?' I replied. 'She's a girl and she's called George.'

Even though I was continuing to make my case, I was becoming less convinced. I turned round to my parents, who both had a slightly pained look on their faces, as though they knew what question I was going to ask them.

'It must be a girl, mustn't it? Why would a man dress up in women's clothing?'

My dad looked at my mum. 'Carole?' he said, hopefully.

'He's your gender,' Mum replied, unhelpfully.

'Right,' said my dad uncomfortably. 'This George chap. Yes. Well. Some men like to wear dresses,' he explained a little unconvincingly.

'Have you ever worn a dress?' I asked.

'Absolutely not.' My father's voice dropped a couple of octaves as he took a long swig from his can of Skol, crunching it in his hand like Popeye with his spinach tin.

'But if this Mr George wants to, then that's good,' Mum continued. 'It's great that he feels comfortable enough with himself to dress like that. And it's great that the BBC are comfortable enough to broadcast it at a time when young families are watching,' she added, in a tone that suggested that it wasn't just not great, but also that the director general would be getting a stiff letter in the morning.

'Right,' I said, still unconvinced but sensing I wasn't going to get anything further out of them at this stage. 'There was just one more thing. What was with the lyrics about wanting someone to hurt him? What was that all about?'

Dad sighed. 'We never had this problem with P. J. Proby.'

I fell in love with pop music at an early age. In the early 1980s a routine developed around Sunday evenings, where everyone else would watch the *Holiday* programme (with Cliff Michelmore) and I would sit in the kitchen, where my father had just mopped the floor, listening religiously to the Top Forty run-down on Radio One (presented by Tommy Vance then, later, my 'mate' Bruno Brookes). I say I was just listening: in fact, so hallowed was this information to me that, like some sort of music-mad mini-Motty, I would write down all the chart positions, complete with arrows and stars to denote whether each song had gone up or down, was a non-mover or a new entry. And as well as writing the charts down, I would record them on a cassette. Some people would spend the entire chart show pausing the recording between songs, to minimize DJ chat to squeeze in some extra music, but I'd just set my C90 tape running at 5.30 p.m., and wait frantically to switch the cassette on to side two at about 6.15 (which was usually just as the Top Ten was about to begin).

Like many people of my generation, the magazine *Smash Hits* was my bible. A bit like *Heat* magazine in the early noughties, *Smash Hits* hit near ubiquity in the 1980s, selling a million copies of every fortnightly issue. Fun, frothy and funny, it struck it Michael

Barrymore-lucky when a new generation of British pop stars, in the shape of Duran Duran, Wham! Spandau Ballet and the like, turned up to write about. The magazine included the requisite posters and song lyrics (even if the song was 'Close to the Edit' by the Art of Noise or Paul McCartney's 'Frog Chorus') but *Smash Hits* also brought to the table an irreverent sense of humour and an idiosyncratic, rather than indie-sycophantic, way of writing. This lexicon of love included phrases such as 'pur-lease!' and 'swingorilliant', 'sniiiiiip!' and 'Back! Back!! BACK!!!' The *Smash Hits* universe featured 'foxtresses' (attractive young females) and Uncle Disgustings (Robert Palmer types who surrounded themselves with said foxtresses). Pop stars were asked not what their new record was about but to tell us, if Wednesday was a colour, what colour it might be. Typical of the magazine was the edition that featured the massively (over) hyped Sigue Sigue Sputnik, who arrived on the music scene with a lot of grand claims and a debut single called 'Love Missile F1-11'. The *Smash Hits* headline simply asked, 'Sigue Sigue Sputnik: the Future of Rock and Roll or a Load of Codswallop?'

If *Smash Hits* was the house magazine of eighties pop, then *Top of the Pops* remained its house programme. By the start of the decade the show had done away with the seventies 'Whole Lotta Love'-based theme (which, although a great song, had always been a slightly odd choice, given how 'the Zep' were very much an albums band and had never released a single in their lives). Instead, the opening credits were handed over to Phil Lynott, whose 'Yellow Pearl' theme was a slightly more synthy affair, full of science-fiction descending 'ooohs' and drum-machine beats. All this while a selection of multicoloured singles sped through space like they were flying saucers, until the camera zoomed in on a flamingo-pink one that proceeded to teardrop explode into a thousand smithereens. (In the late eighties this was replaced by a ghastly plinky-plonk thing called 'The Wizard' by Paul 'N-n-n-n-nineteen' Hardcastle. But let's not dwell too long on that.)

The appearance of Boy George and Culture Club was just one of the decade's many memorable *Top of the Pops* moments. There was Dexys Midnight Runners, who sang their cover of Van Morrison's *Jackie Wilson Said* against a backdrop of a huge photo of the darts player Jocky Wilson (a mix-up or joke, depending on who you listen to). There was the folkie-goth group All About Eve, who couldn't hear their song 'Martha's Harbour' playing so sat silently on their stools rather than miming along. And, right at the end of the decade, there was one of those storming-the-gates editions, when both the Stone Roses ('Fools Gold') and the Happy Mondays ('Hallelujah') made their debuts.

One of the biggest changes to happen to *Top of the Pops* in the eighties was the end of the dancing girls. Since the 1960s the show had boasted a succession of dance troupes who'd fill in with a bit of cheap choreography when a band couldn't make it into the studio. The trend had started with the Go-Jos in the sixties, came into its own with Pan's People (Babs, Flick, Dee Dee, et al) in the early 1970s, then continued with Ruby Flipper, Legs and Co. and finally Zoo.

The reason that the dancers were being given their P45s was the arrival of the pop video. By the early eighties this had gone from being an occasional novelty to something that every single required for success. Suddenly it didn't matter that Kajagoogoo were in New Zealand – not when there was a video to show of Limahl and that bass player with the silly hair going, 'Hush hush, ah you ah'. A glossy three-minute promo seemed an extremely glamorous alternative to bands miming badly in the studio or a group of people dancing along.

The main catalyst for all this was the arrival of the American music channel MTV. This had launched in August 1981 in New York with the simple concept of being like a radio on TV – with VJs playing videos instead of DJs playing records. The first video shown was, appropriately enough (if a little smugly), 'Video Killed the Radio Star' by the Buggles. 'Oh-a oh-a!' indeed. To be honest, the station didn't really impinge on my life much until a few years later, when Sting sang about wanting his MTV on Dire Straits' 'Money for Nothing'. Up until that point I didn't know what it was – and even if I did there was no way our rickety old television set would have picked it up. MTV Europe started broadcasting in 1987 with said Dire Straits song, but most people in Britain wouldn't have noticed.

What I did notice, though, were the effects that the launch of MTV was having on music. Suddenly there was a way for bands to 'break' America without having to spend three years driving around Midwest college towns to 'press the flesh' with a succession of uninterested DJs at KRP and WNK radio. If your video was chosen for the holy grail of 'heavy rotation', then chart success was all but assured. Consequently, pop videos quickly developed into a sort of arty arms race, with record companies throwing pots of money around to ensure that their bands' videos were chosen to be screened.

One of the biggest benefactors was Duran Duran, who found themselves flown to the Caribbean to arse around on yachts for the likes of 'Rio' (that said, they might not have been quite so enamoured with the format by the time of 'Wild Boys' – which involved Simon Le Bon being tied to a giant wheel and repeatedly dunked in water). For their debut single, 'Take on Me', A-Ha found themselves in a cartoon strip. Some of the most memorable videos were the simplest. Robert Palmer's 'Addicted to Love' featured a backing band of identikit lady lovelies; Paul Simon's 'You Can Call Me Al' had Chevy Chase singing along while Simon sulked in the background.

The biggest and the best videos, however, belonged to Michael Jackson. In its early years, MTV followed the classic dividing lines in American music by considering itself a rock station and therefore featuring primarily white artists. To get Michael Jackson on to the station, his record company needed to pull out all the stops – and with 'Thriller', pull out all the stops they did. In came white-rock-friendly names like Eddie Van Halen to squeal some guitar on 'Beat It'. And in came John Landis, director of *An American Werewolf in London*, for the video of 'Thriller'. 'Thriller' was more than just a video: it was a fourteen-minute film with a story and zombies dancing and Jackson turning to the camera at the end with his scary yellow eyes.

While *Top of the Pops* sprinkled a few promos among the live miming, ITV's *The Chart Show* went one better and did away with the performances altogether in favour of just showing the videos: for one hour a week, it was like having a subscription to MTV. There were no presenters − they had been replaced by video-machine-style graphics of 'fast forward' and 'play', 'pause' for the adverts and 'eject' for the end of the programme. The videos themselves would be accompanied by a bit of pseudo-computer graphics, with a Microsoft-type cursor flicking across the screen to open up 'fact boxes' about the bands.

Although *The Chart Show* was ITV's main music rival to *Top of the Pops*, it actually began life on Channel 4. Music was always going to be a natural subject for a television station wanting to be young, edgy and alternative: *The Chart Show* was one of the network's many attempts to present pop music in a new and innovative way. Its launch in 1986 came on the back of two earlier music programmes, one of which was substantially more successful than the other.

The Tube was part of the Channel 4 schedule right from the ready steady go. The programme offered the completely opposite approach to *The Chart Show* in that it was all about live performances from live bands, all shown completely live on a Friday evening. That might not sound like a particularly new idea now, but it was the first time there'd been a live music programme on British TV since Cliff Richard had wiggled his hips at the Hackney Empire on *Oh Boy!* in the 1950s. *Oh Boy!*, however, *The Tube* was not. The title credits depicted a television literally bursting at the seams with bright lights and funky goodness until the set blew its top and *The Tube* logo (the downward stalk of the 'T' spearing the U, a front-and-back Abba-style B, and a similarly mirrored pair of Es), shot out like a space rocket. (In later titles, the logo would be interposed, MTV like, on the Statue of Liberty, the *Titanic*, the moon landing and the parting of the Red Sea).

The Tube was broadcast from the Tyne Tees studios in Newcastle, whose entrance had a long, semicircular tube-like covering – hence the name. The mixture of live music, interviews and magazine features was primarily presented by Jools Holland and Paula Yates, with occasional help from, among others, Muriel Gray and Leslie Ash. Jools Holland and Paula Yates were a world away from the clubby chumminess of the Radio One DJs on *Top of the Pops* (who often appeared with streamers and hats, as though the programme was some sort of giant children's birthday party). They were less Smashy and Nicey and more Shambolic and Naughty: Jools, who had left his first band, Squeeze, for an ongoing relationship with his boogie-woogie piano, ambled about on screen in an amiably amateurish sort of way. Typical of this stance was the 1987 live trailer for the programme broadcast during children's TV, during which he said, 'Be there, or be a completely ungroovy fucker.'

Paula Yates, meanwhile, was unwittingly following in the footsteps of her father, *Opportunity Knocks* presenter Hughie Green. Yates had already seduced herself one rock star in the shape of Boomtown Rats singer Bob Geldof but continued to flirt and flutter with both interviewee and camera. This all sounds a bit tawdry, but Yates was a sharper operator than her peroxide-blonde hair might have suggested, and would wrap the proverbial line round her little finger, rather than crossing it. In one interview with Sting, she said to the Police singer, 'In an interview recently you said that you liked "doing it" on the kitchen table, but when I was at your house the kitchen table didn't look that much bigger than you could have got a couple of bowls of rice on it . . .' Sting, in response, said that he liked Newcastle because it had a 'spunky atmosphere'. That was about right: Paula was frisky as a presenter but never downright rude.

The live-ness of *The Tube* was its litheness; its rawness its roar. It was a staging post for music of its time, offering a *Who's Who* line-up that was snobbery free: anyone who was anyone, from ABC to ZZ Top, turned up to play. Highlights included Madonna performing 'Holiday' at the Manchester club the Hacienda; U2 under a blood-red sky at Red Rocks Amphitheatre in Colorado; the Jam in one of their final television appearances, performing 'Beat Surrender'. The programme wasn't afraid to give space to unknown acts as well. In 1983 an unsigned band from Liverpool, called Frankie Goes to Hollywood, performed their song 'Relax' from Liverpool State Ballroom. I'm guessing that Mike Read wasn't watching – because, given the accompanying semi-clad dancers writhing about with whips and handcuffs, he might just have worked out what the song was about. One person who was watching, however, was record producer Trevor Horn, who signed the band and turned 'Relax' into a smash-hit number one – literally so, in Mike Read's case.

If Mike Read had problems with 'Relax', one can only imagine the steam emanating from his ears when Channel 4 showed their other early music programme, *Mini-Pops*. The idea itself seemed quite innocuous – it was a children's show for children, where young kids sang and danced along to a selection of chart hits. In that sense, it was no different than Disney's long-running and squeaky-clean *Mickey Mouse Club* show, whose roster of child stars have included Justin Timberlake and Britney Spears. In terms of ratings, *Mini-Pops* was one of Channel 4's early successes, pulling in two million plus viewers a week.

All well and good . . . Except that one has slight concerns about who exactly these two million viewers were. For the very young singers were being dressed up in adult clothes, and they had lots of make-up applied to their faces. And the song choices they were being given did not always feel the most appropriate. Like the Rolling Stones' 'Satisfaction' (sung by a young boy, bare-chested underneath his leather waistcoat). Or 'Morning Train' by Sheena Easton, during which a young girl wearing a negligee and dressing gown suggested that night time was the perfect occasion to 'make love'. Or (of all things) 'Baby Love' performed by three young girls wearing tight pink dresses and imitating the Supremes.

'*Mini-Pops* should be called *Mini Whores*. Are you people out of your minds?' suggested one caller to Channel 4's *Right to Reply*. 'Disgusting. It encourages child abuse,' suggested another. In the *Observer*, meanwhile, Julian Barnes described the programme as 'outstandingly repellent', describing one singer as 'thigh-high to a paedophile' and wondering whether the programme was 'kiddyporn' and 'a shop window for junior jailbait'. It says much about the eighties that the stinging nature of the criticism took Channel 4 by surprise. I don't think there was anything sinister in their intentions: just gross naivety as to how the material would be interpreted. And, while the channel was not averse to the odd bit of controversy, this was exactly *not* the sort it was looking for.

The power of television, as Huey Lewis almost sang, is a curious thing. It could make a child sing, in a way the producers of *Mini-Pops* had not intended; but it could also make one man weep. That man was Bob Geldof, and what moved him to tears was Michael Buerk, then a BBC foreign correspondent, reporting on the Ethiopian famine in autumn 1984. The pictures beamed back by satellite were powerful enough, but Buerk's choice of language gave even greater weight to what he (and by extension we) were witnessing: 'As the sun breaks through the piercing chill of night . . . it lights up a biblical famine, now in the twentieth century. This place, say workers here, is the closest thing to hell on earth . . .'

The next time someone says that television is a corrupting influence, just remind them of Michael Buerk's report and everything that resulted from it. In the first instance it inspired Bob Geldof to get Band

Aid together and to write and record 'Do They Know it's Christmas?' – a song, incidentally, whose lyrics are somewhat snidely dismissed as being a bit bombastic but when you think about it feel utterly influenced by and in keeping with the language used in Buerk's original report. Having had the most successful single of all time – until Princess Diana died, anyway – Geldof's attention turned to what was to become the TV music highlight of the decade: Live Aid.

The idea was perfectly simple – a concert starring the great and the good, which would start in London at Wembley Stadium, overlap with a second concert in America, finish the British leg with everyone singing 'Do They Know it's Christmas?', and then continue in America up to a grand finale of the USA for Africa single 'We Are the World'. After months of haggling, including a failed attempt to get the technology sorted for Mick Jagger and David Bowie to sing a transatlantic duet, the date was finally set for Saturday 13 July 1985. For me, a whole day of live music was pretty thrilling stuff – it was a good decade or so before anyone starting televising Glastonbury and other music festivals – and, although other concerts would follow in its wake (the two Nelson Mandela concerts, the Freddie Mercury tribute event), Live Aid was undoubtedly the first and most significant of such outings. It was every bit the eighties Woodstock, except with less mud and a lot more hairspray.

The day itself was blisteringly hot, with the sort of Tory-blue sky that no rain was going to pour from. At one end of Wembley Stadium, crammed to the rafters, was the simple white stage: with its ceiling-high stack of speakers on each side, complete with Live Aid logo and black 'Feed the World' strip across the top, it looked like nothing less than a giant ghetto blaster. First up on Bob Geldof's mix tape was Status Quo. Given some of the criticism Bob Geldof got over the bands he asked to play, that seemed a pertinent choice. Geldof's argument was that he wanted to raise as much money as possible, which meant getting the biggest bands he could persuade to take part: that way more people would watch the show and, hopefully, donate. Hence the Status Quo.

I was more than a little acquainted with the work of the Quo – not through any personal choice, but because that was what the coach driver played day in, day out on the way to school. So, after Rick (bouffant blond hair, bright-pink shirt) and Francis (ponytail, white shirt and waistcoat) had shouted out a few 'All right's, as soon as the pianist starting tinkling away I knew it was going to be 'Rocking All Over the World', even before the guitars had crunched in. And, yes, so the song might never win an NME award, but is the sort of twelve-bar gold that is difficult to listen to without a grin of Marti Pellow proportions spreading across your face. While some bands have the sort of music that can stretch out to fill a stadium, Status Quo achieved the opposite – triumphantly turning Wembley into the back room of a pub.

After Status Quo, the concert was split between the bands who weren't big in America (they went on early) and those who wanted the Stateside coverage (they went on later). In the former batch were the likes of the Style Council, Nik Kershaw, Spandau Ballet and the Boomtown Rats – whose set included an emotional pause during the line in 'I Don't Like Mondays' about how the lesson today was how to die. It was a powerful moment, though perhaps only Bob's second-most memorable line of the day: Geldof never actually said the oft-misquoted, 'Give us your fucking money'; what he did do was tell a television presenter who was trying to read out where to send money to (rather than giving the donations-hotline telephone number) to 'fuck the address, let's get the numbers'.

The day's two standout sets were widely seen as those by U2 and Queen, both of whom saw their records rocket back up the chart in the concert's aftermath. U2, who at this point in their career had released *The Unforgettable Fire* but not yet *The Joshua Tree*, were on the verge of becoming massive. Their planned three-song set ('Sunday Bloody

Sunday', 'Bad' and 'Pride (In the Name of Love)') became just two when, halfway through 'Bad', Bono leaped down from the stage to pull a girl out of the audience. The girl, a fifteen-year-old Wham! fan called Kal Khalique, was passed through the crowd for Bono to hug, kiss and dance with. By the time this was all over, and Bono had managed to scramble his way back on to the stage, the group's allotted time was up and they left without playing 'Pride', their big hit single. Backstage, the rest of the band were furious with Bono for ruining their big chance. Which just goes to show . . .

By complete contrast to Bono's spontaneous moment, Queen's success was down to a minutely planned and tightly rehearsed set. It was as if the group had sat down and thought, 'Right, how many of our hits can we squeeze into our twenty minutes?' The answer was six: 'Bohemian Rhapsody', segueing into 'Radio Ga Ga', 'Hammer to Fall', 'Crazy Little Thing Called Love', a quick bit of 'We Will Rock You' and a closing 'We Are the Champions'. Throughout, Freddie Mercury prowled the set like a caged tiger, strutting away with his half-length microphone stand, leading the audience in a shout-and-recall round of 'Day-oh's. It was a historical performance in a historical show.

After that, it was all artists I'd get into when I was older (David Bowie, The Who, Elton John). Paul McCartney turned up to sing 'Let It Be', complete with microphone problems, before everyone reappeared on stage for a ramshackle rendition of 'Do They Know it's Christmas?'. At which point I went to bed, only catching up on the American leg on video later. Maybe it was because I didn't watch it live, and maybe it was because it was in a slightly random stadium in Philadelphia, but the second half of the show never seemed quite so much fun. What's more, all the bits that stick in the mind are when things went wrong: Led Zeppelin (featuring Phil Collins on drums, fresh from flying over on Concorde) were so ropey that they refused to allow their performance on the subsequent DVD; Duran Duran sang 'A View to a Kill' with a horrendous Simon Le Bum Note; Bob Dylan, meanwhile, turned up with Keith Richards and Ronnie Wood, launched into some very old songs they hadn't rehearsed and mumbled about how it'd be great if some of the money could find its way to hard-up American farmers.

It might be at this point that you're thinking Status Quo, U2, Queen . . . Jesus, what a record collection. And while, yes, it would be cool to tell you that I was the kid at school with the fake hearing aid and bunch of daffodils, clutching a copy of *Meat is Murder* under my arm, my musical tastes were somewhat more hit and miss. In 1984 I was convinced that Frankie Goes to Hollywood were the greatest band in the world. In 1985 I passed this crown over to Tears for Fears. In 1986 I changed my mind again, and decided it was U2. Then I thought it was Prince. Then I heard the Pogues and decided Shane MacGowan was some sort of Guinness-riddled genius. Then I joined the sixth form and starting listening to Bob Dylan and writing poetry like some sort of big soppy ginger twat.

Not that it was enough for me to inflict *Welcome to the Pleasuredome* and *Songs from the Big Chair* on my family at full volume. Having watched and listened to all this music, I decided that I too wanted to become a rock star. In true Bromley fashion, my lobbying for an electric guitar was rewarded with an acoustic one instead (from a second-hand shop in town that I won't name for legal reasons, but put it this way: if you ever get anything nicked in York it's probably worth a visit). For a while, I struggled with some of those *Teach Yourself Rock Guitar* books, attempting to bend my fingers into various unnatural chord shapes and strumming along to various 'arrangements' of 'top rock songs' that had been simplified to the point of being utterly unrecognizable.

Help, to an extent, came in the form of *Rockschool,* a BBC2 series 'that examines how you make music in a rock band'. I draw your attention to the word 'examines' there, which says everything you need to know about the approach of the programme. For the BBC, being in a rock band was a bit like being into science, with lots of exciting new sounds to explore and discover. In a set that looked a bit like a Spectrum 48K computer-game graphic, our guides into this Tomorrow's World were the resident house band: guitarist Deidre Cartwright (who looked a bit like Maggie Philbin); drummer Geoff Nicholls (Howard Stableford); bass player Henry Thomas (Winston Zeddemore from *Ghostbusters*); and keyboardist Alastair Gavin (Rick Moranis). There were also guest spots from such musical luminaries as Midge Ure and Jan Hammer.

The *Rockschool* musicians were a world away from Sid Vicious not knowing which way up he was meant to hit people with his bass guitar. In direct contravention of the punk rules of rock music, each wore the word 'muso' happily around their neck and were the sort of well-meaning people who had practised very hard and didn't go to bed late on a school night. With Henry Thomas' (admittedly impressive) slap bass underpinning the whole thing, the band were nothing less (and nothing more) than an instrumental Level 42. Jean Simmons or Jack Black this wasn't.

Back in York, I'd graduated on to an electric guitar and with my parents able to take no more of my out-of-tune squealings they booked me in for some real *Rockschool*-type guitar lessons. Also in my class was another budding musician, my schoolmate Tom Gladwin. He and I would end up in rival bands at school: my own offerings would be under such awful eighties names as Reflection, and sounded not unlike an instrumental Level 42 (except without the musical virtuosity). Gladwin, who did listen to the Smiths rather than Tears for Fears, ended up with singer Rick Witter in a band called Brockley Haven. Technically they weren't any better (or any worse) than us, but on every other level they were streets ahead: cooler, sharper, edgier, popular, all the important bits about music that *Rockschool* had singularly failed to teach me.

ALL IN THE BEST *POSSIBLE* TASTE

By the time we got to the sixth form there was a bout of musical differences in Brockley Haven and I formed another band with their guitarist, Paul 'Banksy' Banks. Banks was one of those annoying kids at school who didn't do any work because he said he was going to be a rock star. Certainly he was an extremely good, self-taught guitarist: Deidre Cartwright would probably have had kittens to discover he'd taken his first guitar home with a detuned bottom E-string, and had mistakenly assumed that was how it should be strung. Banksy was the world's biggest Simple Minds fan; and, with my liking for U2 and our drummer's love of the Alarm, we became Heartland, purveyors of an expansive sort of stadium rock that didn't work so well in the back room of the Spotted Cow. With talent scouts not exactly hotfooting it to the capital of Yorkshire, Heartland fizzled out. I did the sensible thing and went off to university. And Banksy did exactly what he'd said he would, and rejoined his former Brockley Haven band mates in a new group called Shed Seven.

Having spent the eighties religiously watching *Top of the Pops* and discussing it at school the following day, it was a strange feeling a few years later to watch some of those same people end up on the programme. Shed Seven's success engendered in me that classic Yorkshire response of simultaneously being dead chuffed that one of ours had made it and having a desire to remind them that they were no better than the rest of us. Yes, they might have ended up on the telly and that, but the guitarist will forever be the teenager who swore blind that Nelson Mandela waved to him personally at the second Nelson Mandela concert. And the bassist will always be the boy who asked out the most attractive girl in school and was turned down on the grounds that she wouldn't go out with someone who had a face like a chicken's backside.

After the break, we meet a man who can change into an animal, have a chat with a talking car, and hitch a ride on a helicopter that can fly in silent mode . . .

Ad Break

Levi's

A laundromat, small-town America, the mid-1950s. As Marvin Gaye's 'I Heard It Through the Grapevine' blasts out (at least ten years before it was written, incidentally), a Brylcreemed, Ray-Bans-wearing young man has popped in to do some washing. As two young boys in matching red caps look on, our hero (let's call him Nick Kamen) deposits an entire bag of stones into the washing machine. At which point, he starts taking his clothes off – to the delight of two girls, one of whom is reading a 3D magazine. First to go in is Nick's black T-shirt, followed by his button-fly pair of jeans. Then, still wearing his white boxer shorts and white socks (the guy is wise enough not to mix up colours and whites), Nick finds himself a seat next to a fat sweaty man in a pork-pie hat and reads his magazine . . .

*   *   *

The advert is, of course, for Levi's 501s – the first of many such Americana ads that will make Levi's cool and usher a whole load of re-released classic hits into the charts, such as Percy Sledge's 'When a Man Loves a Woman' and Sam Cooke's 'Wonderful World' (Levi's will later be responsible for inflicting Stiltskin and Babylon Zoo on us, but let's not worry about that right now). Levi's will also make a star of model Nick Kamen: among the many women who'll like the sight of him taking his clothes off is Madonna, who'll write his Top Five single 'Each Time You Break My Heart'.

My problem with this scene is not so much that I'm jealous of Kamen's beefcake-and-beauty-spot looks; it's the whole thing about the stones. Yes, I get the point that he is 'stonewashing' his jeans, but I left a pound coin in my trousers once and it so knackered the drum that I had to buy a new washing machine. Marvin Gaye can't be long into his second verse before the whole laudromat is being shaken by an almighty rumbling sound. At which point, surely, the owner looks up and says, 'All right, which joker puts the rocks in the machine?' And Kamen finds himself flung out on to the street in nothing but his undies: still looking good, but perhaps not quite so smart.

Episode Fifteen

'I love it when a plan comes together'

In the mid 1980s York got its first branch of McDonald's. This was an arrival that, as you might imagine, was greeted with various levels of enthusiasm by different members of the Bromley household. For my parents, this posed a threat to both our physical and moral wellbeing: the latter from what might be called a 'creeping Americanization', except that with Ronald McDonald wandering up and down the street handing out balloons I don't think that you could particularly call it 'creeping'. The liberal grapevine in the city, as you might imagine, was quickly awash with all sorts of rumours about the fast-food chain and its food.

'Apparently [some completely libellous and no doubt factually inaccurate claim that I'm far too sensible to reprint here],' said my mother.

'I've heard that [another urban myth that I'm not going to give the time of day to here],' said my dad.

'Did you know [I'm sure this one was just made up by liberal parents to scare their children],' said Mum, shaking her head in disbelief.

By contrast, the younger generation of Bromleys were slightly more excited by the burger chain's arrival. Up to that point, the only fast food that the city had been able to offer was Wimpy, a brand name which, let's be honest, is a bit Walter the softy. There were also question marks about how fast Wimpy was in fast-food terms, given that you had to wait as they brought the food out to you on proper plates, with proper knives and forks. Equally questionable were some of their menu selections: the teenager's choice, for snigger factor alone, was an extremely long sausage that was curled around in a circle, held in place by a cocktail stick and served in a white floury bap. This was called – oh, my immature sides – a Big Bender in a Bun.

For a teenager, the added bonus of parental disapproval made McDonald's a must-go. In those years before one could get away with being served underage in a pub, it was also somewhere to hang out that was marginally more sophisticated than the swings. On top of that, in those early York-McDonald's years, the chain were running a Trivial Pursuits-based promotion – with every purchase you got a Trivial Pursuit scratchcard, with which you won a prize for every right answer. I don't know what the star prizes were, and no one I knew ever won one. Instead, the prizes you won were things like a free milkshake or a portion of fries, plus another scratchcard. As the questions were not exactly challenging, the result was a regular fast-food chain of free food for York's middle-class teenagers.

The arrival of McDonald's was perhaps the most visible local sign of the ever-increasing influence of American culture at the time, and I certainly was not immune. The look and 1950s feel of the Levi's 501 adverts seemed impossibly cool to my early-teen self. I might have grown out of Clothkits, but clothes were still a sore point with my parents: I wanted to wear Avanti from C&A, or, if I was feeling particularly sophisticated, to shop at Concept Man; unfortunately,

Marks & Spencer had decided to trial a new children's clothes shop in York, called Young Sparks. My parents and I were as far apart in our enthusiasm for this new store as we were over McDonalds, except the other way round.

As well as fashion, American films and music felt equally important: this was the era of Bruce Springsteen's 'Born in the USA', Madonna's 'Like a Virgin' and Prince's 'Purple Rain'. It was also the golden era of John Hughes' wonderful teenage comedies: *Weird Science*, *Pretty in Pink*, *The Breakfast Club* and, above all, *Ferris Bueller's Day Off*, complete with Matthew Broderick in the lead role. I'd already decided that I wanted to be Broderick, when a couple of years earlier he'd played a computer whizzkid in the film *War Games*: in this, Broderick had hacked into the American military network, where he'd almost triggered 'global thermonuclear warfare', but ended up teaching the computer the futility of conflict by playing noughts and crosses with it instead. A couple of years on, Broderick had graduated from IT nerd into the uber-cool Ferris Bueller, a classy, confident kid who gave his headmaster (Ed Rooney) the slip to take the day off with his best mate and girlfriend (the gorgeous Sloane Petersen). Basically, he was everything I was not, and everything I wanted to be.

To be fair to my parents, we did go to McDonald's once. I wasn't allowed a Big Mac as my parents were worried I might keel over and die on the spot and my father, not quite getting the fast-food thing, asked for a knife and fork to eat his with. The highlight of the meal, for the rest of us anyway, was when Dad decided he'd have an apple pie for pudding. Like a McDonald's virgin, he bit down firmly the very first time, to discover that the temperature of the filling was approaching global thermonuclear levels. Turning a Prince shade of purple, he spat the pie out on to the table – a deterioration of eating standards that served only to confirm my mother's suspicions about the restaurant's pernicious influence. Not that my dad was in any position to speak back: having previously complained that his cola was all ice and no drink, he was now grateful to have an entire cup of frozen cubes on hand to pour into his mouth.

We didn't go to McDonald's as a family again.

The other area where American influence was ever-present was, of course, on television. Throughout the decade, there were a string of shows that straddled British TV like some sort of cowboy, kicking its spurs into the sides of the schedule to get the thing to giddy-up. This might not have been anything new – *Kojak* and *Starsky and Hutch*, for example, had both been huge shows in the seventies – but it was in the eighties where the American presence was particularly pronounced, especially on BBC1 and ITV, and especially in terms of police and action shows.

Top of the A-list of these programmes was *The A-Team*. This concerned the ongoing adventures of four former American soldiers who had fought together in Vietnam before being put away for the obligatory 'crime they did not commit'. Having escaped from prison, the four of them now lived in the Los Angeles underground. From here, they worked as soldiers of fortune, their speciality being problems that no one else could help with. All you had to do was work out a way of finding them.

A quick point of order, on the whole 'crime they didn't commit' claim: the crime in question was the robbing of the Bank of Hanoi in 1972, and, as it turned out, the four people who did this job were everyone's favourite crack commando team. The problem was that the commanding officer who'd asked them to do this had actually been killed in the meantime: the result being that by the time they got back with their bags of loot, there was no proof that they had only been following orders. So really, the whole 'crime they didn't commit' thing is a bit of a red herring: they did commit the crime in question; it's just that they were under the impression it wasn't one. Though I'll admit that this more accurate description of events is not quite as snappy as the original.

The A-Team was led by Colonel John 'Hannibal' Smith, who was played by George Peppard. Hannibal was a man with a plan, and he particularly loved it when said schemes came together. He also liked chomping on cigars and dressing up in 'brilliant' disguises. Then there was Lieutenant Templeton 'Faceman' Peck, played by Dirk Benedict, who was the team's resident ladies' man and con-artist (two skills which must have served him well in the Vietnam jungle). Captain H. M. 'Howling Mad' Murdock (Dwight Schultz) was great with a plane, and less good with real life. Again, I don't want to be too pedantic about the set-up, but, given that Murdock resided in a psychiatric hospital, one wonders how much effort the military were really making in going after them.

Last, but by no means least, there was Sergeant Bosco 'BA' Baracus, played by Mr T. BA, which stood for 'Bad Attitude', who was the team's resident hard-man-come-engineer-come-flying-hater. For all Peppard's star quality, a bit like the A-Team van (a black GMC Vandura, complete with red stripe), the programme was very much Mr T's vehicle. T had come into the show following his starring role as 'Clubber' Lang in *Rocky III*, and had a Mohawk hairdo, heavyweight gold jewellery and catchphrases about suckers and not getting on no plane: his most famous phrase was 'I pity the fool', a line that actually originated from his previous role in *Rocky III*.

Apart from this main foursome, the A-Team also featured the occasional add-on team player. To begin with the four were actually five, with the inclusion of Amy Amanda Allen, or Triple A, an undercover reporter. Later on there was a second fifth member in the shape of Dishpan, a man who specialized in special effects and was almost as superfluous. I say almost because, having escaped the clutches of Colonels Lynch and Decker in the first four series, the A-Team were finally caught by General Stockwell in the fifth: Stockwell offered to get their sentence overturned in return for carrying out various secret missions, and Dishpan helped fake their death by firing squad in order to do this (as it turned out, the deal didn't really pan out).

Most of the *A-Team* episodes followed a fairly similar formula. There'd be some downtrodden company like a taxi firm who were getting bullied out of business by an aggressive gun-toting rival. Just when it seemed all was lost, they'd get a strange visit from a man dressed up as an alligator or Elvis, who'd turn out to be Hannibal in cunning disguise. Having taken the job on, Hannibal would puff happily on his cigar, Face would seduce the taxi-firm owner's daughter (I don't know if she was part of the team's fee), Murdock would invent a sock puppet and annoy BA with it, and when BA calmed down he'd solder together an armoured vehicle out of a couple of plant pots and a lawnmower. So inventive was BA that there was probably only one person in the eighties better at making things out of next to nothing, and that was MacGyver. But, as impressive as his skills were, he didn't shout 'Crazy fool'.

All the while, there'd be lots of punch-ups, car chases, shootouts and explosions, during which no one was ever killed. Or badly hurt. Or bruised. Or even bleeding a bit. *The A-Team* was cartoon violence of the *Tom and Jerry* kind, the sort that kept both the body count down and the early-Saturday evening ratings up.

BA and friends weren't the only Americans out there dishing out a version of rough-and ready justice. They weren't even the only ones in Los Angeles, thanks to the presence of the Californian Highway Patrols, or *CHiPs*, as they were more commonly known. Now that would have been a scene, if Francis 'Ponch' Poncherello and Jonathan Baker had pulled over the A-Team van: would Face have smooth-talked their way out of trouble? Or would BA just have rammed their motorbikes off the road? As it was, Ponch and Baker had their work cut out making sure the highways were moving, all while keeping one eye on their boss, Sergeant Getraer, and the other on the ladies of Southern California.

On the eastern side of the country, meanwhile, three very different shows were taking police dramas into new territory. *Cagney and Lacey*, set in New York, was the archetypal crime-fighting-duo format but this time from a female perspective. Not that Christine Cagney (Sharon Gless) and Beth Lacey (Tyne Daly) were soft touches: they couldn't be, as they did battle with both New York's criminals and the sexism within the force itself. Theirs was a world of grind rather than glamour, and a view of police work that was as much slog as it was high-speed car chases. The same again and then some could be said of *Hill Street Blues*: filmed in Chicago, this was again as much interested in the effects of the work on the police themselves as it was on the work they were doing. A bit like its iconic piano theme tune, the show was never flashy or in a hurry – realistic rather than ridiculous, it was as great as it was gritty and arguably the precursor for modern shows such as *The Wire*.

I can see that now, but back then I had eyes only for *Miami Vice*. Jan Hammer probably had a piano in his studio too, but shoved away behind the synthesizers on which he wrote the show's theme music. In fact, you could argue that the contrasts in style between the programmes could be found in the difference between the two instruments. While *Hill Street Blues* had a touch of a more timeless quality, *Miami Vice* wore its era on its rolled-up white jacket sleeve. This was the cop show as Duran Duran video, with thumping music, good-looking leads, high fashion and flash cars. The vehicles in question were eighties super-cars, such as the Ferrari Spider or the Testarossa, in which the lead characters accelerated around Miami under the pitch black of the night sky, all the while listening to something like 'In the Air Tonight' by Phil Collins.

The lead characters, Crockett and Tubbs, were played by Don Johnson and Philip Michael Thomas. Crockett was the marginally more down-at-heel of the two, with a pet alligator called Elvis and a fondness for women who were about to get it. Tubbs, meanwhile, was the sharp-dressed man of the ZZ Top song, down from New York following the death of his brother. The show's producers were so focused on the look and feel of the show that they even had a policy towards colour – 'no earth tones' was the rule. They wanted pink like the flamingos, turquoise like the colour of the sea, and white like the cocaine trade that Crockett and Tubbs were attempting to control. While these colours were in fashion *Miami Vice* looked the part; but when things moved on it rather quickly didn't feel so hip.

Over on Hawaii, meanwhile, the former naval officer Thomas Magnum had got himself a career as a private investigator, and a nice little earner in the process – keeping an eye on the Hawaiian house of novelist Robin Masters. In return, Magnum got an apartment on the seafront and full use of the writer's Ferrari (I can't say I'm familiar with Masters' work, but must have a word with my agent). There was an English servant knocking about, the not-especially-English-sounding Jonathan Quayle Higgins III, who'd been in the army himself and thus wasn't overly impressed with Magnum's methods, but that was about as tricky as Magnum's life got – most of the time it was all burning rubber in the Ferrari, meeting beautiful ladies and solving the occasional case.

The lead role in *Magnum, PI*, was played by Tom Selleck, with a stellar supporting cast consisting of his moustache and chest hair. The part cost him the role of Indiana Jones in *Raiders of the Lost Ark* (the *Magnum* producers famously refused to release him from his contract) but, given that he consequently got to spend most of the eighties in Hawaii, I don't suppose he minded too much. Taking a leaf out of *Dallas'* book, Magnum died at the end of the seventh series but by popular demand for the character to return he was brought back to life in a 'but it was all a dream' way, and carried on as before.

Back on the American mainland, more specifically in the county of Hazzard, Georgia, there were another couple of 'modern-day Robin Hoods', in the form of Bo and Luke Duke. *The Dukes of Hazzard* had originally been done for moonshine and found themselves placed on fairly strict probation: no firearms (which they got round with Robin Hood-style bow and arrows) and no leaving the county (except when broken-down contract negotiations required the characters to disappear for a while). As a result, these good ol' boys made it their business to thwart the bad ol' ways of local bigwig, the white-suited Boss Hogg, and his partner in slightly dodgy crime, Sheriff Roscoe P. Coltrane. Much of this appeared to involve shouting 'Yeeee-haaaaaw!' and driving off ramps in 'General Lee', their red and white 1969 Dodge Charger, while their hot-panted cousin, Daisy Duke, used her feminine ways to uncover useful information. The show also boasted Boss Hogg's 'celebrity speed trap': 'passing' stars would be done for speeding and were given the offer of having their ticket expunged in return for singing at the local bar. Celebrities who just so happened to be driving through Hazzard County included Roy Orbison and Tammy Wynette. You're right: it was probably for the best that Roy was stopped.

Sometimes a character's day job could help them in their fight for justice. Take Colt Seavers – Hollywood stuntman by day, bounty hunter by night. Seavers was *The Fall Guy*, played by Lee Majors, the 'unknown stuntman' who, according to the title song, had stood in for the likes of Redford and Eastwood. Certainly the stunts he did for his films had an uncanny habit of handily reappearing when he was in pursuit of whoever was on the run that week. Equally, there was fashion photographer Dani Reynolds and her good-looking male model Mac Harper, who in *Cover Up* used their photo-shoot cover to uncover all types of dodgy goings on. Harper's role in the series was shorter than anticipated when the actor playing him, Jon-Erik Hexum, was messing around with the prop gun between takes and shot himself: a tragic reminder of the real power of guns, despite what these programmes might have suggested to the contrary.

*   *   *

You'd have thought that, with all these various law-enforcement officers, soldiers of fortune, private investigators, modern-day Robin Hoods, moonlighting stuntmen and undercover photographers, crime might have found itself on the back foot in the American eighties. But oh no – on and on the criminals kept coming, ever nearer and ever more looming, like the wave in *Big Wednesday*. So bad was the situation that not even BA and a soldering iron were going to be enough to hold it back. It was time to bring technology on board in the fight against crime, to go down to the warehouse and pull back the covers on the secret weapon that the boffins had been working on.

The super-vehicle.

That's right: the criminal so-called masterminds had not counted on coming up against a talking car. The car in question was the Knight Industries Two Thousand or KITT for short – which in true Henry Ford fashion you could have in any colour you liked as long as it was black. Unlike your standard Ford, however, KITT was fully computerized, and had a nice little red light that blipped back and forth across the front of the bonnet. Other features that a KITT car salesman might point out would be the ability of the vehicle to talk and to drive itself, that it was bulletproof, bombproof and fireproof, and came with turbo boost as standard, allowing the driver to go from 0–300mph in the blink of an eye. Should you find yourself under attack, there were a range of weapons at your disposal, including oil slicks, smoke screens, flame throwers, tear-gas launchers and magnesium flares. And did I mention the real teak handles and ten-year 'lifetime guarantee'?

KITT was the sturdy steed of Michael Knight in *Knight Rider*. Knight, played by David 'Don't Hassel The Hoff', was, according to the show's introduction (complete with wonderfully blippy soundtrack), 'a man who does not exist'. This was true in a 'crime they did not commit' sort of a way: Michael was Michael Long, a police officer who had almost died in a shootout, only to be saved by millionaire Wilton Knight: he'd then had lots of plastic surgery and changed his surname. Knight (Michael) signed up to Knight (Wilton's) Foundation for Law and Government (or FLAG), on 'a crusade to champion the cause of the innocent, the helpless, the powerless'. The target of this Erin Brockovich with a sports car were those particularly mendacious criminals who operate 'above the law'. Which is a laudable goal, though if one wanted to be a little pedantic that is presumably all of them – criminals who operate within the law are, by definition, not actually criminals.

Michael and KITT were helped in their fight by a two-person back-up team of silver-haired Devon and an attractive mechanic called Bonnie (later Charlene: oh sorry, I'm getting mixed up with *Neighbours*). Devon and Bonnie lived in the back of an articulated lorry, into and out of which Michael would drive whenever he needed instructions and couldn't be bothered to use KITT's various communications devices. To be honest, the whole Michael 'driving' thing was a bit of an unanswered question. If KITT was so absolutely amazing, why did he (it?) need someone to drive him at all? Wouldn't it have been better all round for KITT to drive and give Michael the space and time to do up the buttons on his shirt?

The type of criminals who KITT and Michael came up against were your usual low-down mix of con-artists, smugglers and mercenaries. An unusually high percentage of these seemed to be involved in car racing – thus allowing KITT and Michael to enter various competitions in 'disguise'. In fact, KITT only ever really met his match in the form of other high-tech vehicles. There was Goliath, a truck under the control of Wilton Knight's widow, and the 'Juggernaut', which wasn't actually a juggernaut but rather more of an armoured car with a battering ram. Above all, there was KARR, or Knight Automated Roving Robot, KITT's immediate predecessor: KARR was a bit hacked off to have been superseded by KITT and, having been reactivated by a group of thieves, was determined to stay switched on whatever the cost. Cue lots of KITT v KARR face-offs, at the end of which KARR always ended up looking a total write-off but with its LED display somehow still blinking away, ready to return in a future series.

Given the huge success of *Knight Rider*, it was inevitable that there would be other super-vehicles speeding along in its wake. Like *Street Hawk*. Actually, to be fair, this sort of motorbike version of KITT could also shift at 300mph whenever he decided to use his 'hyper-thrust'. Street Hawk's rider, Jesse Mach, was another of those cops who'd been injured in the line of duty then strong-armed to take part in a secret government project. Street Hawk was 'an all-terrain attack motorcycle, designed to fight urban crime', and was capable of both 'incredible speeds' and 'immense firepower' (or at least as much firepower as you could get on the side of a motorbike).

Meanwhile, in the skies overhead, you couldn't move for high-tech helicopters. There was *Blue Thunder*, a chopper that wasn't actually blue (or, indeed, made of thunder), but came with the usual guff about secret government departments (this time called APEX), amazing speeds (300mph, I'm guessing) and bullet-deflecting armoury. It also had something called 'whisper mode' – a handy little device that basically allowed the helicopter to switch to silent and sneak up on people. I don't know if *Airwolf* could do that but, given that it could fly at supersonic speeds, it probably didn't care. *Airwolf* was so called because it was a military helicopter disguised as a civilian one: a sort of air wolf in sheep's clothing. Its pilot was the preposterously named Stringfellow Hawke, its secret government agency the Firm, and its controller an eye-patched chap by the name of Archangel.

If all these super-vehicles weren't ridiculous enough, there were two further crime-fighters who came with their own unique special powers. The first of these was *Automan*: essentially an electric-blue hologram with a human head. Automan was created by police-officer-come-computer-nerd Walter Nebicher in a '*Weird Science* without a sense of humour' sort of way. Because no one else knew of Automan's existence, Nebicher could take all the credit for all the criminals apprehended by his hologram. In fact, Automan's only flaw was the amount of electricity he needed to exist: so if demand was high (such as the nation reaching for the kettle at the end of *Coronation Street*), he was prone to suddenly disappearing at key moments.

Then there was the strange case of Jonathan Chase, professor in animal behaviour at New York University, and 'master of the secrets that divide man from animal, animal from man'. The result was *Manimal*, a crime-fighting force who could handily change from human being to hawk or panther whenever the situation required. In theory Chase could mutate into any creature he felt like, though in practice it always seemed to be the same two or three. While I don't want to cast aspersions on what could be a particularly impressive icebreaker at parties, is the ability to turn into a lion really that much help against a hardened criminal with a sub-machine gun?

By contrast, back on this side of the Atlantic, attempts to control crime felt just a little bit pedestrian. When Alex Drake (Keeley Hawes) travelled back in time to the early 1980s in BBC1's *Ashes to Ashes*, she found herself in the sort of smart and sassy cop show that, frankly, did not really exist in Britain at the time. The nearest thing to the London that she was now 'living' in was probably *Dempsey and Makepeace*, but she couldn't have ended up there, on account of it being over on ITV.

Dempsey and Makepeace did have a bit of oomph to it, though that was probably to do with having an American cop on board to fling his weight against. Dempsey (Michael Brandon) had ended up in Britain for his own safety (if not always ours) after rooting out various wrongdoings in the New York police force. His British boss, the moustachioed wasp-chewing Chief Superintendent Spikings, teamed him up with the beautiful British blonde detective Harriet Makepeace (Glynis Barber). Makepeace was no dumb blonde: with her Cambridge degree she was as smart as they come, and certainly as smart as smart-arse Dempsey. Cue lots of on/off, 'will they, won't they?'-type tension, which came across as realistic and it was – in real life, the couple made their peace and married in 1989.

Where Keeley Hawes would most likely have ended up was not London at all but the town of Hartley in Lancashire. This was the setting of *Juliet Bravo*, the long-running BBC series about a female inspector who confusingly wasn't actually called Juliet Bravo at all (that was her call sign on police radio). A bit like *Cagney and Lacey*, Inspector Jean Darblay (Stephanie Turner) – and later Kate Longton (Anna Carteret) – found herself battling against both crime and the sexism within the police force. Except in a slightly less hip and urban setting. And without one of those saxophone-filled American theme tunes.

Everywhere you looked, the comparative British crime shows were just not as good as their American counterparts: they had *Street Hawk*; we had *Boon*. In terms of accompanying day jobs, rather than the fashion photographer of *Cover Up* or the Hollywood stuntman of *The Fall Guy*, Britain had Eddie Shoestring, half private detective, half local-radio DJ. The equivalent of *Magnum, PI*, meanwhile, was probably *Bergerac*, with Hawaii swapped for Jersey, the Ferrari replaced by an old Triumph and the leading man's moustache and luxurious chest hair switched for a slightly gammy leg.

Maybe American cop shows were more prolific because there was more American crime to deal with. In a case of life imitating art, the greater the number of criminals that this cast of fictional detectives and vigilantes arrested, so the actual prison population in the United States increased. In fact, it more than doubled throughout the decade, from under 500,000 in 1980 to well over a million by 1990 (a trend that has continued today, culminating in the US having the highest prison population in the world). While bad things happened in Britain, they didn't do so to the same extent – and certainly not to the level that required inventing a talking car to sort them out. Perhaps that is why the American shows of the period were as hot as a McDonald's apple pie and the British ones were just a little bit wimpy.

After the break, we head to York Minster for a good old sing-song, learn how to fly and meet a very peculiar group of doctors . . .

Ad Break

Carling Black Label (Again)

A night at the theatre now, and a production of William Shakespeare's tragedy *Hamlet*. Said Prince of Denmark is in the gravediggers scene, where he finds a skull belonging to Yorick, the former court jester. His discovery is about to lead him into suitably oratorical ruminations about life and death and how we're all going to end up as nothing but a heap of dust so, really, what's the point? As it turns out, Yorick's skull turns into dust sooner than envisaged: as Hamlet says, 'Alas poor Yorick, I knew him well . . .' the skull slips out of his hands and heads head first (head only) towards being smashed into smithereens on the floor.

But wait. Hamlet stretches out his foot and with it catches the skull before it hits the deck. He flicks up the skull and heads it three times, then bounces it from shoulder to shoulder and back down to his feet in true hacky-sack keepy-uppy fashion. Then, from the wings, there is a cry from Hamlet's good friend Horatio.

'My noble Lord Hamlet,' he starts, before beckoning with his hands. 'Over here, son, on my head,' he continues, breaking just a little loose from the original text. In a classic one-two manoeuvre, Hamlet passes the skull across to Horatio; Horatio heads it back to Hamlet, who then bicycle kicks into the box – and, more specifically, on to a lager-drinking man who probably wishes he was *wearing* a box. As Hamlet and Horatio celebrate to cheers from the audience, the skull puts a wager to the lager-drinking man that Hamlet is fond of the Black Label version of the lager beer Carling.

(I should probably say, this being the second time I've mentioned Carling, that other beers are available. Though not many have as consistently good adverts in the eighties. And I haven't even mentioned Carling's three-part magnum opus, in a which a lager-drinking cowboy is pursued by Wild West folk on horseback, first through the subsequent advert for a collection of love songs, and then into a supermarket ad about washing powder . . .)

Episode Sixteen

'Here's where you start paying – in sweat'

One of the television highlights of the decade, it almost goes without saying, was my own much-vaunted small-screen debut. No doubt as you've been reading this book you've been doing so with that nagging thought in the back of your mind: I'm sure that name rings a bell. Wasn't there a Tom Bromley who was some sort of child star back in the early 1980s? In fact, didn't the BBC devote an entire television special to his singing talents, recorded at a packed auditorium in front of thousands of adoring fans?

Well, yes: I don't like to make a big thing about it, but (and you might need to control yourself here, ladies) that is actually correct. Obviously when I say the *entire* television special was devoted to me . . . the BBC felt it unfair to keep the spotlight solely on my talents throughout, so a couple of my support acts might have made it through to the final cut as well. And, all right, when I say packed auditorium, you might be thinking the Royal Albert Hall or the Hammersmith Apollo but we actually did the gig at York Minster – the producers wanted the warmth of that homecoming feel. And, OK, if you want to be really pedantic about it, the thousands of adoring fans were actually the other members of the congregation. It still doesn't alter the fact that the two-second shot of me singing away remains the iconic image from *Songs of Praise* that everyone (in my immediate family) remembers.

To be honest, it would probably have been harder for me not to have appeared on the programme. The BBC had decided that for a Whitsun *Songs of Praise* special they'd fill York Minster with a congregation of schoolchildren. This involved a gathering together of pretty much every primary-school child in the York area. As well as pupils from your own school, there were lots of others who you didn't know yet but would become friends with at secondary school. Possession of the *Songs of Praise* video thus became a sort of teenage trump card, as even the coolest kids in school could be exposed in all their butter-wouldn't-melt glory.

The filming of the programme took place well before Whitsun – well before Easter, in fact. I can say that with some confidence because I kept the programme booklet that the BBC gave everyone with all the hymns in, despite being told that the booklet MUST NOT BE RETAINED (both underlined and in capital letters) – presumably because they had broken every copyright law in the book by printing it. Sorry about that. The booklet itself gave out advice on how to get the most out of the recordings:

To make the programme as effective as possible, will you please

1. Watch the conductor. If you can't see him very well, take the lead from the choir or the organ.
2. Try to ignore the cameras!

Don't be fooled by the jollity of the exclamation mark at the end of the second point. The key phrase was the cross-teacher's voice of 'will you please'. This was clearly written taking into account the producer's previous experiences of dealing with schoolchildren, and his desperate attempts to avoid the recording becoming like that bit in *Grease* when they film the dance competition at Rydell High. In answer to the producer's points:

1. Had I been able to see the conductor, or the choir, or the organ, I would have followed them. However, that was a bit tricky because (presumably in some sort of mix-up) your floor manager decided to stick me down the side behind a pillar.
2. In order for me to ignore the cameras, you need to be turning them in my direction in the first place!

Having given up all hope of fame and fortune, I spent most of the day messing around with my friend Paul and trying to attract the attention of various good-looking girls from the other schools (that was more Paul than me: he was more advanced in such matters, thanks partly to those crumpled magazines that his dad had lent him). So it was something of a surprise all round when, with my family gathered around the television screen, there were Paul and I, captured for posterity, looking all angelic and singing our hearts out. Who says the camera never lies?

One person wasn't fooled, mind. Within a couple of weeks of *Songs of Praise* being broadcast, York Minster was struck by lightning and went up in flames. At the time, some people suggested this was divine retribution for some remarks made by the slightly barking Bishop of Durham – an equally barking theory that seemed to ignore the fact that it wasn't Durham Cathedral that had been hit. I can only think that, if divine retribution *was* the cause, then it was more likely to do with my own off-key rendition of 'O Peter Go Ring Dem Bells'.

*   *   *

There was nowhere in Britain that was big enough for a talent like mine. In fact, there was only one place anywhere capable of handling it: the New York School of the Performing Arts. This was the home of *Fame*, the award-winning film that got turned into a slightly less award-winning television series. Apparently the whole thing was originally going to be called *Hot Lunch,* after one of the songs in the film, but someone sensibly stepped in and changed the name. I don't think Irene Cara would have sounded quite so compelling if she had been singing about leek and potato soup instead of stardom.

Not that the original Irene Cara version was used for the television programme. Although some of the actors featured in both film and TV show (Debbie Allen as taskmaster Lydia Grant, Albert Hague as Mr 'Sho Sho' Shorofsky, Lee Curreri as Leo Sayer lookalike Bruno Martelli and Gene Anthony Ray as electric dancer Leroy), Irene Cara was not among them. Her role of singer/dancer/diva Coco Hernandez was played by Erica Gimpel, who in true Dennis Waterman fashion performed the theme tune to the show as well.

The intro to the programme made the New York School of the Performing Arts look like a very happening place. There were people running down the halls at high speed, people taking piano or ballet classes, practising the cello or spinning round on a sixpence. Most of the students had what appeared to be some sort of twitching disease but was actually them instinctively moving their bodies to the beat and trying their best not to launch into a stop-the-traffic dance routine at every given opportunity. There was a mime artist out on the street who threw his white juggling balls behind him when no one paid him any attention (which probably explained why he was out on the street and not in the school) and a lot of students in leg warmers and leotards who did the splits in mid-air.

There was also, of course, dance instructor Lydia Grant, banging her wooden stick on the floor and reminding the students what the tuition fees were for being a student at the school. Certainly, the currency of stardom had changed since Robert Johnson sold his soul to the devil in return for playing guitar. In the eighties no one was interested in your soul: it was all about paying 'in sweat'. In this unique television currency the single unit is the bead, 100 of which make up a brow and 1000 a 'change of clothes'. For those who thought Lydia Grant was messing around, one only had to be reminded of the real-life success of Dire Straits guitarist Mark Knopfler – it was surely no coincidence that Knopfler was surgically attached to his headband, and that *Brothers In Arms* was one of the bestselling albums of the decade.

Back in class, Leroy, Bruno and Coco were joined by such new talents as thespian Doris Schwartz (Valerie Landsburg), ladies' man Danny Amatullo (Carlo Imperato) and homesick cellist Julie Miller (the *Footloose* and fancy-full Lori Singer). Although Julie and Coco were clearly better-looking, I always found myself drawn more to Doris: this was probably to do with the fact that she was the not-fitting-in, wanting-to-be-more-attractive one with whom any teenager could identify. That and the fact she sang lead vocals to 'Hi Fidelity', the song where the cast took over a music shop and did the show right there.

The shows followed a fairly similar pattern: synthesizer stud Bruno would have a modern/traditional face-off with the more classically minded Shorofsky; Lydia Grant would shout at people; Coco would tell everyone she was brilliant; Danny would cop off with someone; and Leroy would tell Mrs Sherwood that he hadn't done his English homework again. There'd usually be a big song-and-dance number, many of which were repeated when the Kids from Fame started having hit singles and did a tour of sell-out concerts across Britain. In a 'real life imitating art' sort of way, Debbie Allen not only played Lydia Grant but was also the show's choreographer, and found herself dealing with the Kids experimenting with *Fame*'s rewards.

For all the teaching philosophy and first-class tutoring, it has to be said that the success rate of the School of the Performing Arts left a little to be desired: Bruno, supposedly some sort of modern-day Mozart, flounced out; Leroy, the amazingly lithe dancer, ended up teaching at the school; Doris just graduated, though to do what I can't remember (I think I must have blocked it out in order to deal with her leaving). In fact, the only person who achieved anything approaching real stardom was the actress who played the otherwise anonymous Cleo Hewitt in series four: she turned out to be Janet Jackson. Given her success and the general failure of the other characters, maybe the unwitting moral of the show was that fame had less to do with paying 'in sweat' and more to do with who you know.

Back in Britain, the traditional route to superstardom was to try your luck on a TV talent show. In the seventies *New Faces*, together with Hughie Green's *Opportunity Knocks*, had served as the launch pad for much of the light-entertainment establishment in the 1980s. Their many success stories included Russ Abbott, Freddie Starr, Little and Large, Les Dennis, Frank Carson, Lena Zavaroni, Paul Daniels, Bonnie Langford, Tom O'Connor, Lenny Henry, Victoria Wood, Jim Davidson, Gary Wilmot, Michael Barrymore, Roy Walker and the Chuckle Brothers. *Opportunity Knocks* even got it right when it came to the star quality of subsequent *Hi-de-Hi!* actress Su Pollard: she was beaten into second place by a singing dog.

In the mid-1980s the talent shows made a comeback but – as it was with the state of mainstream comedy – the eighties versions were pale in comparison with what had gone on before. Unlike the galaxy of stars that the previous series had thrown up, the combined talent pool of the revised versions amounted to Joe Pasquale. He came second on *New Faces*, which in its new guise was hosted by former winner Marti Caine. Caine, whose stage name was a play on 'tomato cane', was suitably stick-thin with a fiery flick of red hair. Her stunning looks were slightly undermined by her Yorkshire roots, which came to the fore when she yelled her catchphrase at the audience: 'Press your buttons . . . NOW!'

If the eighties talent shows were less actually talent shows and more just, well, shows, they did nonetheless lay the groundwork for future programmes. Many years before Simon Cowell, Craig Revel Horwood, Nigel Lythgoe and Jason Gardiner, there was the original nasty judge: tabloid TV critic and columnist Nina Myskow. Myskow had shown her nasty-judge credentials a few years previously when she was taken to court over a TV review she'd written, in which she described an actress as being both 'ugly' and having a bum that was 'too big'. She was similarly scathing about the contestants on *New Faces*, revelling in the boos from the audience for her rudeness and playing the pantomime-villain role to perfection.

Over on BBC1, meanwhile, *Opportunity Knocks* had been revived as *Bob Says Opportunity Knocks*. The Bob in question was Bob Monkhouse, who smiled his oleaginous smile and said, 'When opportunity comes your way . . . don't knock it!' As with the original programme, the show eschewed the comments of judges. In their place was a computerized version of the original 'clap-o-meter', which had a star wobbling its way across the screen in relation to how hard the audience were applauding. A touch harder than Bob, presumably, whose ten-to-the-dozen claps were more taps than hearty thwacks, and who never looked to me as though he meant it most sincerely. Like *New Faces*, the eighties talent appeared to be washing its hair when Bob came knocking, but the programme's contribution to the cause came in the introduction of telephone voting to choose the winner (in the Hughie Green era, viewers voted via postcards). The shows might not have enjoyed much of a renaissance, but the eighties revamps did at least put all the pieces in place for Simon Cowell later.

*　　*　　*

With the School of the Performing Arts not exactly beating a path to my door, and as I reluctantly concluded that it was not really my place to deprive the world of Joe Pasquale, I ended up ploughing my song-and-dance furrow alone. Despite showing a complete lack of talent in any sort of theatrical discipline, the offers somehow came in. The only ability I possessed was reliability – a useful middle-class trait that meant that teachers and directors could be confident that I'd not only turn up to rehearsal without fail but would do so on time as well.

So when York Minster was holding an early-music festival to coincide with York's mystery-play cycle, who got dragged along to dance in tunic and tights for the American tourists? When my junior school was looking for someone to play the lead role of *Sweeney Todd*, to whom did they turn to hold the tomato ketchup sachets hidden in the cardboard razors? And, despite *Songs of Praise* proving my tone-deafness once and for all, who ended up in the choir for a York Theatre Royal production of *James and the Giant Peach*? A production, I have to add, that 'paid' me for the trouble of performing every other night for three weeks by letting me keep my costume, a bright-yellow tracksuit with peach trimming.

Given all of this early success, it was inevitable that I found myself pushing on with my thespian career. Slightly less choosy in their intake than the New York School of Performing Arts was a local 'youth theatre' group – a phrase that should really strike the fear of God into anyone asked to watch them in action. I found myself going along on Monday nights after school, where I mixed with a succession of Yorkshire luvvies called things like Nova or Vivienne, remarkably confident young things who were not so much out of my league as playing a different sport altogether. This was brought brutally home when I introduced my parents to them at one of our many 'performances'.

'Oh look,' said one of the girls. 'It's thingy.'

I use the word 'performances' in inverted commas because everything the youth theatre attempted to put on was extremely experimental in an eighties sort of a way. For one show we made the audience sit behind desks, as though they were at school, and proceeded to shout at them: not so much to underline the breaking down of the fourth wall in contemporary drama, but more because someone thought it would be funny. In another we attempted to re-enact the blowing up of the Greenpeace ship *Rainbow Warrior* through the medium of dance. At least the director was smart enough on this one to spot my complete inability to move, and made me the bow of the ship: my job was to stand completely stationary while everyone else moved around me.

Given that I was doing all of this appalling drama (maybe *because* I was doing it), it's noticeable how few of the great eighties drama series I settled down to see at the time. *Brideshead Revisited* was just the first of many shows I failed to watch. Next on my list of misses was *Boys from the Blackstuff*, Alan Bleasdale's powerful drama about life on the dole in Liverpool. This starred Bernard Hill as Yosser Hughes, desperate for someone to 'gissa job'. It was a programme that clearly chimed with my parents' thoughts about Thatcherism, so there's no way it wasn't on in our house. And I really like Alan Bleasdale, too – his 1991 drama series *GBH* remains firmly placed in my all-time top ten. All of which can only lead me to conclude that I was just too young to watch *Boys from the Blackstuff* when it was first shown.

I had possibly slightly less excuse, on account of being a few years older, when it came to *The Jewel in the Crown*, ITV's expensive 1984 adaptation of Paul Scott's *Raj Quartet*. I don't think the comparisons with *Brideshead Revisited* helped: the critics might have been making the reference to denote a level of quality and sophistication; I'm ashamed to say that I interpreted it to mean another boring programme about posh people. Indeed, one could even define my tastes at this stage of life as less *Jewel in the Crown* and more *Jewel of the Nile* (a ropey old romcom starring Michael Douglas and Kathleen Turner, for those among you with taste).

What was my excuse two years on again, when the BBC showed Dennis Potter's *The Singing Detective*? On several levels it should have been up my street: it was a great drama, had a young Joanne Whalley dressed as a nurse, and included the sort of sex scenes that had fuming viewers telling Barry Took on *Points of View* that it was 'extraordinarily obscene'. On the other hand, there were the continuous flashbacks and fantasy sequences which meant I never really got to grips with what was going on. Then there was its billing as a musical drama: I like music, and I like drama (despite what you might be getting here), but musicals I've always loathed. Perhaps most crucially of all was the sight of actor Michael Gambon as Philip Marlow, sat in his hospital bed, suffering from as much psoriasis as the BBC make-up department could stick on his face. As a teenage boy struggling to keep his acne under control, I did not consider this entertainment.

Before you mark me down as a complete cultural peasant, there were in fact several significant dramas that I did enjoy. The defining characteristic of these was, I like to think, a sense of prescience in my dramatic choices – spotting stars and writers and programmes that would become bigger names in the nineties and noughties. While I was behind the times in many of my viewing tastes, here, it just so happened, I was marginally ahead.

Although I didn't get on well with *The Singing Detective*, I got on extremely well with Dennis Potter's adaptation of Christabel Bielenberg's memoir, *The Past is Myself*. Christabel Bielenberg was originally Christabel Burton, a vaguely aristocratic young Englishwoman who in the early 1930s married a German law student. Moving to Germany, she found herself trapped on the wrong side of World War Two, looking after their two children while her husband was sent to a concentration camp for working against the Nazis.

Potter's adaptation, simply titled *Christabel*, was the opposite of *The Singing Detective* in terms of its style and, for me, its impact.

The starring role was given to a young and fairly unknown actress called Elizabeth Hurley. Hurley has not always had the most favourable reviews for her acting since then, but her cut-glass vowels and good looks fitted the role perfectly: certainly she had the presence that marked her out for the future.

Another young thespian just beginning to make his way in the world was Hurley's sometime boyfriend Hugh Grant. He turned up playing a preacher in the first series of one of my favourite dramas from the period, *A Very Peculiar Practice*. Hugh's presence, though, was very much a cameo compared to the person for whom the programme was really a calling card. That was the writer Andrew Davies: after this, his first TV series, he went on to write screenplays for such hugely successful programmes as *House of Cards*, *Pride and Prejudice*, *Tipping the Velvet* and *Bleak House*.

Back in the 1980s Davies was in slightly less demand. So much less demand, in fact, that the BBC were asking him for £17,000 that they'd paid him for various scripts that hadn't seen the light of day. Rather than return the money, Davies offered to quite literally 'write off' the debt by coming up with another series instead; this turned out to be *A Very Peculiar Practice*. In a knowing nod to this situation, Davies inserted into the drama a character called Ron Rust, 'Arts Council fellow in creative writing', who also found himself owing the BBC seventeen grand and writing them a script to pay it off.

Ron Rust's serial was a 'sharp, satirical black comedy, with a bit of Chekhovian understated pathos', and Andrew Davies' script wasn't far off being the same. The series was based around a somewhat wonky medical practice at a fictional university (Lowlands). It starred Peter Davison, not as Doctor Who but as Dr Stephen Daker, the new boy on campus. Daker's colleagues were all a bit odd: there was boozy Jock McCannon (Graham Crowden), who was barely in charge, the 'not believing in surnames' feminist Rose Marie (Barbara Flynn), and the fantastically amoral Bob Buzzard (David Troughton). Buzzard was undoubtedly the anti-hero of the show, combining both a Thatcherite streak and unshakeable belief in his own virility: Rose Marie was 'nothing a good rogering wouldn't sort out'; the students were so disgusting they 'were not worth dipping the Buzzard wick'; and 'nookie' with his wife was rigidly on schedule, in every sense of the word.

Peter Davison was extremely good too, in a way that you might not have expected from *All Creatures Great and Small* and *Doctor Who*. Andrew Davies had wanted someone to play a doctor who came across as vulnerable rather than confident, and Davison fitted the role. His character struggled with the surreal quirks of the university while pursuing love interests Lyn Turtle (Amanda Hillwood) in the first series and Grete Grotowska (Joanna Kanska) in the second. There was satire in the mix too – the setting of a practice at a university allowed points to be made about what the Conservatives were doing to health and education – but this was never done in a heavy-handed way. And, just when you thought things couldn't get any weirder, there was a pair of nuns scurrying about in the background, doing naughty things. It was that sort of programme.

Then there were the sorts of dramas that, in decades to come, Hollywood producers would look back on and think, 'You know what, I'm sure we can shoehorn all that complex characterization and slow-build storylines into a two-hour film.' One such drama was *Edge of Darkness*, which was remade in 2010 starring Mel Gibson and Ray Winstone. Back in the day the main character, Yorkshire policeman Ronald Craven, was played by Bob Peck. The story revolved around the killing of Craven's daughter. This initially appeared to have been carried out by Irish terrorists, but, as Craven kept digging, he discovered a far stranger and more sinister chain of events. Craven's daughter was an environmental activist, and further investigation uncovered a secret nuclear-waste dump hidden in an old coal mine. Cue much political intrigue, secret state conspiracy and a bit of mystical belief thrown in for good measure.

None of which particularly does the programme justice: it was a big hit on BBC2, and an even bigger hit when it was transferred to BBC1; in 2000 the BFI placed it fifteenth in their 100 Greatest British Television Programmes; Channel 4 put it third in their 2007 show *Greatest TV Dramas*; and *Broadcast* magazine made it one of only seven dramas in their list of the fifty most influential programmes of all time. I guess, as is the case with any great drama, it chimed with the mood of the time (Cold War paranoia, Chernobyl-style concerns); and it had a great script and performances. But perhaps most of all it just looked brilliant: dark, moody and menacing, it had a big-screen feel in a small-screen setting.

A similar panoramic sweep could also be found in *Traffik*, Channel 4's epic drugs drama that Steven Soderbergh would respell with a final 'c' for multiple-Oscar glory in 2000. The original show's spelling was clever, but was perhaps one of the few unoriginal elements of the programme: the 'c' to 'k' trick had already been done in *Amerika*, a mid-eighties drama series in which the United States had been taken over by the Soviet Union. Otherwise the show was brilliant, interweaving stories from the entire chain of the drugs trade and showing the effects on the various characters involved in each. The starting point was the opium fields of northwest Pakistan, where Fazal and his family were struggling to make ends meet. In Germany, Lindsay Duncan played a sort of Carmela Soprano figure, living the life off the earnings of her dealer husband. Back in Britain, Bill Paterson played the government minister tasked with combating drugs use while attempting to cope with his own daughter's addiction.

The politician's daughter, played by Julia Ormond, was part of a ball-going, well-to-do set at university. I don't know if it was deliberate, but this storyline always struck me as having direct parallels with the real-life story of Olivia Channon, the daughter of the Conservative trade minister Paul Channon. She was very much one of the great and the good at Oxford University in the mid-1980s, and died of a curiously British cocktail of sherry, champagne and heroin after celebrating her finals. This was the class-A world of the modern-day Sebastians, and among its many (equally successful) storylines *Traffik* caught the moment perfectly. It was a fitting, if poignant, way to bookend the decade in television drama – one that began so brightly with *Brideshead Revisited* and closed with this eerie glimpse into its characters' eighties counterparts.

After the break, we go on a blind date, fall in love, get married (twice) and divorced . . .

Ad Break

Nescafe Gold Blend

An apartment block, late evening, and a devilishly good-looking man is working hard at his desk when the doorbell rings. At the door is a pretty blonde lady (Sharon Maughan) wearing a black shoulder-padded top, a necklace that she appears to have borrowed from Mr T and a pair of gold coffee-bean earrings.

'Hello,' she smiles. 'Look, I'm sorry to bother you, but I'm having a dinner party and . . .'

At which point, the man (who turns out to be Anthony Head) raises his eyebrows like a pair of inverted commas. In anticipation, presumably, of the euphemism the woman is about to make.

'. . . and I've run out of coffee.'

This being the eighties, the woman doesn't actually ask if she can borrow some coffee. The mere stating of the fact that she doesn't have any is enough for a fellow sophisticate like Anthony Head to

273

instinctively grasp the severity of her social situation. With the sort of wry chuckle that says, 'Coffee? Or do you mean "coffee"?' he asks her to come in.

As Anthony reaches into the cupboard to lend Sharon a jar of Nescafe Gold Blend, the couple have one of those conversations that on the surface seems to be about coffee but is clearly – judging by the way their eyebrows are going up and down – really about something else. So when Anthony worries that his cock – sorry, his coffee – might be too much for Sharon – sorry, Sharon's guests – she replies, eyebrows to the dozen, that 'they' have 'sophisticated tastes'. Whatever on earth that is supposed to mean.

The irony of the advert is that, if Sharon's dinner-party guests really *do* have sophisticated coffee tastes, they're not going to be fobbed off with a cup of instant. What *would* have been sophisticated, coffee-wise, is if Anthony Head had said, 'Of course you can borrow some coffee. However, I'm afraid all I've got in are these terribly expensive beans, you know the ones that are excreted by that funny little weasel creature in Indonesia. Apparently, there's something in the way that the beans pass through the animal's digestive system that gives them their unique and distinctive flavour. Now, is that going to be too much for your guests?'

At which point Sharon's eyebrows might have decided that they weren't quite sure where this euphemism was heading and they certainly weren't going to hang around to find out.

Episode Seventeen

'Happy Christmas, Ange'

My exploits with the opposite sex in the 1980s, I think it is fair to say, don't exactly amount to a track record that Warren Beatty would recognize. For most of the decade I found myself joining Morrissey in enjoying (if that is the word) a celibate lifestyle – though while his celibacy was through choice, mine was not for want of trying.

In retrospect I think I have to take at least partial responsibility for my lack of action. During my teenage years I inadvertently sent out a number of mixed signals to the young ladies of York, who picked them up far more quickly than I realized I was making them. The first of these occurred at a teenage friend's birthday party. By my mid-teens such get-togethers had developed beyond fairy cakes and Pass the Parcel to a more free-for-all mix of secret cider, Spin the Bottle and heavy petting. On this particular occasion the birthday person invited guests to bring some music with them. It was a request that I was only too happy to oblige, certain in the knowledge that my record collection would be just the thing with which to impress the ladies.

'"I Feel Love"? Oh my God, who brought a seventies disco record with them?'

'Wait, it gets better. This isn't the Donna Summer version. It's a cover by Bronski Beat featuring Marc Almond.'

'Bronski Beat? Marc Almond? If only we knew who brought this single with them. Hang on a second, someone's written their name in large letters on the back . . .'

It's easy to see now how that might have been misinterpreted, but I really wasn't trying to make a statement by taking that single. I actually just liked the song. And to be honest, I probably would have been given the benefit of the doubt, had the party not been followed up soon afterwards by having to give a talk in English. The talk was meant to be about something we felt passionately about; and in true eighties style there was lots of banning the bomb, cruelty against animals, freeing Nelson Mandela and that sort of thing.

'Next up is Tom Bromley,' said my English teacher. 'Tom, what are you going to talk about?'

'Clause 28,' I replied.

Clause 28 was part of a Conservative government bill that banned local councils from 'promoting homosexuality' or 'the acceptability of homosexuality as a pretended family relationship'. A number of Labour councils were marginally more broadminded than the Thatcher government on issues of sexuality, even producing such leaflets as the infamous *Jenny Lives with Eric and Martin*. The Conservatives might not have been able to control all the local councils, but with bills such as this they could control what could and couldn't be said about homosexuality. Clause 28 was, essentially, censorship, born out of nasty old-fashioned prejudice at a time when the AIDS epidemic was big news. It quickly became a cause célèbre for the gay-rights movement and the subject of numerous pieces in the *Guardian*. The more of these I read, the crosser I got, and the more obvious choice it seemed for my English talk.

I can't remember much about giving the talk itself, but I do remember the complete silence as I made my way back to my desk having spoken for twenty minutes about how there was nothing wrong with homosexuality and the importance of gay rights. I also remember my English teacher thanking me for the talk, and telling me it was a 'brave' choice of topic – 'brave' being the word that Sir Humphrey Appleby would use in *Yes, Prime Minister* whenever Jim Hacker had a terrible idea. All around the room, meanwhile, there was the gentle clink of pennies being dropped: 'He's a fan of Bronski Beat, he's banging on about gay rights, doesn't he play the flute as well . . . Why didn't I work that out before?' The talk might have got me a good grade, but in terms of scoring where it really mattered it was going to be even longer before I finally got off the mark.

Television in the eighties had provided me with a succession of women for my teenage self to gaze at both wistfully and lustfully. I'd actually started at an early age, with a particular fondness for various female Hanna Barbera cartoon characters. Daphne from *Scooby Doo* had always struck me as attractive, in a glossy red-haired sort of a way – especially compared to her female rival, the mullet-haired, glasses-wearing Thelma. Then there was Taffy, one of *Captain Caveman*'s trio of female helpers. The girls were known as the 'Teen Angels', which sounds now like some sort of unpleasant site on the internet, but which back then was clearly intended as a knowing nod towards Farrah Fawcett and friends. Taffy, who wasn't Welsh, looked more than a little like Charlie's main Angel and said 'Zowie!' a lot.

As I grew older, I moved on from what counselling has taught me to accept was just a load of pencil-and-crayon drawings. One of the first real people I had a major crush on was Heather Locklear, who played Sammy Jo in *Dynasty*. With her tousled blonde hair and twinkle of naughtiness, Heather was a classic soap-star beauty, but it was as much the character she played that attracted me: Sammy Jo was not only good-looking but also young (to the point that Alexis questioned whether she was old enough to get married). She thought she'd found love in Steven Carrington, and threw herself at him on several given occasions, but Steven was struggling with the same sort of questions concerning his sexuality that I was going to inadvertently raise about myself. With a neat bit of teenage logic, I had managed to convince myself that I could be the one to take Sammy Jo away from all of this. In real life, however, I'm not sure I would have stood much of a chance against Heather's choice of men: Tommy Lee from Mötley Crüe and Richie Sambora from Bon Jovi. Compared to that sort of rock-and-roll pedigree, the spotty teenage guitarist from the school band not quite as good as Shed Seven possibly wasn't that much of a catch.

Another long-standing crush I had was on television presenter Debbie Greenwood. Debbie, whose brunette good looks had won her the title of Miss Great Britain in 1984, had turned up on my screen as the host of the school quiz *First Class*. Here, each team comprised of a second-year, fourth-year and sixth-form pupil, and would go up against another school to answer general-knowledge questions in order to win (I believe for their school) a BBC Micro Computer. It was a crummy prize as prizes go, particularly as the most exciting part of the programme was when the schools did battle on a set of computer arcade games such as *Track and Field* that I, as a not-very-proud owner of a BBC Micro, knew were very much beyond its 32K of processing power.

Female, good-looking and into computers? As far as I was aware, this was the first time such alchemy had happened since Kelly LeBrock in *Weird Science*. If that wasn't enough, I couldn't help noticing that part of Debbie's presentational style was to flirt with the sixth formers (at least, that was how my infatuated imagination saw it). In much the same way as I'd felt that Sammy Jo and I were not far apart in terms of age and thus might stand a chance of getting together, so I was sure that Debbie and I could conceivably have a relationship. That said, in real life Debbie was married to Paul Coia, quiz-show host and the first person ever to speak on Channel 4. Compared to that, my two-second appearance on *Songs of Praise* did not sound that impressive.

Help was at hand, however, for lovesick singles such as myself, in the form of ITV's Saturday-night show *Blind Date*. Launched in 1985, the programme quickly became a staple part of the weekend schedule and didn't leave the stage until 2003. The idea of a dating show was already established in Australia (*Perfect Match*) and America (*The Dating Game*), and ITV built on both of these programmes for their own offering. The original pilot was presented by the comedian Duncan Norvelle. Norvelle, with his 'Chase me!' catchphrase, was not so much camp as a whole branch of Millets. It didn't quite work, so the call went out for someone more family-friendly.

The result was Cilla Black and the coronation of the queen of Saturday night. Cilla was a safe pair of presenting hands and that was what the programme (and ITV) wanted: someone who was going to be warm and soothing rather than smutty and cheap. One only has to look at the succession of dating shows that have come and gone since then to see what happens when you go down this route. Cilla's own roots were as red as one half of her hometown and her language was sprinkled with Liverpudlian idiosyncrasies such as the phrase 'lorra lorra laughs' and addressing the contestants as 'chuck'. (Or maybe all the male contestants were called Chuck – I can't quite remember.)

The format of *Blind Date* was effortlessly simple. On one side of a retractable wall were sat three would-be daters on wine-bar-type stools. Then a member of the opposite sex would sit down on the other side of the wall and ask them a series of questions. According to the answers that were given (complete with 'helpful' reminders from 'Our Graham'), the person asking the questions would choose one of the three contestants as their date. Next they'd be shown the two they'd turned down, which usually amounted to a big fake show of disappointment on all sides, before the wall was pulled back and their 'blind date' revealed. Cilla would then produce a sheath of envelopes containing various date 'options' (in reality, they were all the same) so the couple could pick where they were going; the duo would return to the studio the following week to tell the audience how they'd got on. Or not.

The questions and answers always seemed a bit too neat for the contestants to have come up with, though apparently they were genuine enough – with a bit of 'coaching' from the backstage team. They tended to be of the slightly pseudo pop-psychology variety that you occasionally come across in job interviews: the sort that confirms the job isn't for you as soon as it's asked. So, for example, the female questioner (let's call her Sharon) would say, 'I'm a big fan of looking after myself and keeping fit' – at which point Cilla would interrupt to say, 'And doesn't she look good, fellas?' to whoops and wolf whistles from the audience. Then Sharon, looking faintly embarrassed, would continue, 'and part of my daily regime is to make sure I eat lots of fruit. If you were a piece of fruit, what kind of fruit would that be – and why?'

Then it was down to the three male contestants to try to come up with an answer that was both funny and just a little bit naughty. Number one might try to shoehorn in a reference to their wealth or physical prowess: 'Well, Sharon, as a gymnast I'd have to be a banana. Because when you see me do the banana splits, you'll see how a-peeling I can be.' (Subtext: pick me and I'll give you some seriously supple good loving.) Number two might try to get cute: 'Sharon, if I was a piece of fruit you'd have to be part of it with me. That way, we could be a lovely pair.' (Subtext: I would love to get to first base.) The third contestant, who might be wearing a brightly coloured waistcoat or a Timmy Mallet pair of glasses, would then come in with something completely offbeat and wacky: 'Well, Sharon, if I was a piece of fruit I'd have to be a prickly paw-paw. Because, like Baloo in *The Jungle Book*, I'd love to show you my bare necessities.' (Subtext: I have a restraining order.)

As 'Our Graham' recapped the selection of hilarious answers, Sharon would be racking her brains to work out who she'd least hate to go on a date with. Number three would probably be dismissed out of hand, which would leave her with that perennial female conundrum: the nice guy who's a bit wet, or the exciting guy who's a bit of a knob. Not wanting to look like a complete slapper on national television – particularly as she knew her nan and Auntie Maureen would be watching – Sharon would thus be obliged to turn down the gorgeous contestant number one in favour of weedy contestant number two.

Contestant number two, let's call him Nigel, would then swiftly find that the joy of having been picked by Sharon was to be extremely short-lived. If it wasn't bad enough that he'd picked 'a weekend in Boulogne' out of the possible destinations (Sharon would have been desperately hoping for a few days in the sun at the very least), it would quickly come to light that Nigel's one redeeming feature – the cutesy humour of his 'lovely pair' answer – wasn't even actually for real: he'd been fed the winning line by a member of the production team. Faced with forty-eight hours in a rain-sodden, windswept French ferry port, complete with camera crew sticking their nose in at every given opportunity, Sharon would have to be persuaded firmly by the production team not to reach for the bottle and head for the nearest nightclub.

Back in the studio the following week, Sharon and Nigel would be applauded on to the sofa, where Cilla would ask some gently innocuous questions about how they got on even though she knew full well that the date was a complete disaster. Nigel and Sharon would then make equally simpering noises before their individual recollections of events were played back, with a screen inset showing their date's reaction from the sofa. The scoops would be carefully edited to achieve maximum humiliation for the couple. So sweet Nigel would say, 'From the moment the screen went back, I couldn't believe how lucky I was.' Then Sharon would say, 'From the moment the screen went back, I knew I'd made the wrong choice.' This alternate view of events would then continue throughout the film of the date (Nigel: 'By the end of the first evening, I thought we'd really started to bond'; Sharon: 'I had to have a shower after the first evening, just to get rid of the smell of his awful aftershave'). Eventually some sort of telling final denouement would be reached (Nigel: 'I thought Sharon was a special girl, and would love to carry on seeing her'; Sharon: 'If I never see that weedy idiot again, it will be too soon').

By which point the audience would be booing Sharon and cheering Nigel, even though anyone with half a brain cell could see they were just completely inappropriate for each other. Cilla would stir all this up by saying, 'Oh, Sharon. How could you?' before playing the moment for a lorra laughs by asking, 'I don't suppose I'll be needing to buy myself a hat then?' If I really wanted to analyse the situation, I'd guess that Sharon's rejection wasn't actually about Nigel – it was more about being cross with herself for not having had the guts to pick the cocky-sounding gymnast she really wanted to go out with.

The longer the show went on the more it became clear that, if you were looking for love, *Blind Date* wasn't the place to find it. By the time the programme finished in 2003, there had been 356 episodes. Given that there were two dates per programme, that makes by my maths a total of 712 *Blind Date* couples. And how many times did Cilla have to dust down her hat? Three. That's one successful romance every six years. Or a strike rate of 0.4 per cent. I don't know who said that love is blind, but they clearly weren't tuned into ITV on a Saturday night.

The one marriage that *Blind Date* had a hand in during the eighties was that of Alex Tatham and Sue Middleton. Alex picked Sue to go on a blind date to a medieval banquet in Ireland, and when they got married three years later 4000 people turned up to the church and 17 million tuned in to watch the show. Apart from them, the most memorable contestants from the eighties were all the silly ones: there was posh-voiced Oxford graduate Paul Fox, the first-ever male contestant, who got sent underwear in the post afterwards; window cleaner Paul Nolan, with his Bruce Forsyth impressions; and Claudia Patrice, who sang all her answers to the questions.

In the nineties the contestants were a bit more knowing, with some seeing the show as a potential stepping stone to stardom: Jenni Falconer, Ed Byrne and Amanda Holden were just some of the contestants (the latter, then a nineteen-year-old drama student, turned up wearing nothing underneath her black catsuit). The other memorable moments were all the unpleasant ones: Charlotte Harrison wouldn't go on her date to Nepal, leaving David Smith to go on his own; and Nicola Gill from Guildford, who turned out to be Nicola Gill from *Cosmopolitan* magazine. (Though ironically – at least according to Paul from Nottingham – there was not much, ahem, faking from the fake contestant on the date itself.)

Just as when I was a young boy I'd wanted to know how Paul Daniels did his tricks, I was now intrigued by the magic of the one-liners and wanted to know whether the whole thing was a fix. When the show began introducing the occasional older blind date, people started asking why there was never a gay blind date, or a mixed-age date. By the end of the eighties the little bit of innocence that had originally made the show had started to ebb away: the naughty-but-nice answers to the questions became less cheeky and more crude. As social mores changed, and laddism and *Loaded* arrived, so the contestants seemed less like they were looking for love and more like they were in it for a quick shag. At the same time, the put-downs on the sofa, particularly from the women, became crueller and more bitchy. In the nastier, more-knowing nineties, *Blind Date* became Blind Dated, its belief in old-fashioned romance beginning to look exactly that: just a bit old-fashioned.

* * *

What would you say if I told you things had never changed? You'd probably say, 'Well, Tom, either you need to go back to your therapist about your feelings for that drawing from *Scooby Doo*, or you've quoted me the opening line from that hugely successful eighties comedy *Just Good Friends*.' Unless you're my therapist, you'll be pleased to hear that the answer is the latter. Because no section on romance in the eighties would be complete without the on/off/on/off/on/off relationship between Vince Pinner (played by Paul Nicholas) and Penny Warrender (Jan Francis).

The start of the programme didn't auger well, with the theme song – sung in Denis Waterman fashion by Nicholas – playing out over a sepia-blue background of flowers, like you'd stumbled across an advert for sanitary towels by mistake. But the sitcom itself, written by *Only Fools and Horses* writer John Sullivan, quickly left such misgivings behind. The first series began five years after Vince had stood Penny up at the altar. Having bumped into each other in a pub, the couple quickly ditched their dates for the evening in order to rekindle the recriminations and not get back together when they so clearly should.

One of the reasons the programme was so successful was that its two leads were not exactly unattractive. Paul Nicholas, with his boyish grin and flowing footballer curls, was every bit the eighties heartthrob. With her cropped brunette hair and big brown eyes, meanwhile, Jan Francis had the sort of elfin beauty that quietly sneaked up on you: women everywhere wanted to sleep with Paul and have their hair cut like Jan. Another reason the show worked so well was that, for once in sitcom terms, there was a strong female lead character to balance out the male. In *Blind Date* speak, Penny Warrender was the posh, well-to-do girl asking the questions and Vince Pinner was the cocky and confident contestant number one – good fun, but utterly unreliable. The chance meeting in the pub was Penny's equivalent of sitting on Cilla's sofa, and she wasn't going to hold back on what she thought about him. But as cross as she was trying to be, and as disapproving of Vince as her mother was being, Vince was still making her laugh, and she (and he – and we) could sense that some sort of spark was still there.

'So let's just pretend,' Nicholas sang in the introduction, 'that you and me can be just good friends.' In true Harry-and-Sally fashion, that was never going to be possible, though the original ending to the show might be the opposite to the one you're thinking about. That was intended to be the end of the second series, with Penny telling Vince that they would never get married, kissing him on the cheek and wishing him goodbye. The writer, however, underestimated quite how soppy the British public could be. They didn't want his open-ended, grown-up conclusion to modern love, all of which felt a little too much like real life – the nation wanted romance not realism, which meant Penny and Vince living happily ever after.

So the show returned for a third series and, in the final episode, watched by 20 million viewers on Christmas Day 1986, the couple sidestepped the scheming of Penny's mother and quietly got married in a registry office in Paris. So quiet was the wedding, in fact, that the witnesses were two cleaners whom Vince had pulled off the street.

'What do we do now?' Vince asked.

'Well you could kiss me if you like,' Penny replied.

I don't know if there is a quota for the number of love-hate couples allowed at the BBC, but no sooner had Vince and Penny's on-off relationship finally finished on an 'on' than another iconic on-off couple became decidedly off. Immediately following on from *Just Good Friends* in the schedules on Christmas Day 1986 was *EastEnders*, and a salutary reminder for romantics everywhere that marriage does not always equal happy ever after.

EastEnders had been launched in February 1985 and had, after a slightly wobbly start, quickly established itself as a gritty southern rival to *Coronation Street*. The star of the show was undoubtedly

'Dirty' Den Watts, who not only got to say the first words in the soap ('Stinks in here, dunnit?') but was also the mystery man behind the show's first big plotline – the father of Michelle Fowler's daughter. If that wasn't enough, the actor playing Den – Leslie Grantham – gave the programme its first major controversy when it was revealed that he had spent ten years in prison for murdering a taxi driver.

Back in Albert Square, Den and his wife Angie ran the Queen Vic, one of those soap pubs where all the characters pop in both at lunch and in the evening all the time. Angie was played by Anita Dobbs, who possessed the sort of huge heap of curly black hair that Queen guitarist Brian May would find himself unable to resist. For Den and Angie the bell in the pub was not so much to signify last orders as it was to mark the end of yet another round in their ding-dong relationship. Den's affairs led to Angie developing an ever-growing dependency on the bottle and an increasingly spectacular set of lies – culminating in the perhaps not totally sensible claim that she had only six months to live.

On top of the 20 million who'd tuned in to watch *Just Good Friends*, another 10 million found space on the sofa for what would arguably become the most-watched episode of a programme on British TV (arguably because, as I've already explained, a chunk of this 30-million figure would have been those watching the omnibus the following Sunday). Anyway, it being Christmas, most of the residents of Albert Square were in the pub rather than asleep on the settee like the rest of us. These included Michelle and Pauline Fowler, the latter of whom was about to discover the identity of her granddaughter's father.

Which would have been sensation enough in a normal episode of the soap, but Pauline's discovery was royally trumped by Den asking Angie if he could have a word behind the bar.

'Thank you for the best Christmas ever,' said Angie.

'Our last one,' said Den, a little wistful at the thought of his wife's terminal illness.

The lie, though, it turned out, had even less time to live than Angie supposedly had, as Den revealed with that murderous snarl of his that he knew all about it.

'That has got to be the sickest joke you've ever played, and Den Watts fell for it,' he growled. 'Well now the joke's on you.' At which point, sourly calling his wife 'my sweet', Den handed over a solicitor's letter, telling her he was filing for divorce.

'Happy Christmas, Ange,' he growled, giving her possibly the worst gift since the Soviet Union got Afghanistan 'an invasion' for Christmas back in 1979.

With Penny and Vince married, and Den and Angie decidedly not, the mantle of television's leading on-off couple found itself in the hands of Bruce Willis and Cybill Shepherd in *Moonlighting*. Willis and Shepherd played David Addison and Maddie Hayes, who respectively worked at and owned the Blue Moon Detective Agency in Los Angeles. It was a match made in purgatory: he, the good-looking, unshaven, know-it-all detective; she, the good-looking, bossy, know-it-all blonde. Theirs was big-screen presence in a small-screen show, and the series lit up as a result.

The programme was like all the best bits of one of those black-and-white screwball-comedy films, the sort starring Cary Grant or Katherine Hepburn. Indeed, it was as if Michael J. Fox had come back from the past in *Back to the Future* and brought with him the stolen reels of what was on at the cinema. Coupled with this classic-comedy feel was a Woody Allen-style approach to messing with the format: actors would break out of character to talk directly to camera; members of the crew would walk into shot to move props or scenery around; or the whole thing might mutate into a spoof Shakespeare play, complete with costumes and rhyming couplets.

Moonlighting was crackers and crackled at the same time. Right from the word go, David and Maddie were the sort of characters who got on each other's wick so absolutely that there was always a thin, wisecracking line between hate and love. As with the characters in *Just*

Good Friends, and as with Katherine Hepburn giving Cary Grant as good as she got many years before, the relationship worked because the female lead was strong rather than simpering. Cybill Shepherd as Maddie was a force of nature, happy to spar the full twelve rounds with her partner. Insults flew back and forth like Freddie Laker across the Atlantic. 'If there was a close-down sale on human beings, you'd be the last one to sell!' Maddie would yell. 'You oughta know,' David would retort, 'you're the sort of person who goes through life looking at the price tags, not the merchandise.'

Towards the end of series three, the simmering reached boiling-point.

'I'm sick of this,' David told Maddie. 'Two years of is you is, or is you ain't.'

'Two years of a man who believes culture is dark beer,' Maddie responded.

'Bitch,' said David.

'Bastard,' said Maddie.

She slapped him firmly across the face. David, though, didn't move. Maddie slapped him again. Still David didn't move. When she raised her hand for a third time, David grabbed her firmly by the wrist. For a moment all was silent and still. Then David pulled Maddie slowly towards him, 'Be My Baby' by the Ronettes started playing, and the couple finally kissed.

All of which, like *Just Good Friends*, made for great television. Unlike *Just Good Friends*, however, the clinch didn't come at the programme's end (it didn't even come at the end of the series). There were other factors thrown into the mix as well, but as soon as the couple started to kiss *Moonlighting* started down the long slow slide of losing its mojo. The arguing might have continued, but the anticipation had all gone: as Shepherd and Willis fell out behind the scenes, so the nation fell out of love with their characters too.

* * *

Meanwhile, over in a quiet residential street in Melbourne, a game of cricket was just getting underway. Opening the bowl was the very medium pace of Robinson (Jim), coming round the wicket to the opening batsman, the right-handed Robinson (Paul). Robinson (Jim) had set an attacking field with two slips and Daniels (Helen) behind the stumps – a fielding arrangement that the gentle pace of his bowling perhaps did not quite justify. And certainly Robinson (Paul) made immediate use of the huge empty spaces, taking the attack to the bowler and clubbing the ball immediately through the window of number 32.

This scene was, of course, from the opening credits to the Australian soap *Neighbours*. Originally bought by the BBC as a mainstay for their newly developed daytime schedule, it quickly became a hit with students and school children taking a sickie. This was largely thanks to the fact that the soap didn't look like a traditional British one: the weather was sunny rather than rainy; the mood was upbeat rather than down; and the characters were, Mrs Mangle apart, predominantly young and good-looking. At the heart of the show were the exploits of a small group of friends: Scott Robinson (played by Jason Donovan), Charlene Mitchell (Kylie Minogue), Mike Young (Guy Pearce) and Jane Harris (Annie Jones). Before long, the BBC realized the show's potential and moved the programme's repeat to an early-evening slot: the hour between the end of children's TV and the start of *The Six O'Clock News*.

It says much about the comparative moods of *EastEnders* and *Neighbours* that their most memorable eighties moments were a divorce for the former and a wedding for the latter. The *Neighbours* nuptials were between Scott and Charlene in an episode that was originally shown in Australia in 1987 but only made it on to British screens (playing 'catch-up', as *Going for Gold* would put it) in November the following year. It was a fictional relationship that was reinforced by rumours of a real one between the actors off screen and a huge (and sickly) single, *Especially for You*, released shortly afterwards.

Unlike a typical soap-opera wedding, for Scott and Charlene every-thing went right. The sky was as clear blue as it had been for Charles and Diana. Jason, looking a bit like a snooker player with his bog-brush hair and morning suit and bow tie, turned up at the church to be greeted by what appeared to the band A Flock of Seagulls but actu-ally turned out to be a group of friends saying, 'Good on you.' There followed a bit of fake 'What if Charlene doesn't turn up?' which was swiftly swatted away by his fellow 'snooker players', Guy Pearce and Stefan Dennis.

Considering how many people watched the wedding back in the UK, the actual attendance in the church was really rather small. So small, in fact, that I'm not even convinced that all of Jason's so-called friends even bothered to make it inside. Anyway, as the vicar prompted the congregation to be upstanding, Jason turned to look back down the aisle. The doors swung open (I'm not sure who pushed them, but let's not spoil the moment) and in walked Kylie on the arm of Craig McLachlan.

At which point normal wedding etiquette went flying out of the stained-glass window. Rather than walking in to 'Here Comes the Bride' or Pachelbel's *Canon in D*, Kylie and Jason instead chose the little-known song 'Suddenly' as sung by Australian singer Angry Anderson (Anderson was a Castlemaine XXXX version of Phil Collins and I really don't know what he had to be angry about – to be honest, he should be pretty chuffed, considering his ropey old ballad became a Top Ten single). Anyway, not only was the choice of music unconventional, but also the poor vicar found himself having to strug-gle through the service while Angry was still wailing away.

Angry's song served to dominate the wedding. As he sung on and on, everyone gave up trying to speak and simply resorted, depending on where their character's story arc was at that point, to looking either happy, tearful, wistful, or about to crap themselves. Halfway through, the vicar realized that Angry had stopped singing and, while the guitar solo went on, took the opportunity to get Jason and Kylie to say their vows before the caterwauling started up again. Cue more tilting of heads, Kylie lifting her veil and the newlyweds helping themselves to a thirsty old snog.

The *Neighbours* wedding was soap opera as pop video. Perhaps the producers had judged that the alternative to making on-screen relationships ruder was to go to the opposite extreme and saccharine things up. Perhaps they decided it would be better for the emotion to be displayed through music than to risk their cast having a crack at it. What they delivered as a result was one of those moments that across the country teenage girls rushed to record, and to re-watch again and again until the video cassette was worn out.

I don't know if it was by accident or design, but the producers decided that Scott and Charlene's relationship was one they were not going to mess with. When Kylie left the series, Charlene found herself heading to Brisbane for an apprenticeship. When Jason left, the following year, Scott followed her, getting a job at a newspaper there. And that, in soap land, is where they have stayed: still apparently happily married more than twenty years later, with two children called Daniel and Madison. In this instance, at least, someone really did get to live happily ever after. For ever and ever. The end.

After the break, we meet an MP who's a bit of a B'stard, stick a deck-chair up our nose, and, due to broadcasting restrictions, have our words spoken by an actor . . .

Ad Break

Cornetto

To the waterways of Venice, international capital of love. A be-permed young man is sat alone in a gondola when he notices another gondola is about to pass, containing a young lady. He blows the lady a kiss, and in true romantic fashion serenades her with a song. The tune he chooses is an old Neopolitan song, 'O Sole Mio', though he eschews the original words (which translate as 'My Sun') for his own rewritten lyrics.

The object of the man's infatuation, it turns out, is not the young lady after all. It's not that she's unattractive – she's nice in a Janet Ellis sort of a way. It's just that she is eating a particular brand of ice-cream cone. The man – and you have to admire his directness here – wants her Cornetto: 'Give eeet to me,' he croons. The woman, who obviously isn't paying too much attention to the words, closes her eyes and relaxes into the sheer pleasure that only a Cornetto can provide. At which point her suitor leans across and nicks her ice cream.

Our singer is correct, by the way, to suggest that the Cornetto is an Italian ice cream. The name and concept actually originated with the Italian firm Spica, who worked out that by putting a layer of chocolate between the ice cream and the wafer cone they could stop the latter going soggy. However, I am slightly less correct to call him 'our singer' because, for all our ice-cream Romeo's good looks, his words are actually sung by Renato Pagliari. Renato will later go on to team up with Renee (real name Hilary) for their huge Number One single 'Save Your Love'.

Given his romantic credentials, why aren't we allowed to see Renato singing the song himself? Perhaps it's because of the fact that, like any proper Italian singer, Renato is a man of Pavarotti proportions: as a result, not only would the phrase 'just one Cornetto' ring a little falsely, but also the sight of the gondola wobbling as he grabbed an innocent woman's ice cream was probably not what the ad agency were after.

Episode Eighteen

'Shut your mouth and look at my wad!'

In April 1988 the Pogues were one of the guest bands on Ben Elton's *Friday Night Live*. There was Shane MacGowan, shambling about in a pair of sunglasses, and there was the usual *Friday Night Live* backdrop of large white hands wobbling behind, like someone had borrowed them from Kenny Everett's preacher character, Brother Lee Love. The first song they played was 'Fiesta', essentially the band's Spanish-tinged party song – an uncontroversial number that would ultimately end up in a car advert (for the Vauxhall Tigra, bizarrely, rather than the Ford Fiesta).

By 1988 the Pogues had nudged out Tears for Fears and U2 for position as my favourite band in the world. I'd been to see them the previous year at the Manchester Apollo – my first-ever gig. That might sound quite late for a first gig, and also quite a long way to go to watch one, but you can blame Bob Geldof for that. Back in 1983 a raucous Boomtown Rats gig had led to bands being banned from York University, depriving the city of its one proper gig-sized venue. Bob Geldof might have fed the world, but he'd also left teenagers like me having to travel to places like the Manchester Apollo and Nottingham Rock City if I wanted to watch anyone half decent play live. Anyway, the Pogues gig remains fondly and firmly imprinted in my memory: the band's row of pints across the front of the stage, all gone by the end of the gig; Kirsty MacColl turning up to sing 'Fairytale of New York'; my ears still ringing with it all the following morning.

Shane MacGowan, so I was fond of telling anyone who would listen, was some kind of lyrical genius and should have been getting the same sort of adulation that Morrissey was being given with the Smiths. He matched the romance of an Irish poet with a novelistic sense of place, be it a rainy night in Soho or a Christmas Eve in New York. The Pogues never wore it heavy, but there was also a touch of politics to their proceedings too. The standout song on their second album, *Rum Sodomy & the Lash*, was a cover of the Eric Bogle folk song 'And the Band Played Waltzing Matilda' in which a First World War soldier recounts his experiences at the Battle of Gallipoli – an anti-war message that at fifteen I was only too happy to lap up.

Back on *Friday Night Live*, the Pogues had followed 'Fiesta' with a slightly more controversial choice from their new album. 'Streets of Sorrow/Birmingham Six' starts off with a delicate lament by Pogue Terry Woods about living through the Irish Troubles, before Shane MacGowan's contribution kicks angrily in – the focus of his fury is the convictions of the so-called Guildford Four and Birmingham Six: the ten people found guilty of planting two huge IRA bombs in the 1970s. MacGowan's song echoed what many people thought about their dubious convictions: that the only thing the ten were guilty of was 'being Irish in the wrong place and at the wrong time'.

As it turned out, you had to be a Pogues fan like me to know all this, because barely had the band begun the 'Birmingham Six' section of the song than the performance was cut off; the *Friday Night Live* logo appeared and the programme cut to an unexpected advert break. Quite why this happened has never been made entirely clear. The official line from the IBA was that the programme was overrunning and its makers, London Weekend Television, were contractually obliged to go to the advertisements – even if that meant chopping off the song. Personally speaking, I've always erred towards cock-up rather than conspiracy theory (in every sense, unfortunately). And that's true of my thoughts even here, where evidence gives weight to the notion that the powers that be knew full well what Shane MacGowan was going to sing about and pulled the plug on 'Birmingham Six' accordingly. What is beyond doubt is that a few months later the IBA officially blacklisted the song from all its television and radio stations.

The ban was in response to new government restrictions on broadcasting about Northern Ireland, something that the IBA decided applied to the Pogues' song: 'The song alleges some convicted terrorists are not guilty,' they declared, 'and goes on to suggest that Irish people are at a disadvantage in British courts of law. That allegation might support, or solicit or incite support for an organization proscribed by the Home Secretary's directive'. No one appeared to consider the possibility that the Pogues were not in fact singing in support of terrorism, but were just banging the drum for two miscarriages of justice.

The Pogues' song was just one victim of the broadcasting ban announced by Home Secretary Douglas Hurd. Margaret Thatcher had long been critical of the 'oxygen of publicity' that Irish terrorists and their apologists got in news coverage, and the government responded after a bomb on a coach had killed a number of soldiers in autumn 1988. All such groups were now placed under the ban, and their voices were no longer allowed to be heard on television or radio. By starving them of their publicity 'oxygen', so the theory went, groups such as Sinn Fein would find themselves struggling for breath at the ballot box.

It wasn't the most watertight ban in the world, in that the people it affected could still chat away to newspaper reporters as much as they liked. And, although they couldn't speak on television or radio, the ban could be circumvented by using actors to speak their words instead. Which led to the bizarre late-eighties spectacle of Gerry Adams and Martin McGuinness sounding more deep-voiced and dramatic than they actually were, all the while coming across as though they were taking part in a badly dubbed movie. The ban became a cushy little number for a small pool of Irish actors, including *The Crying Game*'s Stephen Rea, who got paid up to £120 an hour for lip-synching whatever the interviewee was saying.

The ban was — as bans often are — as counterproductive as it was clumsy. While appearances by Sinn Fein et al did decrease in its wake, any media coverage lost was made up for by their becoming cause célèbres for human-rights campaigners. Terrorist sympathizers were suddenly figureheads in the fight for freedom of speech – that old adage of hating what certain people say but defending their right to say it. The hoped-for reduction in influence, meanwhile, never materialized: in fact, by 1993 Sinn Fein's share of the vote in Northern Ireland had actually increased.

It wasn't the only ban that had failed. By then, too, Shane MacGowan's blacklisted lyrics had turned out to be something far more dangerous than inflammatory: it seemed they were true. In 1989 the Guildford Four had their convictions quashed by the Court of Appeal; in 1991 the Birmingham Six were similarly released. As the men left the courtroom to huge cheers from the crowds outside, the celebrations drowned out the slightly less prominent sound of the authorities quietly lifting the ban on the Pogues' song.

Friday Night Live was hosted by Ben Elton, complete with spangly suit and regular sprinklings of 'Yes indeed's and his 'little bit of politics'. Ben actually talked about politics more than a little bit, and it was a rare episode of the programme where he didn't go off on one about the prime minister – or 'Mrs Thatch', as he not-particularly affectionately called her. (Elton has always had a strange habit of shortening words – future reductions would include describing his novels as 'novs' and 'Bohemian Rhapsody' as 'Bo Rap'.)

Ben wasn't the only person to take a stab at satirical comedy in the eighties, though he was perhaps the only person to do so dressed in Bacofoil. Another regular on *Friday Night Live* was Harry Enfield, whose most enduring character was Stavros the kebab-shop owner ('Hello, matey peeps!'). In the later eighties Enfield came up with another character, a brash and garish invention called Loadsamoney. Loadsamoney was all the worst bits of Thatcher's Britain – boorish and confident, and flaunting his money at any given opportunity. Waving a roll of notes around, he'd shout his name at the audience and say: 'Shut your mouth and look at my wad!' However, not everyone got the joke, and some of the people Loadsamoney was meant to be lampooning treated him as some sort of folk hero instead. Enfield wisely killed him off.

Over on the BBC, Jasper Carrott beefed up his various Saturday-night shows (*Carrott's Lib*, *Carrott Confidential*) with a smattering of more Brummie-accented satire. Carrott has always been a slightly odd vegetable in the history of British comedy, sitting neither with the old-school performers nor the alternative-comedy scene. Instead, his engaging everyman persona had originally built up a substantial live following in the seventies, which he'd then translated into viewing figures in the eighties. Carrott's take on, say, the arrival of nuclear missiles at Greenham Common, was to worry about how they'd be deployed during a Soviet attack, and in particular how they'd navigate the roadworks at Newport Pagnell on the M1.

I knew Jasper Carrott's work well because of my dad's collection of cassette tapes of his seventies show. Another cassette that I all but wore out was that of *Not the Nine O'Clock News*. This programme, featuring Rowan Atkinson, Mel Smith, Griff Rhys Jones and Pamela Stephenson, was really where much of the eighties strand of topical comedy came from. The show, which actually began at the end of the 1970s, was irreverent and razor-sharp in a way that hadn't really been done since *That Was the Week that Was* was over a decade before: classic sketches included a parody of the Church's anger over the Monty Python film *Life of Brian*, in which Python worshippers were furious about a film called *Life of Christ*; 'The Ayatollah Song', in which Pamela Stephenson sang about fancying the religious leader and warning him not to 'Khomeni' closer; and a spoof of *Game for a Laugh* in which the Beadle-style prank involved surprising their victim by cutting his wife's head off.

Not the Nine O'Clock News opened doors, in terms of both what television comedy could be about and the fact that the producers would now consider material from anyone: consequently the programme gave many of the comedy writers of the eighties their first big break. Some of the subsequently famous names who contributed material were Richard Curtis, Clive Anderson, Ruby Wax, Rory McGrath, Andy Hamilton, Nigel Planer and Douglas Adams. The programme's producer was John Lloyd, who would also be at the helm for the decade's next big satirical comedy.

Spitting Image was predominantly the brainchild of Peter Fluck and Roger Law: two artists who had made a name for themselves creating puppet caricatures for newspapers such as *The Sunday Times*. Beginning in 1984, the programme (whose alternative titles included *Hands Up Mrs Thatcher* and *Rubber News*) spent the rest of the decade viciously lampooning celebrities and politicians, left, right and SDP Liberal Alliance.

Bringing these caricatures to life was no easy (or indeed cheap) task. The latex puppets cost £2000 a go to make and could require up to three puppeteers to work each one; each was two feet long, with a larger-than-life head (the puppets, that is, not the puppeteers). Each half-hour episode took at least three days to make, at an estimated cost of £250,000 a show. As well as the puppeteers, Fluck and Law employed a huge supporting cast: writers on the show included Richard Curtis, Ben Elton, Rob Grant and Doug Naylor (who would go on to write *Red Dwarf*), Ian Hislop, John O'Farrell, Andy Parsons and Jo Brand; impressionists, meanwhile, included Chris Barrie, Rory Bremner, Steve Coogan, Jon Culshaw, Hugh Dennis, Harry Enfield, Alistair McGowan and John Sessions. Actually, when you look at all the comedy talent that was involved, 250 grand suddenly doesn't seem so bad.

Well written, well spoken and well latexed, *Spitting Image* treated politicians, celebrities and royalty in a way that had never been seen on British television. Here were politicians as vicious caricatures: Margaret Thatcher as a deep-voiced man, Kenneth Baker as a slug, Norman Tebbit as a bovver boy, Edwina Currie as a vampire; on the opposition benches, Roy Hattersley's puppet more than put the spit into *Spitting Image*, while Denis Healey's eyebrows were the size of small badgers. The royal family, meanwhile, were given anything but the red-carpet treatment: Prince Philip was a gun-toting Greek, Prince Andrew a well-hung Lothario (the *Spitting Image* book included a naked double-page spread, complete with carefully positioned chipolatas); both the Queen Mother and Princess Margaret, meanwhile, were depicted as being just a little partial to the occasional swig or two. And foreign dignitaries were treated with no more reverence: the Pope was a sunglasses-wearing dude; Gorbachev's birthmark on his forehead became a hammer and sickle; Ronald Reagan's caricature, with his colouring-in books and children's toys, made even George W. Bush look like the school swot.

I loved *Spitting Image* when it started out, and I was certainly not alone. Although the programme had been aimed at an older and sophisticated audience, what it actually got was something much younger: the over-55s thought it was in bad taste, while the 12–34 age group loved it. It was this 'youth' profile that saved the programme from being cancelled, when the initial high costs and low viewing figures kept everything in the balance.

Soon the programme was so successful it was venturing out into all sorts of spin-offs: the accompanying book sold almost half a million copies; 120,000 rubber Margaret Thatchers for dogs to chew on were shifted; and then there was 'The Chicken Song', the single about putting deckchairs up your noses and pretending your name was Keith, which not only successfully spoofed Black Lace's 'Agadoo' but also ended up achieving what Black Lace never quite managed by reaching Number One. Refreshingly, the comedy songs were actually quite funny: the B-side to 'The Chicken Song' was the quite wonderful 'I've Never Met a Nice South African'. And who could forget the classic ZZ Top pastiche 'We've Got Beards'? Or the show marking the 1987 Conservative election victory with a group of brown-shirts singing the *Cabaret* number 'Tomorrow Belongs to Me'.

Even with all the talent at the producer's disposal, the sheer length of time it took to put the programme together meant that only so much topicality could be squeezed into the show; hence the songs and, as the series went on, the inclusion of an ever-increasing number of celebrities. That, combined with the fact that the initial shock factor had inevitably faded away, led to the perception by the end of the eighties that the programme wasn't quite as good as it used to be. One could argue that the writing wasn't as good as it had been at the beginning: certainly some of the key names had left the show by then, but at the same time those who were left were faced with the great task of upping the ante just as the big hitters of British politics (Nigel Lawson, Norman Tebbit) were making way for a tail order of talent (David Waddington, John Major). Satire is all about pricking the pomposity of those in power – and by the end of the decade *Spitting Image* had pretty much done all the big pricks. What followed afterwards was therefore always going to be a bit of a dead rubber.

There was only one case where the *Spitting Image* parodies had a particularly detrimental effect in the real world, and that concerned the Liberal leader David Steel and the SDP leader David Owen. David Steel was depicted as so diminutive he squeaked away and sat in David Owen's pocket; Owen, meanwhile, was portrayed as being unscrupulous and pulling the wool over his coalition partner's eyes at every given opportunity. This caricature made David Steel come across as both weak and the junior partner in their relationship: John O'Farrell, one of the programme's writers, suggested that this 'was one of the most important factors in the Liberal leader's decision to assert himself so vigorously after the 1987 general election and to try to force David Owen into a merger of the two parties'. This overcompensation led to the two men falling out and, ultimately, to the falling apart of their alliance.

This, however, was the exception. For all the having the Michael royally taken out of them, politicians by and large liked to appear on *Spitting Image*. The fact that a puppet had been made of them was seen as a symbol of public recognition: far better to be lampooned than not to be parodied at all. Indeed, several politicians so liked the satire they went as far as offering to help: Jeffrey Archer, for example, sent in tapes of himself speaking in order to improve the quality of the impressions of him; Michael Heseltine, meanwhile, got so many people asking him the whereabouts of his flak jacket (this being what his puppet always wore) that he tried to buy his puppet. After some negotiation, the programme agreed that he could have it for £7300 but only if he made the cheque payable to the Labour Party. Heseltine, unsurprisingly, refused.

Given how much politicians liked seeing themselves on the television, it always seems somehow surprising that they resisted letting cameras into the House of Commons for so long. It had first been trialled when Labour were in power back in 1964: for a fixed period cameras duly recorded proceedings, but MPs watched the footage and decided not to show it to the public. From then on, the issue of televising parliament came up repeatedly (eleven times over the next two decades) and was rejected every time. The main argument against was not dissimilar to the one that parents give to children about watching too much TV: that it would have a detrimental effect on the behaviour of those concerned. 'Parliament is a wonderful and unique institution,' said Quintin Hogg in one of the many debates. 'It is different in character after television is brought in.' The result, so it was said, would be the trivialization of parliament, with proceedings becoming 'info-tainment' as MPs hammed it up and played to the gallery. Television, another MP argued, would focus on the party leaders, with backbenchers ending up as little more than 'Cecil B. de Mille's chorus from *Samson and Delilah*'. Another concern was that the Commons would be turned into a television studio stuffed with lights, making the chamber incredibly and uncomfortably hot.

The counterargument, of course, was that MPs were our elected representatives and we had a right to watch what they got up to on our behalf, rather than having to rely on those nice crayon drawings you still get to show what's happened in court. By the end of the 1980s Britain was the only country in the European Community, as it was then, who did not televise parliamentary proceedings. Indeed, more than fifty countries across the world had already allowed the cameras in, including such liberal states as Communist China. ITN pointed out that the public gallery seated only 65 people; by contrast *News at Ten* got 12 million viewers. So televising it would mean that another 11,999,935 people got to see what was going on. Or, to put it another way, televising would be equivalent to filling the public gallery for the next 1300 years.

In February 1988 parliament finally voted to allow cameras in. After further debate and wrangling, a date was set — for the State Opening of Parliament on 21 November 1989. It was another of those 'historic' moments in eighties TV – though it was the sort of 'historic' moment that only BBC2 and Channel 4 found space in the schedules for (over on BBC1 was an old black-and-white Western; ITV, meanwhile, went with a quiz called *Tell the Truth* and the latest episode of the Australian soap *The Young Doctors*). Which felt a bit like television, having got what it wanted, was putting parliament in its place for taking so long.

The first person to speak on television in parliament was the back-bench Conservative MP Ian Gow. He marked the occasion by (a little uncharitably) making it clear he didn't think that the television cameras should be there: 'I have always voted against the televising of proceedings of this House, and expect that I always will.' He then talked about a letter he had received from an image consultancy, which in selling their services suggested that the impression one makes on television is due firstly to image (55 per cent), then body language (38 per cent) and finally what one is actually saying (7 per cent). Gow dismissed this as a 'preposterous assertion', but it doesn't seem that preposterous to me – rather like actually quite useful advice. Gow went on to quote from the letter, in which the consultancy guaranteed 'to improve your appearance through a personal and confidential image consultation. You will learn if you need a new hairstyle – and where to get it.'

At which point the House rocked with laughter, and for the first time viewers were allowed in on the joke. Ian Gow, you see, had even less hair than the man in the Hamlet cigar advert desperately trying to comb over his last remaining strands as he had his picture taken in a photo booth. The theme of hair (or lack thereof) was picked up by Labour leader Neil Kinnock, who admitted that he also suffered 'from a certain tonsorial difficulty'. He used the presence of the cameras to the full by pulling out of his pocket the first-ever parliamentary prop: 'I have been given something called *papier-poudre*, which looks to me like cerebral blotting papers, which apparently are for mopping one's head.' He offered this to Ian Gow as a 'fraternal' gesture and said that, should he ever be worried about being bald, he should remember that the deputy prime minister, the chancellor of the exchequer and the home secretary were proof that 'luxuriant grey hair is not necessarily evidence of wisdom'.

There was no doubt that the arrival of the cameras meant that MPs were more aware of how they came across. Ian Gow might not have taken up the image consultancy's offer, but more than 100 Tory MPs did take advice from one public-relations firm on how to appear 'concise, interesting and sincere'. Meanwhile a mirror appeared in the whip's office of the Liberal Democrats, so that MPs could check themselves before they went in. And female MPs competed with each other to wear the most eye-catching colours. On the opening day, Margaret Thatcher wore royal blue (and made a noticeable effort to come across as nice and listening), while six of her fellow female Tory MPs wore bright-red outfits, one wore yellow and another (Teresa Gorman) turned up in purple. Not that you'd know about the latter – no gentleman on the Tory benches was willing to offer her his seat, and she ended up standing at the back out of the way of the cameras.

All this aside, it soon became clear that the initial concerns about televising parliament were largely unfounded. The cameras might have distorted things a little in the beginning but, as the Bucks Fizz song put it, they never lied. The bright colours of the women's outfits might have been chosen for a bit of self-promotion, but they also served to highlight how predominantly white and male the House of Commons was. And, though MPs attempted to 'doughnut' people who were speaking (sitting round them in a circle, to make the chamber looked packed), the cutaway shots revealed just how empty the chamber was – and how often. Which showed why some MPs didn't want it televised and exactly why it should be.

Some MPs may have been concerned about how they were to look on TV, but they could at least take comfort in the fact that they would never come across quite as appallingly as the Conservative MP for the (then) fictional Yorkshire constituency of Haltemprice. The MP in question was Alan Beresford B'Stard, played by Rik Mayall in the ITV comedy *The New Statesman*. B'Stard was the youngest MP in the Commons and the one with the biggest majority – the latter being because both the Labour and SDP candidates were on life-support machines following a somewhat suspicious car accident.

Alan, as his name suggested, was a bit of a B'Stard, a character made up of all the worst excesses of Thatcherism. It wasn't his constituents he served, it was himself, at every given opportunity. His political views made Norman Tebbit look like Michael Foot: he was treasurer of the Keep Britain Nuclear group and secretary of Friends of South Africa; his *Who's Who* entry listed his pastimes as 'Dining out on other people's expenses' and 'Grinding the face of the poor'; his view on abortion was that 'ugly, stupid, poor people should not be allowed to have children'; and among his many campaigns was one to re-legalize slavery.

The show brought a bit of bite to television satire just as that of *Spitting Image* was beginning to fade. In fact, studio audiences found *The New Statesman* so funny that the recordings of the early shows repeatedly overran because of the amount of laughter. The show was consequently re-scripted to last just nineteen minutes, leaving five full minutes of laughter space in each episode. Preceding the televising of parliament, *The New Statesman* brought an educational element to proceedings, too, showing viewers what the House of Commons looked like. The programme's model chamber had originally been built for the TV version of Jeffrey Archer's *First Among Equals*, and had been hastily snapped up by the show's producers just as it was about to be dismantled.

A slightly older statesman, and an ever so slightly more subtle political caricature, was Jim Hacker MP, star of *Yes, Minister* and *Yes, Prime Minister*. The battleground here was less the House of Commons and more the corridors of Whitehall, the subject of the show being the eternal struggle between minister and mandarin. Jim Hacker, played by Paul Eddington, was the man in power – in theory. In practice the strings were pulled by his permanent secretary, Sir Humphrey Appleby, played brilliantly by Nigel Hawthorne, with private secretary Bernard Woolley (Derek Fowlds) usually the political piggy in the middle.

The programme followed a regular pattern of Jim Hacker trying to achieve something (say, an initiative on open government) and Sir Humphrey outmanoeuvring him and restoring the status quo. It was acutely well observed, and so hit home that it became one of Margaret Thatcher's favourite programmes. The prime minister and her press secretary even wrote a sketch themselves, which Paul Eddington and Nigel Hawthorne found themselves press-ganged into performing with her at an awards ceremony in 1984.

For me, *Yes, Minister* was always the pick of the political comedies, though that might have been partly because I never quite forgave Rik Mayall for *Filthy, Rich and Catflap*. So sharp was the writing of *Yes, Minister* that the shows were developed into a series of wonderful companion books, with the scripts redrawn as memos and letters and minutes of meetings (*The New Statesman* equivalent was just a collection of the scripts). It was this attention to detail that helps explain why Sir Humphrey has lasted as shorthand for civil servants, while expenses-fiddling MPs are just called bastards, rather than B'Stards.

Satire is at its best when there is something substantial to aim at: the same is true of investigative journalism. At the beginning of the 1980s the Thatcher government had found itself at loggerheads with the BBC over the Falklands War. As the decade neared its end, its ire had switched to a different station and coverage of a different conflict. By 1988 ITV had already emphasized the independent part of its name by being unafraid to ruffle political feathers with *Spitting Image* and *The*

New Statesman. This same independent spirit was displayed when it broadcast perhaps the most controversial documentary of the decade, on a subject that was anything but a laughing matter.

Death on the Rock was a special edition of *This Week*, ITV's long-running *Panorama*-style current-affairs programme, which was made by the network's London weekday-television company, Thames Television. The edition was the culmination of a seven-week investigation into the events of 6 March 1988, when three members of the IRA – Danny McCann, Sean Savage and Mairéad Farrell – were shot dead by the SAS.

The following bare bones of the story are among the few details that remained uncontested. McCann, Savage and Farrell were, it was claimed, plotting to set off a huge car bomb in Gibraltar – its target being the changing of the guard outside the Convent, the official residence of the Governor of Gibraltar. Having crossed the border from Spain, the trio had set up the first part of the operation: Savage left a white Renault car near where the ceremony would take place, in order to ensure that they had a parking space they could use for the car-bomb car (back in Spain, the trio had a hire car hidden in the basement of a multi-storey car park, packed with explosives, ready for the switch). Having parked the car, Savage then met up with McCann and Farrell, who had entered Gibraltar separately, and the trio began their way back to the border on foot. As they reached the forecourt of a (closed) Shell petrol station, a number of cars pulled up and the trio were intercepted by the SAS. Within minutes the three had been shot dead, and the British special-service unit was being whisked away as quickly as it had arrived.

The official version of events is simple in its clarity. Having checked out the white Renault once Savage was out of sight, intelligence officers were convinced that this was the car that contained the bomb. When approached by the SAS, the IRA members made 'threatening movements' – moving hands towards pockets and handbags. The assumption was that the IRA members were probably not only armed, but also concealing a remote-control 'button' that when pressed would detonate the explosives. As such, the SAS had no choice but to shoot them immediately, rather than go through the palaver of attempting to arrest them.

As Thames Television started to research the documentary, however, they came across what they felt were a number of significant problems in the official version of events. Firstly the white Renault: it was initially claimed that it contained a 500lb car bomb, but it was discovered to have no explosives hidden in it at all. What is more, it was unclear how the intelligence officers could have come to the conclusion that the car had contained such a device. The quick check here was to see how weighted down the car was — if the boot was packed with explosives, then the body of the car would be sitting low against the wheels. The white Renault, however, not only contained no explosives but also did not look like a car that might contain any explosives.

Secondly, even had the car contained the explosives, the chances of the IRA members having a workable remote-control detonator on them was in itself remote. By the time the SAS caught up with them, the trio were well out of range for such a device to work — especially given the hilly and built-up terrain between them and the car. Perhaps unsurprisingly, given that there was no bomb in the car, no such 'button' was found on the IRA members. And the trio had no weapons of any description on them: it transpired that they were completely unarmed.

As for the shootings themselves, the programme-makers tracked down a number of eyewitnesses, and their versions of events differed markedly from the official account. Geoffrey Howe, then foreign secretary, told the House of Commons that the IRA members had 'made movements which led the military personnel . . . to conclude their own lives and the lives of others were at risk'. By contrast, none of the eyewitnesses that Thames had tracked down had seen any such 'movements'. In fact they saw the exact opposite: one witness saw Farrell and McCann raise their hands up, as if in surrender, before being shot dead. Savage, meanwhile, was seen gunned down from behind as he attempted to escape.

By speaking to experts and corroborating the accounts of independent witnesses at the scene, Thames had discovered that the official version of events was at best confused in a 'fog of war' sort of a way, and at worst somewhat profligate with the truth. The implication of their findings was that British officers were acting under a 'shoot-to-kill' policy, something that contravened all sorts of conventions and tenets of natural justice, and was not the sort of thing that democratic governments were meant to get up to. *Death on the Rock*, therefore, had all the hallmarks of high-quality, hard-hitting television journalism – first-hand testimony and juicy revelations that would make any democratic government deeply uncomfortable.

The government response to the programme was to attempt to stop it being broadcast. Geoffrey Howe rang the chairman of the IBA and asked him to pull the programme. His argument was that *Death on the Rock* amounted to trial by television and would prejudice an inquest that had been set up in Gibraltar to examine the killings. However, the IBA robustly turned the request down on the grounds of free speech, arguing that it was confident the programme had been properly made and that broadcasting it would not prejudice the inquest. Firstly, the programme wasn't being shown in Gibraltar, where the inquest was taking place, and anyway, an inquest is not the same thing as a trial: with no one being charged with anything, the government's attempts to stop the programme looked more than a little bit wobbly.

Reaction to *Death on the Rock* was as wide apart as the two competing accounts of events. The government was absolutely furious, condemned its broadcast roundly, and was strongly backed up by its supporters in the press. The *Sun* was one of several Tory-supporting papers who attempted to destroy the credibility of one of the programme's main witnesses, Carmen Proetta, who it described as 'the tart of Gib' and claimed she'd made up what she'd seen because she hated the British (Proetta would go on to successfully sue the newspaper for libel, and won substantial damages). The television industry, by contrast, awarded the programme-makers the BAFTA for Documentary of the Year.

The split verdict of events rumbled on. The inquest that Geoffrey Howe had been so worried about in Gibraltar backed up the official version of events. Thames Television, meanwhile, set up its own inquiry into the making of the programme, led by a former cabinet minister and leading QC. Their report vindicated the programme-makers, describing them as acting 'in good faith' and their research as 'painstaking'. The government 'utterly rejected' the findings of the report. Many years later, in *The Defence of the Realm: The Authorized History of MI5*, author Christopher Andrews promised to reveal 'what really happened . . . in Gibraltar in March 1988'. His book, however, merely backed up the original government account.

There was one final casualty in the story of the Gibraltar killings – that of Thames Television itself. The programme, and the IBA's defiance in broadcasting it, was seen by some commentators as the catalyst behind the government's subsequent decision to shake up the ITV network. In 1991 the company lost its long-running London franchise to Carlton Television, a process described by Peter Kellner in the *Independent* as 'an exercise in ideological vengeance . . . to punish the company that made *Death on the Rock*'. Or maybe they just didn't bid enough money. Whichever was true, one of the great names of British broadcasting had disappeared.

All of which sounds rather serious, and I think it probably is. Because one of the things that is essential in making a democratic society tick is free speech and the freedom of the media – however uncomfortable that might be for the government of the day. Once we have cabinet ministers leaning on broadcasters to pull programmes, we're at the top of a slope that starts with the truth getting trampled on and ends up with censorship. It's true that in the case of *Death on the Rock* the three people who were shot were IRA members plotting to kill scores of people. But the people who get shot in such situations are not always the right ones: in 2005 the police followed Jean Charles de Menezes and shot him dead at Stockwell tube station. The official version of what happened that day sounded eerily similar to that of the Gibraltar killings: the suspect was acting suspiciously and resisting arrest; the police were worried that he had a remote-control device with which he could detonate a bomb at any second. And, also like the Gibraltar killings, there were plenty of eyewitness accounts that diverged substantially from what the authorities were presenting to the media.

There was, of course, one huge difference between the two cases: Jean Charles de Menezes was not a terrorist – he was an ordinary member of the public. Not only had the police made a tragic mistake by targeting him, but they then compounded that mistake by offering an account that was at odds with what actually happened. The fact that such incidents can still occur, and that the official response to them remains to deny and disseminate, is precisely why it is so important that there are people making investigative programmes like *Death on the Rock* – and why the freedom to broadcast them is not something with which a government should ever try to interfere.

After the break, we discover a shocking piece of vandalism in the garden, get the hiccups from some 'fast-food TV', and wonder whether the dish of the day is going to be round or square . . .

Ad Break

Real Fires

Home sweet home, and the sitting room is aglow with the warmth of a real fire. As 'Will You Still Love Me Tomorrow?' plays softly in the background, the door opens and in walks a soppy sort of bulldog, who waddles over to sit in front of the fire, gazing adoringly at its flames. Before long, the door is opening again: this time it is the house cat, a black fur-ball of a moggy, the sort with the glint in its eye that tells us who is really in charge. Rather than there being any time-honoured cat/dog face-off, however, over she pads and, with an affectionate peck on the cheek, settles down next to him. Hold on a second – the ark is still unloading: scuttling across the floor now is a small white mouse. So seduced is the cat by the glow of the fire that she leans forwards to give the mouse a kiss too. 'Now you know what people see in a real fire,' is the closing strap-line.

*　　*　　*

ctually, no. I don't really know what people see in a real fire, because I haven't actually seen any people – just a dog, a cat and a mouse. And I'm not even convinced that this reaction is representative of what such animals see in a real fire. I've got a real fire and a cat and, should a mouse be foolish enough to scuttle across towards her in the hope of a kiss, I'm pretty sure he'd be sent away not so much empty-handed as emptied generally.

All I can think is that this real fire isn't in just any old house. The only possible reason for the animals behaving as they are must be that this is the home of Barbara Woodhouse, eighties animal-trainer extra-ordinaire. No one, and certainly no animal, messes with Woodhouse. If she snaps, 'Walkies!' you walk. If she orders, 'Sit!' you sit. And that's just the owners. In this instance, Barbara must be in the kitchen off camera, shouting, 'Fireplace!' and 'Kiss!' to her furry friends. It's just fortunate that the cameramen were all headphoned up and couldn't hear her – otherwise Channel 4 might have had to get out one of their red triangles.

Episode Nineteen

'I'll have an E please, Bob'

What B best sums up how television changed in the 1980s? That'll be *Blockbusters*, Bob. Beginning in 1983, the programme was an early-evening general-knowledge quiz programme, in which – for reasons that always seemed rather spurious – two sixth-formers did battle against one. Apparently this was 'to test the old adage that two heads are better than one', except that the one head had to get only four questions right to the two heads' five in order to win. So quite how that was meant to be a scientific test I'm not entirely sure. The idea probably made more sense in its original version in America, where the duos were usually related rather than just friends.

The host of *Blockbusters* was Bob Holness, who sat underneath a large polystyrene effigy of Zeus and looked a bit like William G. Stewart would if he'd been through a mangle. Holness, it was widely and erroneously claimed, played the saxophone solo in Gerry

Rafferty's 'Baker Street'. The claim actually started out as a joke in the *NME*, but slowly snowballed into 'truth' as it got passed on – its urban-legend status helped by the fact that there was no credit for the solo on the record itself, and that the presenter of *Blockbusters* in America was also called Rafferty. (The solo, if you're interested, was actually played by someone called Raphael Ravenscroft. He got paid £27 and the cheque bounced.)

Back on *Blockbusters*, the contestants sat under more polystyrene effigies (these varied, but included worthy figures like Isambard Kingdom Brunel and Mother Teresa) and tried not to worry about them falling down as they did battle over a grid of twenty hexagons. Each yellow hexagon contained a letter of the alphabet, which was the initial letter of the answer to the question. So, to give the example of the very first question ever asked on *Blockbusters*, 'What S is the correct name for the pedal of the piano, sometimes called the damper pedal?' Actually, Bob didn't even get as far as saying 'damper pedal', because at that point Ruth from Felixstowe buzzed in to give the correct answer, which is 'sustaining pedal'. No, I didn't know that either. As Ruth was part of the duo, the hexagon went blue and formed the first link in what they'd hope would be a winning line of five from left to right. Had the single contestant, Alasdair from Newbury, got the right answer, the hexagon would have gone white and he'd have made a start in trying to make a line of four from top to bottom.

Each correct answer won the contestant £5. Which in theory meant that you could go all the way round the board, picking up as much cash as possible, though no one ever seemed to do this. Perhaps the prize for winning was too great – get through this stage of the game and you'd be given a shot at the 'Gold Run'. Here you had sixty seconds to get a line across the board from left to right to win yourself a prize. Rather than single letters, these hexagons had a few letters in each to make things more interesting. So you might get ESC – what quiz show was hosted by Paul Daniels? – or COD – what phrase was shouted out to contestants on *The Price is Right*? – or TB – what would Bob Holness say when you got across the board? The Gold Run was great television in that players got only one shot at each hexagon: get a wrong answer and the hexagon would disappear, which meant having to attempt a more circuitous route in an ever-decreasing amount of time. Contestants were allowed to play a total of five Gold Runs before being made to retire, and the prizes would get significantly better with each one – usually culminating in a holiday abroad.

For the most part *Blockbusters* was a quiz for the clever ones from school, coupled with just a cloying tinge of cuteness. As with Sebastian in *Brideshead Revisited*, contestants would happily bring with them a teddy bear or fluffy toy as a lucky mascot. As the programme's closing credits ran, the studio audience would partake in something called the 'Hand Jive': an embarrassing little Pat-a-Cake-style routine that consisted of clapping hands on knees, clapping hands, then wafting one hand over the other, a bit of one potato, two potato, three potato, four, and finally twirling the index finger of one hand round while that arm's elbow rested in the palm of the other hand (the second half of this routine being directly lifted from the one Bucks Fizz did for 'Making Your Mind Up').

Even more than this, what summed up the innocence of the programme were the laughs that came from the audience if one of the contestants asked, 'Can I have a P please, Bob?' No contestant worth their salt would have felt their *Blockbusters* experience complete without having asked Bob this. But, as the decade went on, there became a second letter that also elicited a laugh from the audience. It was a different sort of laugh to the one that the P joke generated: it was coming from a smaller section of the audience, and was both lower and a little bit more knowing – schoolboy puerility having been overtaken by a savvier, more streetwise sense of humour. For the cooler contestants, the thing to say now was: 'I'll have an E please, Bob?'

*   *   *

It wasn't just me who grew up in the 1980s: it seemed childhood did too. The innocence of early youth was less lasting and the real world was more impinging. This became apparent in the most innocuous of places, even in such hallowed television sanctuaries as the *Blue Peter* garden. In one famous episode in the mid-1980s, mumsy presenter Janet Ellis addressed the audience with the sort of severe-teacher's look that let you know as soon as you saw it that someone was about to get it big time – and you just hoped it wasn't you.

'Vandals broke into the *Blue Peter* garden,' Janet announced, adding in true Enid Blyton fashion: 'and caused rather a lot of damage.' These hooligans were clearly without scruples: 'One really cruel thing they did was to pour fuel oil into the fishpond . . . If that wasn't enough they trampled on the bedding plants as well.'

Not the bedding plants as well? The bastards.

Fellow presenter Peter Duncan continued the bad news: 'The vandals then broke our lovely ornamental urn given to us by Mr Taylor from Barnet, and then smashed up our sundial and callously threw it into the pond.'

I love the use of the word 'callously' there, which – if I might be so bold – was a little bit of editorializing on the part of Peter Duncan. I'd personally wager that the sundial was thrown into the pond *with* feeling rather than without.

'It's very sad,' Janet commented, 'to think that some people take such pleasure from harming their fellow human beings.'

It is very sad indeed, Janet, to think that some people take pleasure from harming their fellow human beings. However, as far as I am aware, no human beings were actually hurt in this bout of vandalism. Their feelings maybe; their bodies not.

Meanwhile Percy Thrower, the *Blue Peter* gardener, was slightly less reserved on the subject of what had happened: 'People who do this sort of thing must be mentally ill, mustn't they, Janet?'

Well, I'm no expert on mental illness myself, Percy, so can't really comment from a position of authority. But then I'd also hazard a guess that you're not speaking about mental illness from a position of authority either, in which case my opinion is no less valid than yours. So, for what it's worth, I don't suppose the people who vandalized the garden were mentally ill: they were probably just a bit bored. Unfortunately, as the culprits of this crime have never been brought to light, I don't think that it is possible to verify this one way or another. Years later, there was a suggestion that Premier League footballers Les Ferdinand and Dennis Wise, both of whom grew up in West London, might have been involved. This suggestion actually came from Les Ferdinand himself, who in an interview said that he helped the culprits over the wall. However, he claimed in a subsequent interview that he'd only said this as a joke. So who knows?

What the attack did symbolize was the way in which the modern world was making its presence felt, whether television liked it or not. The cocoon of innocence that television created for children was creaking itself open, and reality was beginning to creep in. Then again, maybe the truth was that the cruelties of adult life had always been there but had just been brushed under the carpet until now. After all, one of the few things in the garden that the vandals didn't touch was the statue of Petra, the long-standing *Blue Peter* dog, who'd died in 1977. Except, of course, that Petra hadn't died in 1977 at all. She'd actually snuffed it shortly after being introduced to the *Blue Peter* audience as a puppy. Rather than upset the nation's children, the programme had simply buried the puppy quietly (and without a large bronze statue), and scoured London until they'd found a similar-looking replacement.

Which begs an interesting question: if the *Blue Peter* garden had been vandalized in the early 1960s, would the BBC have protected the nation's children and not told them? And if a newly introduced *Blue Peter* puppy had suddenly died in the 1980s, would Janet Ellis have sat down for another straight-to-camera piece? Maybe it wasn't just children but also adults' attitudes to them that were changing.

Another part of children's television that came up, quite literally, smack against the adult world was that of *Grange Hill*. The long-running school drama series had always been a little bit controversial, featuring run-of-the mill school issues like bullying or whether people who ate free school meals had to sit at separate tables. One episode I vividly remember watching was when pupil Jeremy Irvine died in a swimming-pool accident, his dead body floating lifelessly at the bottom of the water. There was a touch of the seventies public-information film about it – see what happens when you mess around unsupervised? – but it was undoubtedly a haunting and shocking scene.

The pupil who had been messing around with Jeremy Irvine was a young Zammo MacGuire. I don't think the link was ever made between that accident and his subsequent and controversial battle with heroin addiction, but looking back it feels difficult not to see the latter as a coping mechanism for dealing with the drowning. Heck, *I* still had the willies about the incident, and I was only watching it on the telly. Zammo was right there, and probably had to deal with freaking out every time he had a bath. No wonder he started smack-ing up.

When word got out that *Grange Hill* was going to have its very own heroin addict, the papers were both outraged ('TV fury over *Grange Hill* junkie') and inquisitive ('Who will the junkie be?'). There followed something of a chicken-and-egg debate between teachers and the BBC about who influenced who. The teachers claimed that the programme spread 'bad practices': 'The schoolchildren end up behaving like the ones they see on TV,' one teachers' union told the *Sunday Mirror*. The BBC's response was that they were reflecting real life: 'We want to get to the kids before the pushers reach them at school gates.'

Maybe it was different down in London, but certainly in York the programmers beat the pushers by a country-bumpkin mile. I've got to be honest and say that, when *Grange Hill* started the whole heroin storyline, I didn't know the first thing about drugs. I'd thought that Grandmaster Flash's song 'White Lines (Don't Do It)' was about the perils of overtaking on a dangerous road. When the rappers shouted 'Freebase!' I'd assumed it was the signal for the bass player to improvise. And, while there was always a bit of moistness behind my ears when growing up (it pains me to tell you that until he died I didn't actually know that Freddie Mercury was gay), when it came to drugs I was certainly not the only one. I still remember the day a couple of years later when two classmates got caught smoking joints outside school. As they were being roundly reprimanded, it quickly became clear that the issue was that they were smoking – not what they were puffing away on. The teachers who'd caught them simply did not have a clue what cannabis was.

All of which perhaps proves *Grange Hill's* point, but undoubtedly the heroin storyline was a shot in the arm for my drugs education. In years gone by, the powers that be had hidden away dead puppies so as not to alarm the younger generations. Now this self-same childhood innocence was being re-branded as dangerous ignorance. And, as I knew from those adverts on the telly about AIDS, you could die from that in the eighties. It all felt rather unfair: barely had my parents finished explaining about the birds and the bees before I was being told in no uncertain terms to steer clear of the birds or face certain death: 'There is now a danger that has become a threat to us all,' boomed the government advert. 'It is a deadly disease for which there is no known cure . . .' The only unknown left in my scared new world was whether the virus or the addiction was going to do for me first.

As it turned out, it was possible to have sex or take drugs without handing over your life in the process. For all the strength of the *Grange Hill* storyline (and it was undoubtedly powerful and hard-hitting TV), it was fatally undermined by the sheer naffness of the accompanying 'Just Say No' campaign and (s)hit single – complete with middle section (c)rap. The BBC's supplier of this was a notorious American Mrs Big (real name Nancy Reagan), who had already pushed her product to schoolchildren in America and was now keen to expand into new markets. 'Just say no' was a simple message but, by painting drugs as such a black-and-white issue, it also seemed a dreadfully simplistic one. It treated children like children, just when children were starting to be something else. As the subsequent sniggers on *Blockbusters* demonstrated, it was a campaign that did not succeed.

The person who did know how to attract the attention of young people was not Nancy Reagan but Janet Street-Porter. Janet Street-Porter in those days came across as a sort of punky version of Esther Rantzen: she'd conducted the first-ever television interview with the Sex Pistols on *The London Weekend Show* and had co-hosted both *The Six O'Clock Show* with Michael Aspel and *Saturday Night People* with Russell Harty. By 1985 she was going out with Tony James, who used to be the bass player in Billy Idol's punk band, Generation X, and was about to inflict on the world his new musical outfit, Sigue Sigue Sputnik. Sporting brightly coloured streaks in her hair and rubber mini-skirts, Street-Porter was a regular at the band's concerts.

In answer to that *Smash Hits* question, the nation had quickly decided that Sigue Sigue Sputnik were very much codswallop rather than the future of rock and roll. And yet, while the band might not have nudged popular music any further forwards, something of their approach did live on – just in a different medium. For ultimately the music mattered less than the style: theirs was an image that drew on films such as *Blade Runner* and *A Clockwork Orange*; their videos, meanwhile, were programmes on 'Sputnik Network Television' and were superimposed with a mixture of computer graphics, logos and slogans; their songwriting had a similar cut-and-paste approach, which included samples from all corners of popular culture; they attempted to reinvent things in what they thought was a modern way, such as putting adverts between the songs on their albums; all of which was carried out in a blaze of hype and publicity directed by their Ray-Bans-wearing publicist, Magenta de Vine.

While Sputnik Network Television didn't take off, Janet Street-Porter's *Network 7*, hosted by Magenta De Vine, did. This youth (or 'yoof') programme was a self-styled 'channel within a channel', where 'news is entertainment and entertainment is news'. Another one of their slogans was 'Tomorrow's news today', which basically suggested that tomorrow's news (i.e., news now) would all be entertainment. Which, as it turns out, wasn't far off the mark. Filmed from a former banana warehouse by the Thames, which would eventually be knocked down to make way for Canary Wharf, *Network 7* went out on Sunday mornings on Channel 4 and was an attempt to tackle topical topics in a way that would appeal to a younger audience. This involved what then seemed like an innovative mix of fast-cutting camera shots, often from unusual and wonky angles, lots of music, and so many graphics it was almost like there was a permanent ticker-tape of trivia flashing across the screen. It was fast-moving, fast-paced and dismissed by some as 'fast-food TV'. Janet Street-Porter dismissed that criticism, saying, 'When people complain about that I just tell them they're too old.'

What the criticism was about, and what the style was drawing on, were two areas that connected directly with a younger, rather than an older audience: computer games and pop videos. The switchback style also chimed with the beginnings of a flicking culture: the arrival of the remote control meant that people were now zapping between channels instead of resting on one; the launch of the compact disc again meant that people could flick through to the song they wanted rather than listening to the whole side of an album before changing over. Not for the last time, there were mumblings about this leading to shorter attention spans, which – also not for the last time – missed the point: there was still plenty of information being presented; it was just being packaged in a different way.

The 'electronic tabloid' labels were perhaps more accurate in terms of what *Network 7* was actually showing: the programme wasn't afraid to tackle difficult issues, with results that were often shocking in more than one sense of the word. On one occasion the programme featured a woman having cosmetic surgery live. On another they interviewed a man on Death Row in Louisiana, and ran a phone vote among viewers asking whether or not they thought he should be killed. (They did.) But for every interview with teenage prostitutes in Swindon there was an idea such as leaving a group of celebrities in the middle of a tropical nowhere to see whether they'd survive or shout, 'Get me out of here!'

Network 7 was one of those programmes whose influence was far bigger than its actual audience. It wasn't long before Janet Street-Porter was poached to be Youth Programmes Editor by the BBC. At the time, the BBC had put the nation's teenagers in the hands of Jonathan King, with his shows *Entertainment USA* and (in retrospect) the unfortunately titled *No Limits*. Street Porter cancelled these and set up another of her channels within a channel: *Def II*, complete with barcode logo. Magenta de Vine came across from Channel 4 to join her, and programmes ranged from the *Rough Guide* travel shows to the harder-hitting *Reportage* and music programmes such as *Snub* and Antoine de Caunes' *Rapido*.

Back on Channel 4, Yoof TV was spreading its teenage tentacles into the late evening. In 1989 it launched *Club X*, a programme that promised 'ninety power-packed minutes of music, art, drama, fashion and culture'. What we actually got was '*The South Bank Show* in Stringfellow's', as one newspaper put it. The show was broadcast live from the self-styled Club X, and – like in any nightclub – you couldn't hear properly what anyone was saying. Unable to comprehend the reasoning behind, say, a visual-art performance of naked women daubing themselves in blue paint, the viewing public saw less of a visual-art performance and more just some naked women, daubing themselves in blue paint. Which did sort of work as late-night TV, though not perhaps as Channel 4 had originally intended.

For all the deriding of Yoof TV as a concept, its influence has survived long after the original programmes had bitten the dust. It paved the way for a good chunk of television in the early 1990s, from Terry Christian and *The Word* to Chris Evans and *The Big Breakfast*, and its influence can be felt in all manner of programmes, be that in the way that presenters walk about when talking on camera or the increasing interest in popular culture as proper news. And as for the suggestion that it has reduced the attention spans of the audience, all I can say is . . . Hang on – I'm sure it'll come back to me in a second.

There was one other aspect of the direction in which television was heading that *Network 7* also managed to correctly predict. The show's title sequence (and also its logo) was based around a satellite dish – in the opening credits to the show it was orbiting the earth, sending back down a selection of images in a crackly electric-blue beam of the sort that a Ghostbuster might zap a Stay-Puft Marshmallow Man with. As the decade drew to a close, it did so with two rival companies offering to make this title sequence a reality and beam television programmes down from space.

One day at breakfast in 1989, I was flicking through the *Guardian* when I spotted a full-page advert headed 'Four ways of persuading your parents to pay for a channel they'll hate'. The advert was pushing a music channel called The Power Station, and in true Yoof TV style was sticking it to traditional TV: 'From Merseybeat to heavy metal, glam rock to punk, Britain has originated most of music's main trends,' the advert suggested, perhaps overplaying its hand a fraction (the blues? Soul? Rock and roll, anyone?). 'Which makes it all the more surprising that we've put up with music that has all the freshness and vitality of a re-released compilation.'

The advert did have a point there. In 1989 the Brit Awards had been hosted by Fleetwood Mac drummer Mick Fleetwood and page-three model turned pop 'singer' Sam Fox. It had been excruciating: a new Little and Large double act who were every bit as unfunny as the real thing.

'Isn't it about time,' the advert continued, appealing directly to the cooler part of the *Blockbusters* audience, 'that house music was given a fair hearing?'

I wasn't too sure about that myself, but a brand-new music channel had to be a good thing. Apart from the house music, it was going to play 'pop not pap' and lots of British bands because European music was 'bland'. The Power Station wouldn't 'just be endless videos back to back' – that's a shame, I thought, before being flattered to be told that 'you've got too much between the ears for that'. Not much more, I thought, dreaming wistfully about having MTV pumped into my living room.

So how did I pick up this amazing new channel? The Power Station was one of five channels being launched by a new company called British Satellite Broadcasting. BSB were about to start broadcasting a whole handful of new channels, which would be transmitted via satellite to a dish on the side of your house. The advert's wheeze was that, as a music-loving teenager, I should deny the existence of The Power Station and simply tell my parents about the other four channels on offer (Galaxy, the entertainment channel; Now, a 'channel for living', whatever that was; The Movie Channel, which was dedicated to movies; and The Sports Channel, which, well, you've probably got the idea by now). Hmm, I thought, considering the advert's suggested tactics for a moment. What were the chances of getting my parents to agree to a big white dish on the front of the house, and to sign off not only on having more television in the house but to pay for the privilege as well? My one attempt at persuading parents on the merits of satellite television lasted all of four words.

'Dad, could we—'

'No.'

As so often happens when it comes to new technology, British Satellite Broadcasting weren't the only satellite network trying in vain for the Bromley's shilling. In February 1989 Rupert Murdoch had launched his own company, Sky Television. This was offering four channels – Eurosport instead of The Sports Channel, Sky Movies instead of The Movies Channel, Sky Channel instead of Galaxy and Sky News in place of a 'channel for living' (whatever that was). Not only was the choice of channels not quite as good (Rupert was clearly not a fan of house music), but neither was the picture quality. As well as that, the size of dish with which you needed to embarrass your-selves on the front of your house was far bigger: BSB's receiver, by contrast, wasn't just smaller – in fact it wasn't even a dish at all but a 'square aerial' or 'squarial', which would look a bit like someone had mistakenly stuck a bathroom tile on the side of your house.

Television in the eighties was ending the decade as it had begun, with a battle between competing formats. At the start of the eight-ies, the fight had been between the two rival video recorders on offer – Betamax and VHS. Betamax was the critic's choice, with the perception being that it offered superior recording quality (in fact, the difference between the two was fairly minimal, especially on an aver-age television: the perceived difference was as much to do with the relative advertising campaigns). The one actual difference between the two formats had been in the length of tapes originally on offer – Betamax cassettes were only an hour long, compared to two for VHS, which meant that the latter became the preferred choice for video rentals as you could usually get a whole film on one cassette. By the eighties the tape-length difference between the formats had disap-peared, but by then the damage had been done: VHS had its nose in front (about 70 per cent to 30 per cent), a fact reflected in the number of films on offer at your local Blockbuster.

There is a second anecdotal argument for VHS's success, which is that (as with many technological innovations) pornography played its role – apparently it was widely available on VHS but not on Betamax. I don't really know about that, but I don't think that pornography had much to do with Sky's success over BSB. In this case it was more to do with the fact that, while BSB – a bit like Betamax – had the perceived better package, technical problems with the squarial delayed the launch. By the time BSB finally began, its cheaper VHS of a rival had already made a head start. There followed one of those extremely expensive stand-offs, as most of the nation waited to see who was going to win before taking the plunge. Ultimately the result went Rupert's way: having both lost eye-watering sums of money, the two companies agreed to merge. In November 1990 BSB and Sky became BSkyB. Which might sound like a draw, but the new company was to be marketed as Sky and, with the two satellite formats incompatible, the squarial was dropped in favour of Rupert's dish.

From wanting a P to wanting an E, television was growing up. It was simply growing too – as well as the new channels on offer from satellite, there was more television on terrestrial TV than ever before. Gone were the days when daytime television was dominated by schools programmes and *Pages from Ceefax*. Now BBC and ITV were running competing viewer-friendly schedules, with rival live studio debates (*Kilroy* versus *The Time The Place*), rival coffee-morning magazine shows (*Good Morning with Anne and Nick* versus *This Morning with Richard and Judy*) and rival game shows (*Going for Gold* versus, er, *Lucky Ladders*).

Gone, too, were the nights when all that happened was that the national anthem would be played and you had to go to bed. Channel 4's discussion show *After Dark* continued on and on until either the debate dried up or Oliver Reed embarrassed himself with one of the other guests. Meanwhile, in 1988, ITV began broadcasting through the night for the first time: it might not always have been great televi-sion (*America's Top Ten*? *Videopix*? *Jobfinder*?) but it was nice to see the insomniacs thrown a bone at last.

Since 1980 television had taken me from being a small child to being someone on the verge — in theory at least — of adulthood. We'd been through a lot together: royal weddings and greasy squat thrusts, shoulder pads and pre-teen pop stars, Stetson hats and breakfast rodents, Jump Jets and talking cars. The rickety old Bromley set had been the family equivalent of the fifth Beatle: a four-channelled friend who'd never let us down. For ten years we had relentlessly switched from BBC1 to BBC2, from ITV to Channel 4 and every combination in between. As we'd flicked back and forth, like we were Janet Street-Porter directing *Network 7*, the TV had always been there to do our bidding. Until, with the decade over, it decided it could take no more.

For my seventeenth birthday, in December 1989, my parents (with a slightly anguished look in their eyes) gave me driving lessons as a present. There followed a succession of shouty late evenings in empty superstore car parks as my father tried to stop me burning out his clutch. After a few lessons he reluctantly agreed to let me loose on the open road, which would involve me stop-starting round the block and him clinging to the handle above the passenger door as though his life depended on it.

On one particular evening, I'd just turned into our street when I noticed a fire engine, lights flashing and siren blaring, doing the same at the opposite end of the road.

'You'll have to pull over and let it through,' Dad said, pointing to a space.

I did what I was told, pulled over to the pavement on the left, and waited. And waited. For, rather than bombing past us in a blaze of red and blue, the fire engine was actually slowing down. In fact, it had stopped in the middle of the road. About half the way down the street. Directly outside our house.

'Shit,' my father said, for once in his life eschewing 'sugarooney' as his choice of swear word. He jumped out of the car and I followed suit. The first thing we saw was my mother, running down the road towards us like a suburban version of Edvard Munch's *The Scream*. Behind her, our house had turned itself into the set of *London's Burning*. There was the regulation small crowd of onlookers gathering to watch, a succession of firemen readying themselves with oxygen masks, and our home doing its best impression of one of Hannibal Smith's cigars.

The good news was that everyone had got out alive. Helen and Katherine were both fine, if a little bit on the chilly side. Joff was out at 'basketball practice' (I say 'basketball practice' because he wasn't actually at basketball practice at all. But that's another story). Everyone was accounted for, with one important exception.

'It's the television,' Helen explained. 'It caught fire.'

The Bromleys, it transpired, had changed channels once too often. The endless flicking had finally been too much for the telly – with one of its internal components starting to smell funny, then starting to smoke, then bursting into flames. Although the fireman had stopped the house burning down, there was nothing they could do for the TV, which, in a defiant final closedown (and one without a playing of the national anthem), had taken the sitting room with it. So fierce had been its white-dot fury that the light switch on the other side of the room had completely melted. Gone were the chairs I grew up watching TV on, gone too was the video recorder and my fledgling VHS collection. My mother's entire collection of literature, which had always looked down on the TV with disdain, had been reduced to nothing but a few burned pages.

As it turned out, our television, a bit like San Francisco, had been built on a fault. We learned later that the manufacturer in question had put one of those recall adverts in the newspapers, but we'd been too busy watching the TV to notice it. The day after the fire, we had the company's UK managing director on the phone. He sounded quite keen that we didn't ring Anne Robinson on *Watchdog* or anything, and in return was offering us a blank cheque to redecorate the house and a brand-new state-of-the-art television as a replacement.

To begin with my mother did not want anything made by that manufacturer in the house ever again. I could see her point, but on the other hand this was a far nicer television set than any my dad would have bought. It had – gasp! – a remote control. And – double gasp! – Ceefax. The Bromleys had a chance to enter the nineties without being a decade behind the rest of the country, and it was one I wasn't going to turn down.

'If we have a television remote control,' I casually suggested, 'then we won't be doing all the flicking that caused the old television to catch fire.'

This, it so happened, was the winning argument. Mum got a new book collection and the rest of us got a new set to 'Ooh' and 'Aah' at. The set was so fancy that to start with it didn't feel like part of the family. But then the sliding bit on the back of the remote control, where the batteries go in, got broken from being repeatedly played around with. Dad got his black masking tape out to stick it back together, and it started to feel like one of us. We'd finally joined the modern world, and found ourselves pondering perennial modern-world questions, such as why the remote control is always tidied away on to the top of the TV.

That, then, was the eighties that was. As the Bromleys settled down on their new sofa, in their newly painted sitting room, gathered round their new television set, we were ready to watch a new decade of television: *Gladiators, GBH, This Life* and *Cold Feet; Eldorado* and *TFI Friday; Alan Partridge, Pride and Prejudice,* Diana's funeral and *Friends; Our Friends in the North* and *Men Behaving Badly; Noel's House Party* and *The Big Breakfast; The Word, The Day Today,* the launch of Channel 5 and . . .

But that's for another series.

Closedown

Well, as you might have gathered, we've now come to the end of this particular book. If this was the closedown of an evening's viewing on eighties television, it would be at this point that the continuity announcer would talk you through some of the highlights of tomorrow's schedule, and then there'd perhaps be a quick weather forecast. Though why anyone would need a weather forecast just before they went to bed was always a little beyond me.

Then a clock would appear on screen, ticking its way towards midnight or whatever unfeasibly late hour it was. The announcer would remind viewers that various radio stations were broadcasting throughout the night, for those who were not yet ready for sleep or who wanted some company during the small hours. If you were watching BBC1, the image on screen would then be the channel's trademark revolving globe for the duration of the national anthem, before everything faded to black.

So this just leaves me to thank you for your company for the last few hundred pages. I wish you a warm farewell, and hope that you'll join me again for some further writing in the future. Goodbye for now.

Pages from Ceefax

(To be read to the accompaniment of light, noodling incidental music)

Ten programmes that ushered in the eighties on 31 December 1979
Ten programmes that ushered out the eighties on 31 December 1989
The ten most-watched programmes on eighties TV
Ten TV things that nearly happened in the eighties
Ten great television theme tunes of the eighties
The big Christmas films of the eighties
Ten great eighties romances
Ten people I fancied in the eighties . . .
. . . And ten for the ladies
Ten long-running programmes that began in the eighties
Ten great eighties catchphrases
Ten great eighties villains
Ten eighties winners of the BBC Sports Personality of the Year
Eight Hosts of the Brit Awards
And finally . . . My ten favourite television moments of the eighties

TOM BROMLEY

Ten programmes that ushered in the eighties on 31 December 1979

Blue Peter Review of the Year (BBC1). Including the Great Blue Peter Bring
   and Buy Sale, James Callaghan and eighty pantomime horses.
Larry Grayson's Generation Game (BBC1). With Isla St Clair.
Murder on the Orient Express (BBC1). A 'star-studded' film version of Agatha
   Christie's novel.
The 70s Stop Here (BBC1). The best and worst of seventies TV, with Penelope
   Keith.
Things to Come (BBC2). A discussion of 'the spiritual prospects for the 1980s'.
The Old Grey Whistle Test (BBC2). Featuring Blondie.
Give Us a Clue (ITV). Featuring Una Stubbs, Lionel Blair and Roy Hudd.
Max with Love (ITV). Max Bygraves special, featuring Geoff Love and Lorraine
   Chase.
Carry on Dick (ITV). 'Classic' *Carry On* fun.
The 'Will Kenny Everett Make it to 1980?' Show (ITV). With Cliff Richard, the
   Boomtown Rats and Hot Gossip.

Ten programmes that ushered out the eighties on 31 December 1989

A Question of Sport – A Celebration of 20 Years (BBC1).
A Hazard of Hearts (BBC1). Regency romp starring Helena Bonham Carter.
Clive James on the 80s (BBC1). With Jerry Hall.
Chris Evert's Wimbledon Farewell (BBC2). With Chris Evert.
Rab C. Nesbitt's Seasonal Greet (BBC2). With Gregor Fisher.
The Karen Carpenter Story (ITV). Biopic of the saccharine seventies singer.
Cilla's Goodbye to the Eighties (ITV). With Phil Collins and Jason Donovan.
Granpa (Channel 4). *Snowman*-type adaptation of a popular children's book.
The Pirates of Penzance (Channel 4). Film version of the musical, starring
   Kevin Kline and Linda Ronstadt.
Sticky New Year with Julian Clary (Channel 4). Seeing the new decade
   in . . . nuendo.

The ten most-watched programmes on eighties TV

EastEnders (BBC1, 25 December 1986) 30.15 million
Royal Wedding (BBC and ITV, 29 July 1981) 28:4 million
Coronation Street (ITV, 19 March 1989) 26.93 million

ALL IN THE BEST *POSSIBLE* TASTE

Dallas (BBC1, 22 November 1980) 21.6 million
To the Manor Born (BBC1, 9 November 1980) 21.55 million
Bread (BBC1, 4 December 1988) 20.97 million
Neighbours (BBC1 4 April 1989) 20.92 million
Just Good Friends (25 December 1986) 20.75 million
BBC News (BBC1, 25 November 1984, the day Band Aid was recorded) 20.42 million
Only Fools and Horses (BBC1, 25 December 1989) 20.12 million
(Source: bfi.org.uk; though note my earlier comments about *EastEnders* and the
   omnibus edition)

Ten TV things that nearly happened in the eighties

Dynasty was originally called *Oil*.
George Peppard was the first choice to play Blake Carrington.
Roly in *EastEnders* was meant to be an Alsatian.
The role of Del Boy in *Only Fools and Horses* was offered to Jim Broadbent.
Just Good Friends was meant to finish with the downbeat ending at the end of series two.
Spitting Image was nearly called *Rubber News* (another possible title was
   Hands Up Mrs Thatcher).
Argentina almost won the Falklands War.
Blackadder was almost cancelled after series one.
David Bowie and Mick Jagger's abandoned transatlantic duet during the Live
   Aid concert – they couldn't get it to work.
Dirty Den was almost properly killed off on *EastEnders* – the BBC1 controller
   overruled the producers and took out the final shot of his dead body, in order to
   leave open the possibility of the character's return.

Ten great television theme tunes of the eighties

Hill Street Blues
Cagney and Lacey
Knight Rider
Magnum PI
Ulysses 31
Moonlighting
Miami Vice
Dallas
Battle of the Planets
Jamie and the Magic Torch

TOM BROMLEY

The big Christmas films of the eighties

1980: *20,000 Leagues Under the Sea* (BBC1) versus *George and Mildred: the Movie* (ITV).

1981: *Dr No* (ITV).

1982: *International Velvet* (BBC1) versus *The Parent Trap* (ITV).

1983: *Superman* (ITV).

1984: *Mary Poppins* (BBC1) versus *The Man with the Golden Gun* (ITV).

1985: *Moonraker* (ITV).

1986: *Annie the Musical* (BBC1) versus *Dumbo* (ITV).

1987: *Indiana Jones and the Temple of Doom* (BBC1) versus *Alice in Wonderland* (ITV).

1988: *Back to the Future* (BBC1) versus *The Empire Strikes Back* (ITV).

1989: *The BFG* (ITV).

(Films shown following the Queen's speech on Christmas Day: in 1981, 1983, 1985 and 1989, BBC1 showed Christmas specials from the likes of *Blankety Blank* and *Bread*)

Ten great eighties romances

Scott and Charlene (*Neighbours*)

David and Maddie (*Moonlighting*)

Penny and Vince (*Just Good Friends*)

Den and Angie (*EastEnders*)

Peter Davison and Sandra Dickinson

Charles and Diana

Roland Rat and Glenis the Guinea Pig

Dempsey and Makepeace

John and Kate (*Dear John*)

René and Yvette (*'Allo 'Allo*)

Ten people I fancied in the eighties . . .

Daphne (*Scooby Doo*)

Taffy (*Captain Caveman*)

Valerie Landsburg (Doris from *Fame*)

Heather Locklear (*Dynasty*)

Debbie Greenwood (*First Class*)

ALL IN THE BEST *POSSIBLE* TASTE

Glynis Barber (Harriet Makepeace)
Elizabeth Hurley (*Christabel*)
Cherie Lunghi (*The Manageress*)
Catherine Bach (Daisy Duke)
Vicki Michelle (Yvette in *'Allo 'Allo*)

. . . And ten for the ladies

Nick Kamen (Levi's 501 ad)
Paul Nicholas (*Just Good Friends*)
Patrick Duffy (*Dallas*)
Michael Nader (Dex Dexter in *Dynasty*)
Michael Praed (*Robin of Sherwood*)
Jason Donovan
Nick Berry (*EastEnders*)
Peter Howitt (Joey in *Bread*)
Karl Howman (*Brush Strokes*)
Tom Selleck (*Magnum, PI*)

Ten long-running programmes that began in the eighties

Newsnight (1980)
Family Fortunes (1980)
Countdown (1982)
Channel 4 News (1982)
Taggart (1983)
EastEnders (1985)
Neighbours (1986)
Casualty (1986)
This Morning (1988)
Home and Away (1989)

Ten great eighties catchphrases

'All done in the best *possible* taste'
'Lovely jubbly'

'I have a cunning plan'
'I love it when a plan comes together'
'See what you say and say what you see'
'By the power of Greyskull, I have the power'
'Here's Our Graham with a little reminder'
'What do points make? Prizes . . .'
'Come on down!'
'You'll like this − not a lot, but you'll like it'

Ten great eighties villains

Alexis Colby
JR Ewing
Dirty Den
Skeletor
Jeremy Beadle
Boss Hog
The Interceptor
KARR
Zoltar
General Galtieri

Ten eighties winners of the BBC Sports Personality of the Year

1980: Robin Cousins
1981: Ian Botham
1982: Daley Thompson
1983: Steve Cram
1984: Torvill and Dean
1985: Barry McGuigan
1986: Nigel Mansell
1987: Fatima Whitbread
1988: Steve Davis
1989: Nick Faldo

ALL IN THE BEST *POSSIBLE* TASTE

Eight hosts of the Brit Awards

1980: no awards
1981: no awards
1982: David Jacobs (Best British Male: Cliff Richard)
1983: Tim Rice (Best International Solo Artist: Kid Creole)
1984: Tim Rice (Best Comedy Record: Neil)
1985: Noel Edmonds (Best Female: Alison Moyet)
1986: Noel Edmonds (Best Newcomer: Go West)
1987: Jonathan King (Best British Group: Five Star)
1988: Noel Edmonds (Best British Newcomer: Wet Wet Wet)
1989: Mick Fleetwood and Samantha Fox (Best Album: Fairground Attraction)
(Note: the Brit Awards started in 1977 and then stopped again.)

And finally . . . My ten favourite television moments of the eighties

Kenny Everett bending Terry Wogan's microphone on *Blankety Blank*
The final scene of *Blackadder Goes Forth*
Del Boy falling over in the wine bar on *Only Fools and Horses*
Five Star being sworn at on *Going Live!*
The vandalizing of the *Blue Peter* garden
The Sammy Jo and Fallon mud fight on *Dynasty*
The start of Channel 4
Queen at Live Aid
Ricky Villa's goal for Tottenham in the 1981 FA Cup final replay
The Robin Day–John Nott interview

Sources and Bibliography

Television

It might not surprise you to hear that much of the research for writing this book has been done by means of re-watching various old television programmes. Some of these can be found propping up the schedules on channels such as G.O.L.D., ITV3 and Challenge TV. A large number of the more popular ones are currently available on DVD (as listed below) should you feel like investigating further; a further *tranche* can be tracked down on old VHS cassettes, for which eBay is your best hunting ground.

(Note: my definition of 'currently available' is based on what's listed as 'in stock' at amazon.co.uk. A few of the programmes on the 'not available' list have been released on DVD in the past but have since been deleted and/or might be reissued in the future. Thus they might be available from other sellers, but at substantially higher prices because of their scarcity. In terms of the available DVDs, I have listed complete collections where possible: where only individual series (or American 'seasons') are available, I have listed the details for series one and marked how many of the subsequent series are available. All information is correct at the time of writing, but please remember that future availability can go up as well as down.)

Currently available on DVD

Airwolf, Series 1–3 Box Set (Universal, 2007)
All Creatures Great and Small, Series 1–7/Christmas Specials (Universal, 2009)
'Allo 'Allo!, Complete Series (Universal, 2009)
A-Team, The, Complete Collection (Universal, 2007)
Bagpuss: The Complete (UCA, 2005)
Battle of the Planets, Mega Box Set (Playback, 2004)
Bergerac, Complete Collection (2 Entertain, 2009)
Blackadder, Complete Collection (2 Entertain, 2005)
Blake's 7, Series 1 (2 Entertain, 2004); Series 1–4 available
Boon, Series 1 (Network 2005); Series 1–3 available
Boys from the Blackstuff (2 Entertain, 2003)
Bread, Series 1 and 2 (Playback, 2003); Series 3 available
Brideshead Revisited, Complete Series (ITV Studios, 2008)
Brush Strokes, Series 1 and 2 (Playback, 2004)
Buck Rogers in the 25th Century, Series 1 (Playback 2004); Series 2 available
Cagney and Lacey – The True Beginning (20th Century Fox, 2007)
CHiPs, Complete Season 1 (Warner, 2007); Series 2 available
Comic Strip Presents, Complete Collection (4DVD, 2007)
Dallas, Complete Series 1 and 2 (Warner, 2004); Series 1–12 available
Dangermouse, 25th-Anniversary Box Set (Fremantle, 2006)
Day of the Triffids, The (2 Entertain, 2005)
Dear John, Series 1 (Acorn Media, 2010)
Dempsey and Makepeace, Complete (Network, 2008)
Doctor Who, numerous DVDs available, even from the Sylvester McCoy years (2 Entertain)
Dogtanian, Complete First Series (Revelation, 2004); Series 2 available
Dukes of Hazzard, Series 1 (Warner, 2005) Series 1–7 available
Dynasty, Season 1 (Paramount, 2009); Series 1–5 available

Edge of Darkness (2 Entertain, 2003)

Emmerdale – The Best of Emmerdale (Network, 2007)

Fall Guy, The, Season 1 (20th Century Fox, 2007); Season 2 available

Fame, Season 1 (MGM, 2006); Season 2 available

Filthy, Rich and Catflap, Series 1 (Playback, 2004)

Fingerbobs, The Complete (E1 Entertainment, 2007)

Game for a Laugh, The Best of, Series 1 (Network, 2010)

Grange Hill, Complete Series 3 and 4 (2 Entertain, 2007); Series 1 and 2 available, though trickier to get hold of

Heidi, Series 1 (Universal, 2004); Series 2 available

He-Man and the Masters of the Universe, Complete Season One Box Set (Contender, 2007)

Hi-de-hi!, Complete Series (Universal, 2009)

Hill Street Blues, Series 1 (Channel 4 DVD, 2006); Series 2 available

Hitchhiker's Guide to the Galaxy, The (2 Entertain, 2005)

Ivor the Engine, The Complete (UCA, 2006)

Jamie and the Magic Torch, – The Complete, Series 1 (Fremantle, 2009); Series 2 available

Jewel in the Crown, The, Complete Series (ITV, 2009)

Juliet Bravo, Series 1 (Cinema Club, 2005); Series 1–6 available

Knight Rider, Complete Box Set (Universal, 2006)

Knots Landing, Complete First Season (Warner, 2007)

Last of the Summer Wine, Series 1 and 2 (Playback, 2002); Series 1–16 available

Live Aid (Warner, 2004); Led Zeppelin excepted

Magnum, PI, The Best of (Playback 2003); Series 1–8 available

Miami Vice, Complete Collection (Universal, 2007)

Minder, Complete Collection (Fremantle, 2009)

Moonlighting, Series 1–5 Complete (Sony, 2009)

Mysterious Cities of Gold, Complete Series (Fabulous, 2008)

Neighbours: The Iconic Episodes, Volume 1 (Fremantle, 2008); Volume 2 available, as well as *Neighbours: The Defining Moments*

New Statesman, The, Complete Series Box Set (Network, 2006)

Not the Nine O'Clock News, The Best of, Volume 1 (2 Entertain, 2003); Volume 2 available

One Man and His Dog, 30 Years of (Acorn Media, 2006)

Only Fools and Horses, Complete Collection (2 Entertain, 2006)

Open All Hours, Complete, Series 1–4 (2 Entertain, 2009)

Saturday Live, The Best of, Series 1 (Network, 2007); Series 2 and *The Very Best of Friday Night Live* available

Singing Detective, The (2 Entertain, 2004)

Snowman, The (Universal, 2008)

Sorry!, Series 1 (2 Entertain, 2007); Series 2 and 3 available

Spitting Image, Series 1–7 Complete (Network, 2009); Series 1–8 individually available

Street Hawk, Complete Series (Fabulous, 2010)
Superstars, The Best of (2 Entertain, 2003)
Terry and June, Series 1 (Cinema Club, 2005) Series 1-9 available
Top of the Pops 40th Anniversary (2 Entertain, 2004)
Tube, The, Series 1 (2 Entertain, 2006)
Two Ronnies, The Best of the (2 Entertain, 2001)
Ulysses 31, Complete (E1 Entertainment, 2004)
Willo the Wisp, Complete (E1 Entertainment, 2000)
Willy Fog, Complete Collection (Revelation, 2005)
Yes, Minister and *Yes, Prime Minister, Complete,* Box Set (2 Entertain, 2006)
Young Ones, The, Complete Series 1 and 2 (2 Entertain, 2007)

Currently unavailable on DVD

Adventure Game, The
Automan
A Very Peculiar Practice
Beadle's About
Blankety Blank (DVD game available)
Blind Date
Blockbusters (DVD game available)
Bob's Full House
Brookside (selected episodes available on 4oD)
Bruce Forsyth's Play Your Cards Right
Bullseye (DVD game available)
Cannon and Ball (Live DVD available)
Captain Caveman
Catchphrase (DVD game available)
Christabel (available on import)
Colbys, The
Family Fortunes (DVD game available, with Vernon Kay)
Fifteen-to-One
Going for Gold
Happy Families
Just Good Friends
Keith Harris Show, The
Kenny Everett Television Show, The
Late, Late Breakfast Show
Les Dennis Laughter Show
Little and Large
Manimal

Paul Daniels Magic Show
Price is Right, The (DVD game available, with Joe Pasquale)
Roland Rat
Russ Abbot's Madhouse
Telly Addicts (DVD game available)
That's My Dog
3-2-1
Traffik (available on 4oD)
Treasure Hunt
Triangle
Ultra Quiz

The internet

The internet is also a fertile hunting ground for old programmes. The first port of call are the official websites, such as Channel 4's 4oD, on which you can watch various classic programmes for free: selected episodes from *Brookside* are there for your viewing pleasure, for example, as is the entire series of *Traffik*.

Then there are video websites, most predominantly YouTube, on to which numerous kind and dedicated souls have uploaded all sorts of weird and wonderful television clips from the period. This is a great treasure trove if you want to relive a classic theme tune or track down a specific television memory. You can also watch some complete eighties programmes here, as long as you don't mind watching them in two-minute bursts.

Thirdly, depending on how legally and ethically minded you are feeling, there are also multiple file-sharing websites from which you can download assorted programmes, a resource I utilized in no way whatsoever during the course of writing this book.

Select websites

BBC.co.uk
Channel4.com/4oD
Childofthe1980s.com
Digitalspy.co.uk
Grangehillfans.co.uk
He-man.org
Kaleidoscope.org.uk
Kidsfromfamemedia.blogspot.com
Mililibrary.com
Ofah.net (*Only Fools and Horses*)
Offthetelly.co.uk
Ratfans.com
Remembertheeighties.com
Transdiffusion.org
TV-Ark.org.uk
TVbite.com
TVCream.com
TVWhirl.co.uk
UKgameshows.com
UltimateDallas.com
UltimateDynasty.net
Watchwithmothers.net
Yes-Minister.com
YouTube.com

Books, Newspapers and Magazines

Television has always been blessed with some wonderful writers, and the 1980s was no exception. This was the era of columns by the likes of Clive James and Julian Barnes in the *Observer*, a young Mark Lawson at the *Independent*, and the perennially brilliant Nancy Banks-Smith in the *Guardian*. I can only doff my cap to their excellence, and hope that my own writing on the era has not damaged their rich tradition too much.

As well as re-watching television programmes, I spent many pleasurable hours reading various books about television and the eighties and trawling through various newspapers and magazines for columns and articles. In terms of newspapers, *The Times*, *The Sunday Times*, the *Guardian* and the *Observer* were my main references, though I looked to other newspapers as and when appropriate. In terms of magazines, of particular use were the *Radio Times*, the *TV Times*, the *Listener*, *Look-In*, *Smash Hits* and my decaying collection of early copies of *Q* (which I always knew would come in handy someday).

Select bibliography

Andrew, Christopher, *The Defence of the Realm: The Authorised History of MI5* (Allen Lane, 2009)

Barfe, Louis, *Turned Out Nice Again* (Atlantic, 2008)

Beadle, Jeremy, *Watch Out! My Autobiography* (Century, 1998)

Boyce, D. George, *The Falklands War* (Palgrave Macmillan, 2005)

Bradford, Sara, *Diana* (Viking, 2006)

Briggs, Raymond, *The Tin-Pot Foreign General and the Old Iron Woman* (Hamish Hamilton, 1984)

Chester, Lewis, *Tooth and Claw: The Inside Story of Spitting Image* (Faber and Faber, 1986)

Chippendale, Peter, and Chris Horrie, *Stick it Up Your Punter!* (William Heinemann, 1990)

Clarke, Steve, *The Only Fools and Horses Story* (BBC, 1998)

Daniels, Paul, *Under No Illusion* (Blake, 2000)

Day-Lewis, Sean, *One Day in the Life of Television* (Grafton, 1989)

Dennis, Les, *Must the Show Go On?* (Orion, 2008)

Donovan, Jason, *Between the Lines* (Harper Collins, 2007)

Dyke, Greg, *Inside Story* (Harper Collins, 2004)

Edmondson, Adrian, *How to Be a Complete Bastard* (Virgin, 1986)

Edward, HRH Prince, *Knockout: The Grand Charity Tournament* (Collins, 1987)

Evans, Jeff, *The Penguin TV Companion*, Third Edition (Penguin, 2006)

Fisher, John, *Tommy Cooper: Always Leave Them Laughing* (Harper Collins, 2006)

Franklin, Bob, *Packaging Politics* (Edward Arnold, 1994)

Frith, Mark, *The Best of Smash Hits* (Little, Brown, 2006)

Geldof, Bob, *Is That It?* (Sidgwick and Jackson, 1986)

Hagman, Larry, *Hello Darlin'* (Simon and Schuster, 2001)

Hanrahan, Brian, and Robert Fox, *I Counted Them All Out and I Counted Them All Back* (BBC, 1982)

Harris, Robert, *The Media Trilogy* (Faber and Faber, 1994)

Holland, Jools, *Barefaced Lies and Boogie-Woogie Boasts* (Michael Joseph, 2007)

Horrie, Chris, and Steve Clarke, *Fuzzy Monsters: Fear and Loathing at the BBC* (William Heinemann, 1994)

James, Clive, *Glued to the Box* (Jonathan Cape, 1983)

Jones, Ian, *Morning Glory: A History of Breakfast Television* (Kelly Publications, 2004)

Kibble-White, Graham, *Look-In: The Best of the Eighties* (Carlton, 2008)

Kingsley, Hilary, and Geoff Tibbals, *Box of Delights* (Macmillan, 1989)

Lewis, Richard, *The Encyclopedia of Cult Children's TV* (Allison and Busby, 2001)

Lewisohn, Mark, *Radio Times Guide to TV Comedy* (BBC, 1998)

Marks, Lawrence, and Maurice Gran, *The New Statesman* (Andre Deutsch, 1992)

Postgate, Oliver, *Seeing Things: A Memoir* (Sidgwick and Jackson, 2000)

Royle, Trevor, *War Report: The War Correspondent's View of Battle from the Crimea to the Falklands* (Mainstream, 1987)

Turner, Alwyn, *Crisis, What Crisis?* (Aurum, 2008)

Viner, Brian, *Nice to See It, to See It Nice* (Simon and Schuster, 2009)

Whiteley, Richard, *Himoff! The Memoirs of a TV Matinee Idol* (Orion, 2000)

Windlesham, Lord, and Richard Rampton, *The Windlesham/Rampton Report on Death on the Rock* (Faber and Faber, 1989)

Young, Hugo, *One of Us* (Macmillan, 1989)

Acknowledgements

Many thanks to everyone who has helped in the course of writing this book. Particular thanks to Mike Jones, Rory Scarfe, Dawn Burnett and all at Simon and Schuster, Simon Trewin at United Agents, Monica O'Connell, Ian Allen, Andrew John, my parents (both for bringing me up and being good sports) and especially my wife, Joanna, for giving me the time, space and confidence to write this.

Index